BBC

DOCTOR WHO

THE TENTH DOCTOR

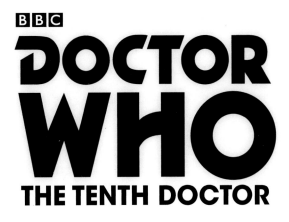

VOL 1: REVOLUTIONS OF TERROR

"A lot of fun!"
COMIC BOOK RESOURCES

"An atmospheric story, with rich characterization."
COMICS WORTH READING

"Would make a great addition to any comic library – not just a fan's!"
GEEKY GIRL PROJECT

"Top marks for the artwork!"
SCI-FI MAFIA

"Absolutely blown away by the artwork."
POP CULTS

"Go buy this!"
COMICS VERSE

"Whovians will not be disappointed."
FLICKERING MYTH

"It really captures the feel of Russell T. Davies' era of *Who*."
NERD LIKE YOU

"Perfectly captures the spirit of *Doctor Who*!"
KABOOOOOM!

"Fully embracing the spirit of the series, all Whovians will find themselves shouting, 'Allons-y!'"
NEWSARAMA

"10 out of 10!"
PROJECT FANDOM

"For fans of the TV show, this is a must buy, especially if you miss David Tennant's portrayal."
PANELS AND PIXELS

"The artwork is superb."
COMIC BOOK THERAPY

"Nick Abadzis' dialogue for the Doctor is fantastic."
DEN OF GEEK

"The artwork is stunning."
GEEK SYNDICATE

"The *Doctor Who* comic fans have always deserved."
BLOODY DISGUSTING

"If you've missed the skinny one with the sandshoes, then you'll enjoy this."
SCIFI BULLETIN

TITAN COMICS

SENIOR EDITOR
Steve White

TITAN COMICS EDITORIAL
Lizzie Kaye,
Kirsten Murray,
Tom Williams

PRODUCTION SUPERVISORS
Maria Pearson,
Jackie Flook

PRODUCTION CONTROLLER
Obi Onuora

STUDIO MANAGER
Emma Smith

CIRCULATION MANAGER
Steve Tothill

SENIOR MARKETING & PRESS OFFICER
Owen Johnson

MARKETING MANAGER
Ricky Claydon

ADVERTISING MANAGER
Michelle Fairlamb

PUBLISHING MANAGER
Darryl Tothill

PUBLISHING DIRECTOR
Chris Teather

OPERATIONS DIRECTOR
Leigh Baulch

EXECUTIVE DIRECTOR
Vivian Cheung

PUBLISHER
Nick Landau

Special thanks to
Steven Moffat, Brian Minchin,
Matt Nicholls, Georgie Britton,
Edward Russell, Derek Ritchie,
Scott Handcock, Kate Bush,
Julia Nocciolino, Ed Casey,
Marcus Wilson and Richard
Cookson for their invaluable
assistance.

DOCTOR WHO: THE TENTH DOCTOR VOL 1:
REVOLUTIONS OF TERROR
HB ISBN: 9781782761730 SB ISBN: 9781782763826

Published by Titan Comics, a division of
Titan Publishing Group, Ltd. 144 Southwark Street,
London, SE1 0UP.

BBC, DOCTOR WHO (word marks, logos and devices) and TARDIS are
trade marks of the British Broadcasting Corporation and are used
under license. BBC logo © BBC 1996. Doctor Who logo © BBC 2009.
TARDIS image © BBC 1963. Cybermen image © BBC/Kit Pedler/
Gerry Davis 1966.

With the exception of artwork used for review
purposes, no portion of this book may be reproduced
or transmitted in any form or by any means, without the
express permission of the publisher Titan Comics
or the BBC.

Names, characters, places and incidents featured in
this publication are either the product of the author's
imagination or used fictitiously. Any resemblance to
actual persons, living or dead (except for satirical
purposes), is entirely coincidental.

A CIP catalogue record for this title is available from
the British Library. First edition: April 2015.

10 9 8 7 6 5 4 3 2 1

Printed in China. TC0273.

Titan Comics does not read or
accept unsolicited DOCTOR WHO
submissions of ideas, stories
or artwork.

www.titan-comics.com

BBC

DOCTOR WHO
THE TENTH DOCTOR

VOL 1: REVOLUTIONS OF TERROR

WRITER: NICK ABADZIS

ARTIST: ELENA CASAGRANDE

COLORIST: ARIANNA FLOREAN

**LETTERS: RICHARD STARKINGS
AND COMICRAFT'S
JIMMY BETANCOURT**

**EDITOR:
ANDREW JAMES**

**DESIGNER:
ROB FARMER**

BBC

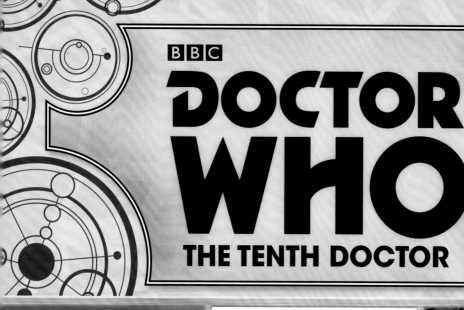

DOCTOR WHO

THE TENTH DOCTOR

POLICE BOX

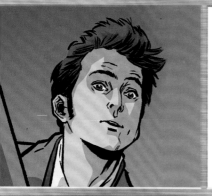

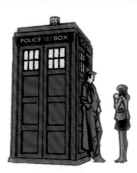

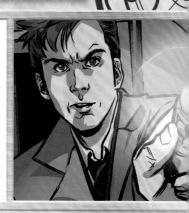

THE DOCTOR

An alien who walks like a man. Last of the Time Lords of Gallifrey. Never cruel or cowardly, he champions the oppressed across time and space. Forever traveling, the Doctor lives to see the universe anew through the eyes of his human companions!

THE TARDIS

'Time and Relative Dimension in Space'. Bigger on the inside, this unassuming blue box is your ticket to unforgettable adventure! The Doctor likes to think he's in control, but more often than not, the TARDIS takes him where and when he needs to be...

THE SONIC

An engineering marvel, the Sonic Screwdriver is a tool that scans, detects, unlocks and – yes! – unscrews. Vulnerable to deadlock seals and wood, it's still one of the Doctor's most useful possessions. His current model accessorizes a blue tip with a coral handle.

PREVIOUSLY...

It can be wonderful to explore all of time and space at the Doctor's side, but the universe can also be a dark and dangerous place – as the Doctor's most recent companion, Donna Noble, found to her cost. Forced to leave her behind, the Doctor has since been wandering alone. But no matter how far he travels, or how long, something always brings him back to Earth...

When you've finished reading this collection, please email your thoughts to doctorwhocomic@titanemail.com

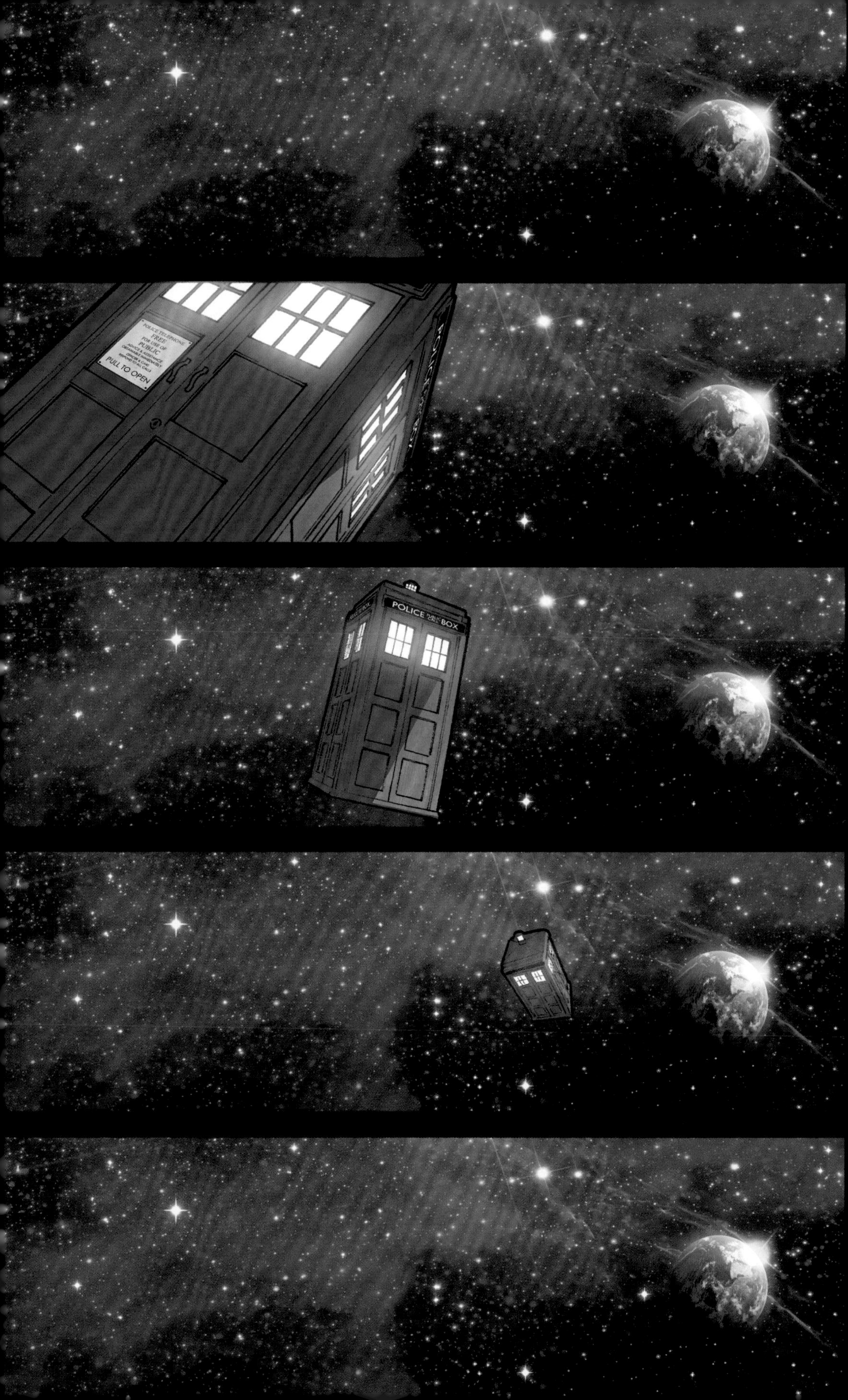
POLICE TELEPHONE
FREE
FOR USE OF
PUBLIC
PULL TO OPEN
POLICE BOX

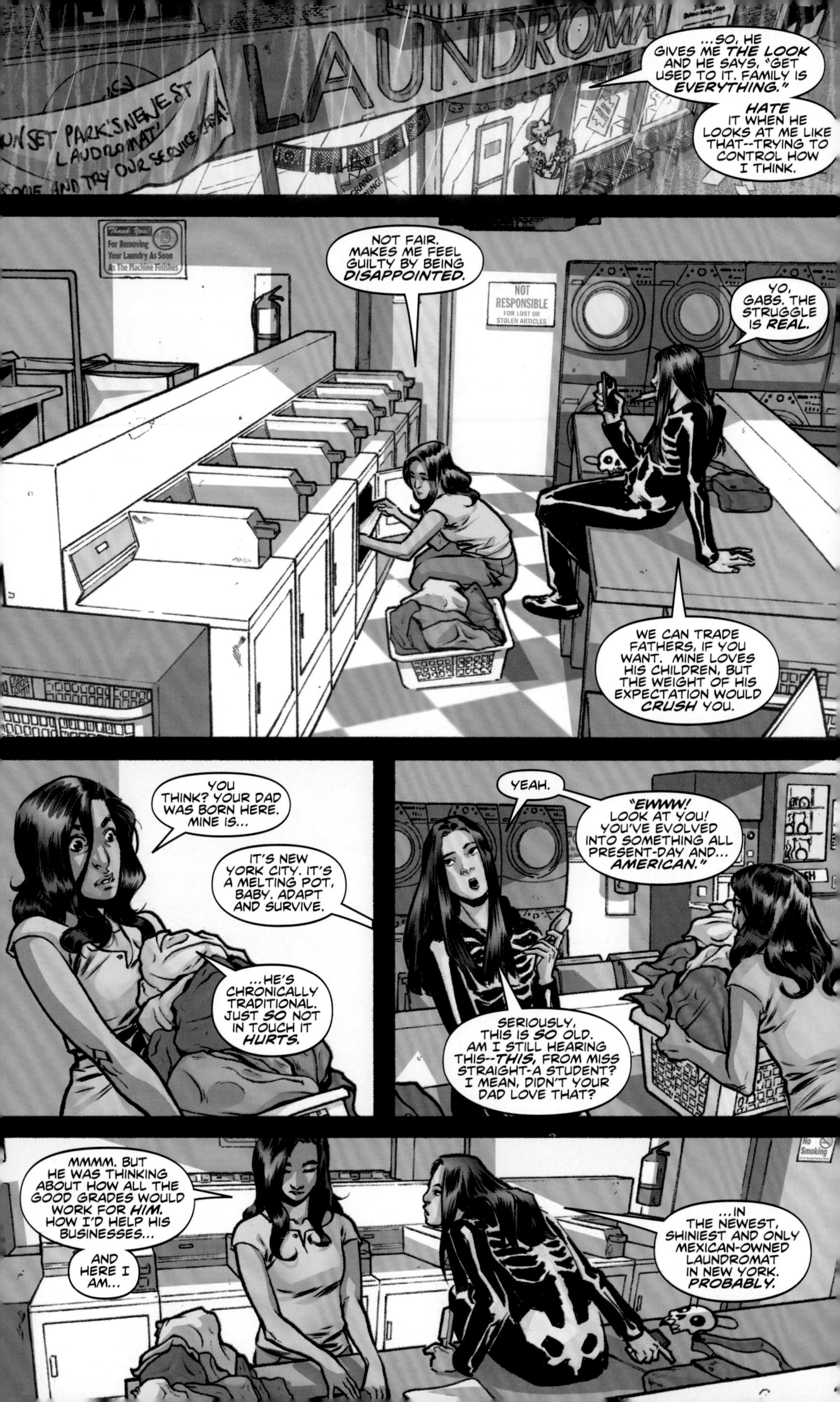

LAUNDROMAT
...SO, HE GIVES ME **THE LOOK** AND HE SAYS, "GET USED TO IT. FAMILY IS **EVERYTHING.**"
HATE IT WHEN HE LOOKS AT ME LIKE THAT--TRYING TO CONTROL HOW I THINK.
Thank You! For Removing Your Laundry As Soon As The Machine Finishes
NOT FAIR. MAKES ME FEEL GUILTY BY BEING **DISAPPOINTED.**
NOT RESPONSIBLE FOR LOST OR STOLEN ARTICLES
YO, GABS. THE STRUGGLE IS **REAL.**
WE CAN TRADE FATHERS, IF YOU WANT. MINE LOVES HIS CHILDREN, BUT THE WEIGHT OF HIS EXPECTATION WOULD **CRUSH** YOU.
YOU THINK? YOUR DAD WAS BORN HERE. MINE IS...
IT'S NEW YORK CITY. IT'S A MELTING POT, BABY. ADAPT AND SURVIVE.
...HE'S CHRONICALLY TRADITIONAL. JUST **SO** NOT IN TOUCH IT **HURTS.**
YEAH.
"EWWW! LOOK AT YOU! YOU'VE EVOLVED INTO SOMETHING ALL PRESENT-DAY AND... **AMERICAN."**
SERIOUSLY, THIS IS **SO** OLD. AM I STILL HEARING THIS--**THIS,** FROM MISS STRAIGHT-A STUDENT? I MEAN, DIDN'T YOUR DAD LOVE THAT?
MMMM. BUT HE WAS THINKING ABOUT HOW ALL THE GOOD GRADES WOULD WORK FOR **HIM.** HOW I'D HELP HIS BUSINESSES...
AND HERE I AM...
...IN THE NEWEST, SHINIEST AND ONLY MEXICAN-OWNED LAUNDROMAT IN NEW YORK. **PROBABLY.**
No Smoking

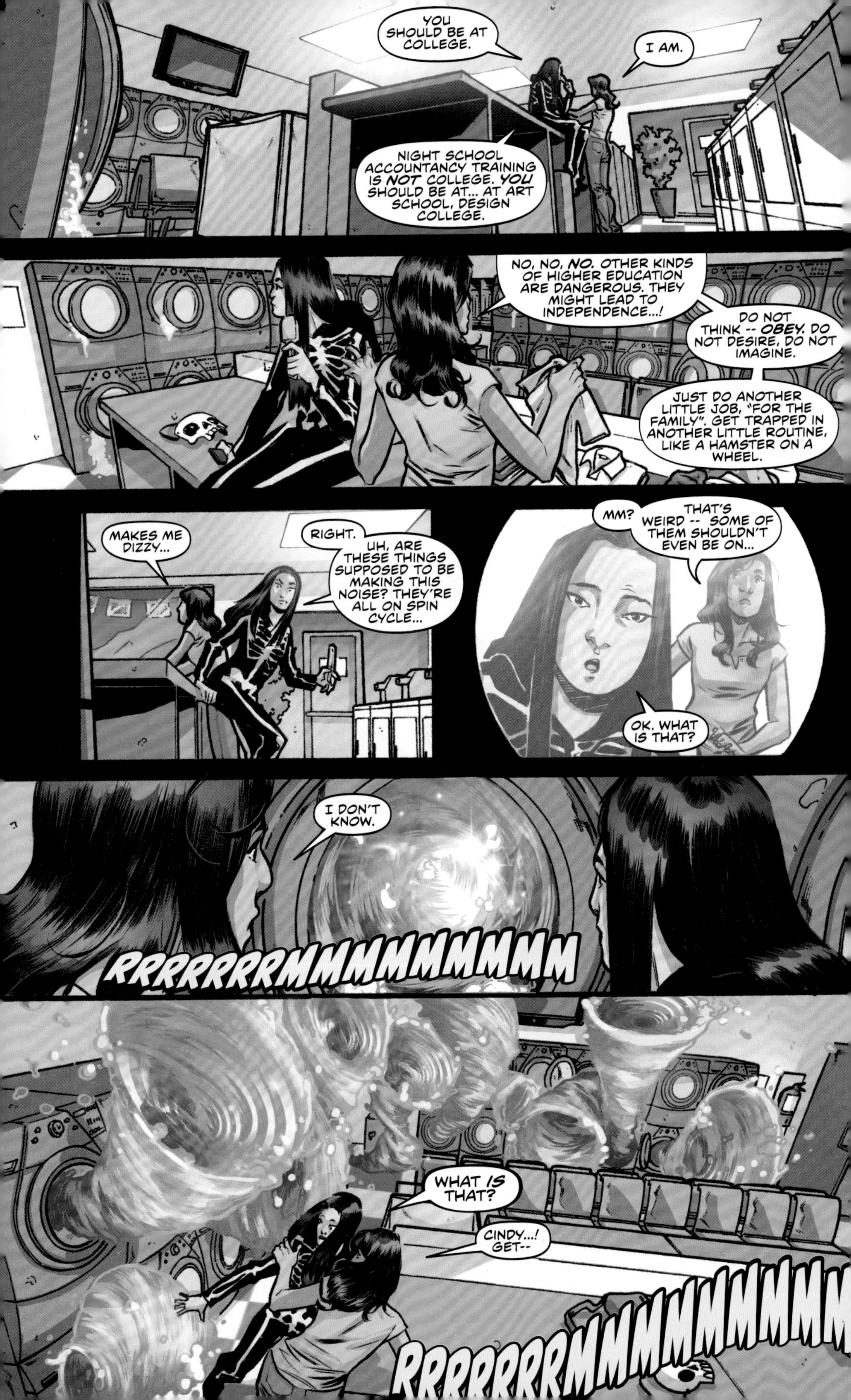
YOU SHOULD BE AT COLLEGE.
I AM.
NIGHT SCHOOL ACCOUNTANCY TRAINING IS *NOT* COLLEGE. *YOU* SHOULD BE AT... AT ART SCHOOL, DESIGN COLLEGE.
NO, NO, *NO*. OTHER KINDS OF HIGHER EDUCATION ARE DANGEROUS. THEY MIGHT LEAD TO INDEPENDENCE...!
DO NOT THINK -- *OBEY*. DO NOT DESIRE, DO NOT IMAGINE.
JUST DO ANOTHER LITTLE JOB, "FOR THE FAMILY". GET TRAPPED IN ANOTHER LITTLE ROUTINE, LIKE A HAMSTER ON A WHEEL.
MAKES ME DIZZY...
RIGHT.
UH, ARE THESE THINGS SUPPOSED TO BE MAKING THIS NOISE? THEY'RE ALL ON SPIN CYCLE...
MM?
THAT'S WEIRD -- SOME OF THEM SHOULDN'T EVEN BE ON...
OK. WHAT IS THAT?
I DON'T KNOW.
RRRRRRRMMMMMMMMMM
WHAT *IS* THAT?
CINDY...! GET--
RRRRRRRMMMMMMMMMMMM

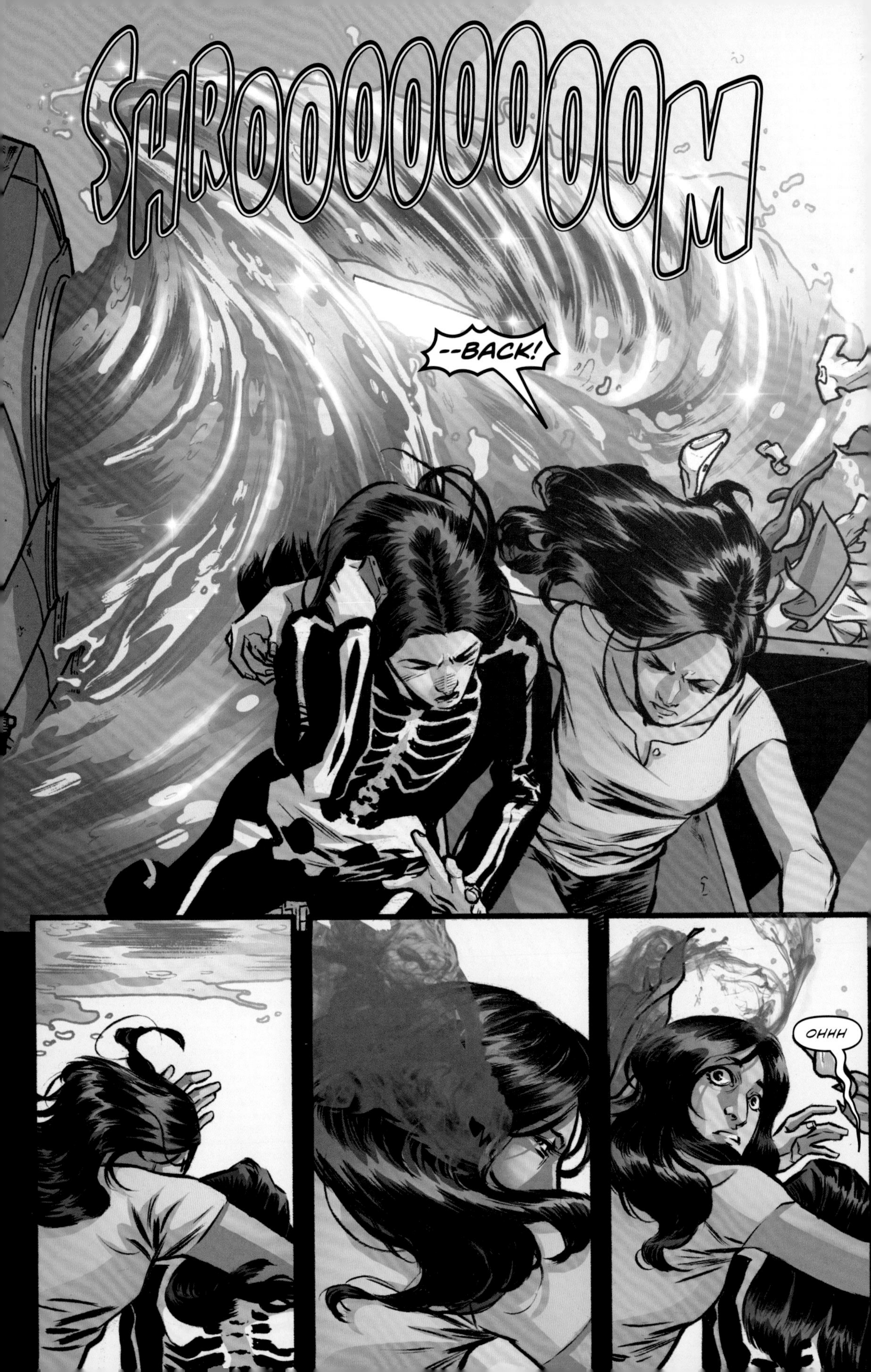
SHROOOOOOOOOM
--BACK!
OHHH

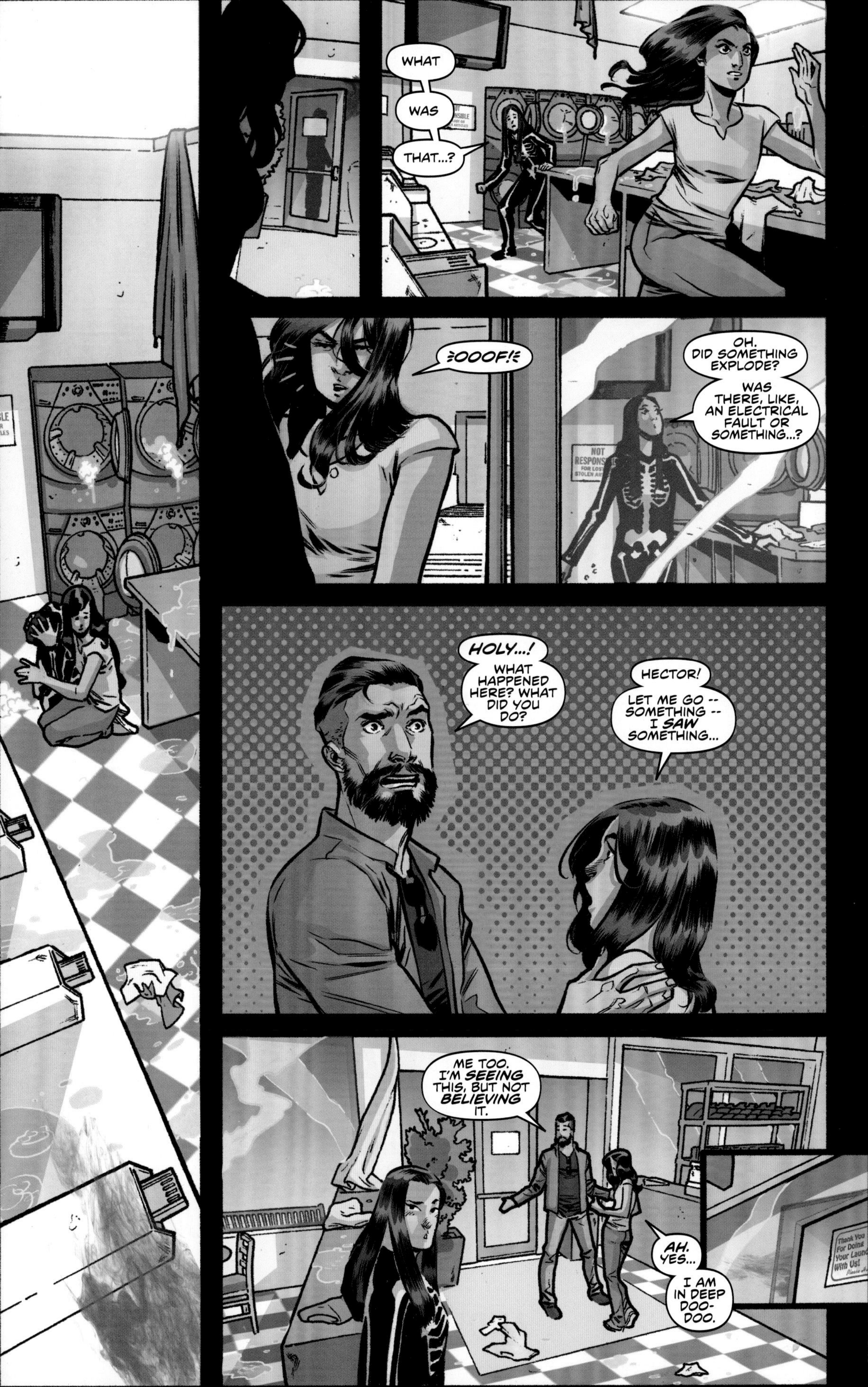
WHAT
WAS
THAT...?
OOOF!
OH. DID SOMETHING EXPLODE?
WAS THERE, LIKE, AN ELECTRICAL FAULT OR SOMETHING...?
HOLY...!
WHAT HAPPENED HERE? WHAT DID YOU DO?
HECTOR!
LET ME GO -- SOMETHING -- I SAW SOMETHING...
ME TOO. I'M SEEING THIS, BUT NOT BELIEVING IT.
AH. YES...
I AM IN DEEP DOO-DOO.

BBC

DOC
WH

THE TENT
REVOLUTION

WRITER
NICK ABADZIS

LETTERER
**RICHARD STARKINGS AND
COMICRAFT'S JIMMY BETANCOURT**

EDITOR
ANDREW JAMES

TOR 10

DOCTOR

S OF TERROR

ARTIST
ELENA CASAGRANDE
WITH MICHELE PASTA • SPECIAL THANKS TO PAOLO VILLANELLI AND LUCA LAMBERTI

COLORIST
ARIANNA FLOREAN
WITH CLAUDIA SG, FABIOLA IENNE, VALENTINA CUOMO, AZZURRA FLOREAN

DESIGNER
ROB FARMER

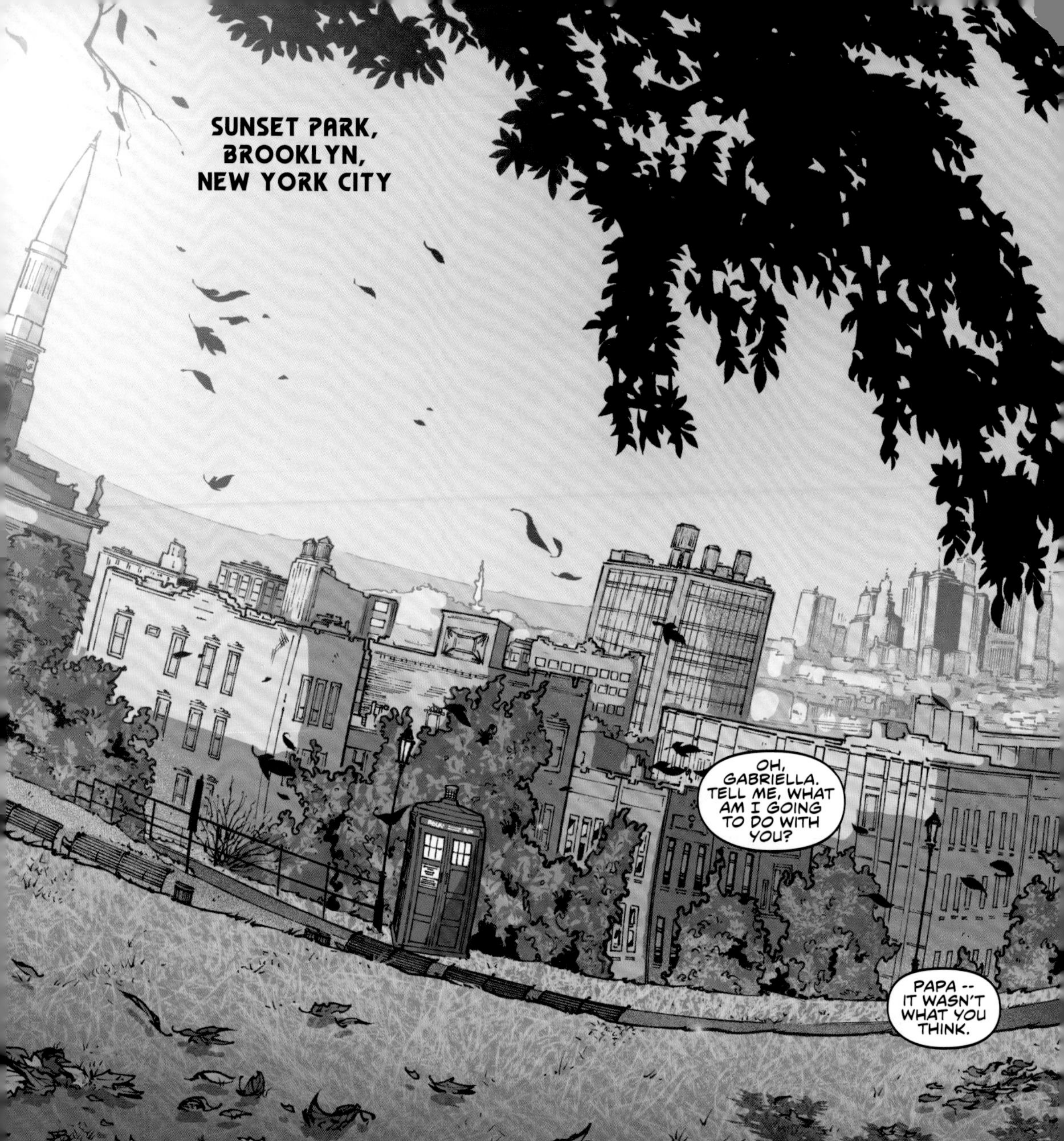
SUNSET PARK, BROOKLYN, NEW YORK CITY
OH, GABRIELLA. TELL ME, WHAT AM I GOING TO DO WITH YOU?
PAPA -- IT WASN'T WHAT YOU THINK.

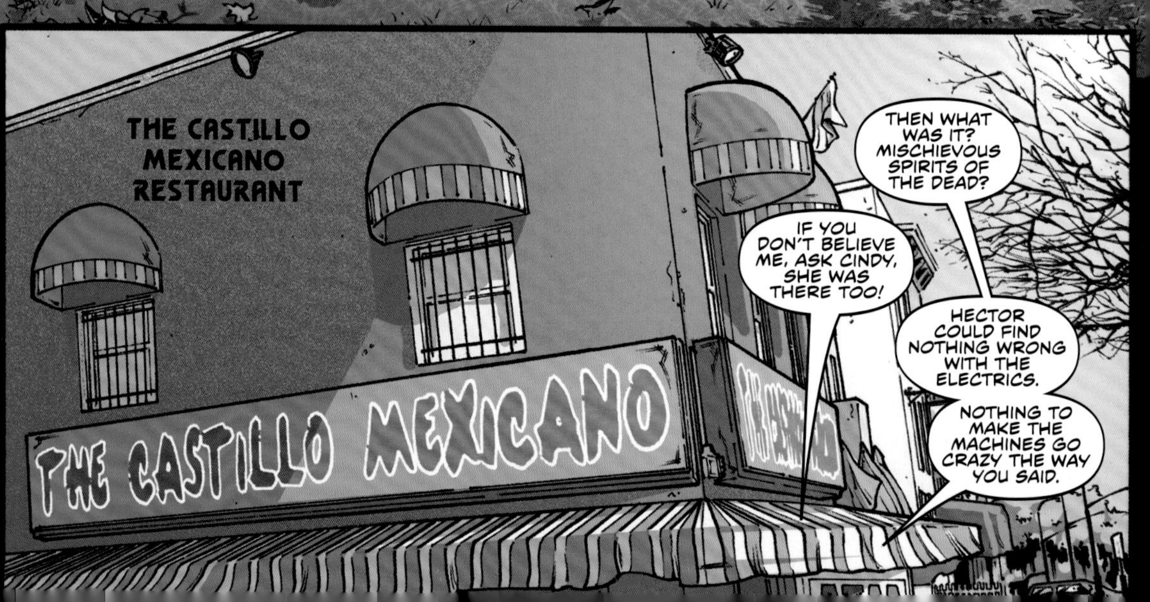
THE CASTILLO MEXICANO RESTAURANT
THE CASTILLO MEXICANO
THEN WHAT WAS IT? MISCHIEVOUS SPIRITS OF THE DEAD?
IF YOU DON'T BELIEVE ME, ASK CINDY, SHE WAS THERE TOO!
HECTOR COULD FIND NOTHING WRONG WITH THE ELECTRICS.
NOTHING TO MAKE THE MACHINES GO CRAZY THE WAY YOU SAID.

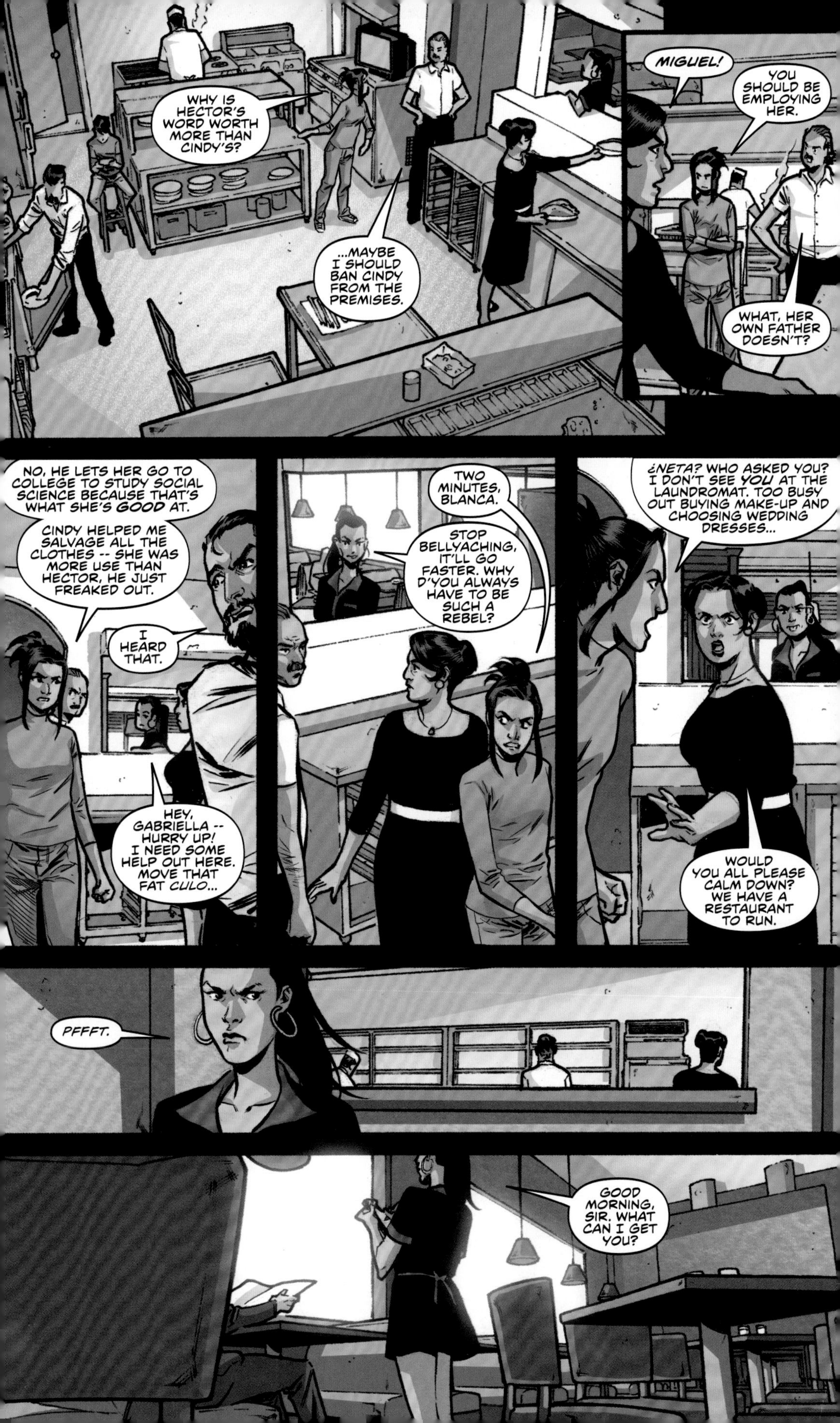
WHY IS HECTOR'S WORD WORTH MORE THAN CINDY'S?
...MAYBE I SHOULD BAN CINDY FROM THE PREMISES.
MIGUEL!
YOU SHOULD BE EMPLOYING HER.
WHAT, HER OWN FATHER DOESN'T?
NO, HE LETS HER GO TO COLLEGE TO STUDY SOCIAL SCIENCE BECAUSE THAT'S WHAT SHE'S *GOOD* AT.
CINDY HELPED ME SALVAGE ALL THE CLOTHES -- SHE WAS MORE USE THAN HECTOR, HE JUST FREAKED OUT.
I HEARD THAT.
HEY, GABRIELLA -- HURRY UP! I NEED SOME HELP OUT HERE. MOVE THAT FAT *CULO*...
TWO MINUTES, BLANCA.
STOP BELLYACHING, IT'LL GO FASTER. WHY D'YOU ALWAYS HAVE TO BE SUCH A REBEL?
¿NETA? WHO ASKED YOU? I DON'T SEE *YOU* AT THE LAUNDROMAT. TOO BUSY OUT BUYING MAKE-UP AND CHOOSING WEDDING DRESSES...
WOULD YOU ALL PLEASE CALM DOWN? WE HAVE A RESTAURANT TO RUN.
PFFFT.
GOOD MORNING, SIR. WHAT CAN I GET YOU?

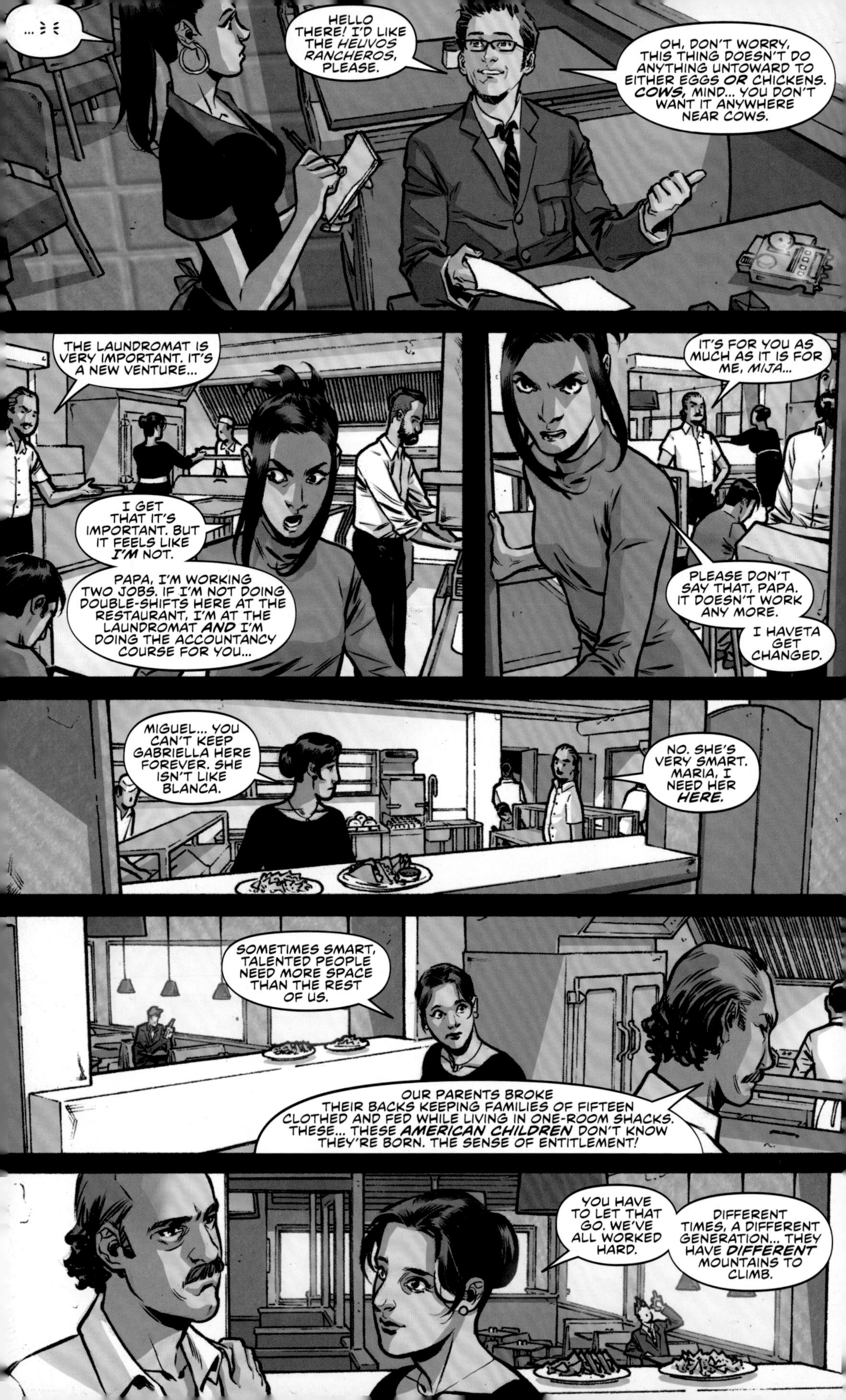
...!!
HELLO THERE! I'D LIKE THE *HEUVOS RANCHEROS*, PLEASE.
OH, DON'T WORRY, THIS THING DOESN'T DO ANYTHING UNTOWARD TO EITHER EGGS ***OR*** CHICKENS. ***COWS,*** MIND... YOU DON'T WANT IT ANYWHERE NEAR COWS.
THE LAUNDROMAT IS VERY IMPORTANT. IT'S A NEW VENTURE...
I GET THAT IT'S IMPORTANT. BUT IT FEELS LIKE ***I'M*** NOT.
PAPA, I'M WORKING TWO JOBS. IF I'M NOT DOING DOUBLE-SHIFTS HERE AT THE RESTAURANT, I'M AT THE LAUNDROMAT ***AND*** I'M DOING THE ACCOUNTANCY COURSE FOR YOU...
IT'S FOR YOU AS MUCH AS IT IS FOR ME, *MIJA*...
PLEASE DON'T SAY THAT, PAPA. IT DOESN'T WORK ANY MORE.
I HAVETA GET CHANGED.
MIGUEL... YOU CAN'T KEEP GABRIELLA HERE FOREVER. SHE ISN'T LIKE BLANCA.
NO. SHE'S VERY SMART. MARIA, I NEED HER ***HERE.***
SOMETIMES SMART, TALENTED PEOPLE NEED MORE SPACE THAN THE REST OF US.
OUR PARENTS BROKE THEIR BACKS KEEPING FAMILIES OF FIFTEEN CLOTHED AND FED WHILE LIVING IN ONE-ROOM SHACKS. THESE... THESE ***AMERICAN CHILDREN*** DON'T KNOW THEY'RE BORN. THE SENSE OF ENTITLEMENT!
YOU HAVE TO LET THAT GO. WE'VE ALL WORKED HARD.
DIFFERENT TIMES, A DIFFERENT GENERATION... THEY HAVE ***DIFFERENT*** MOUNTAINS TO CLIMB.

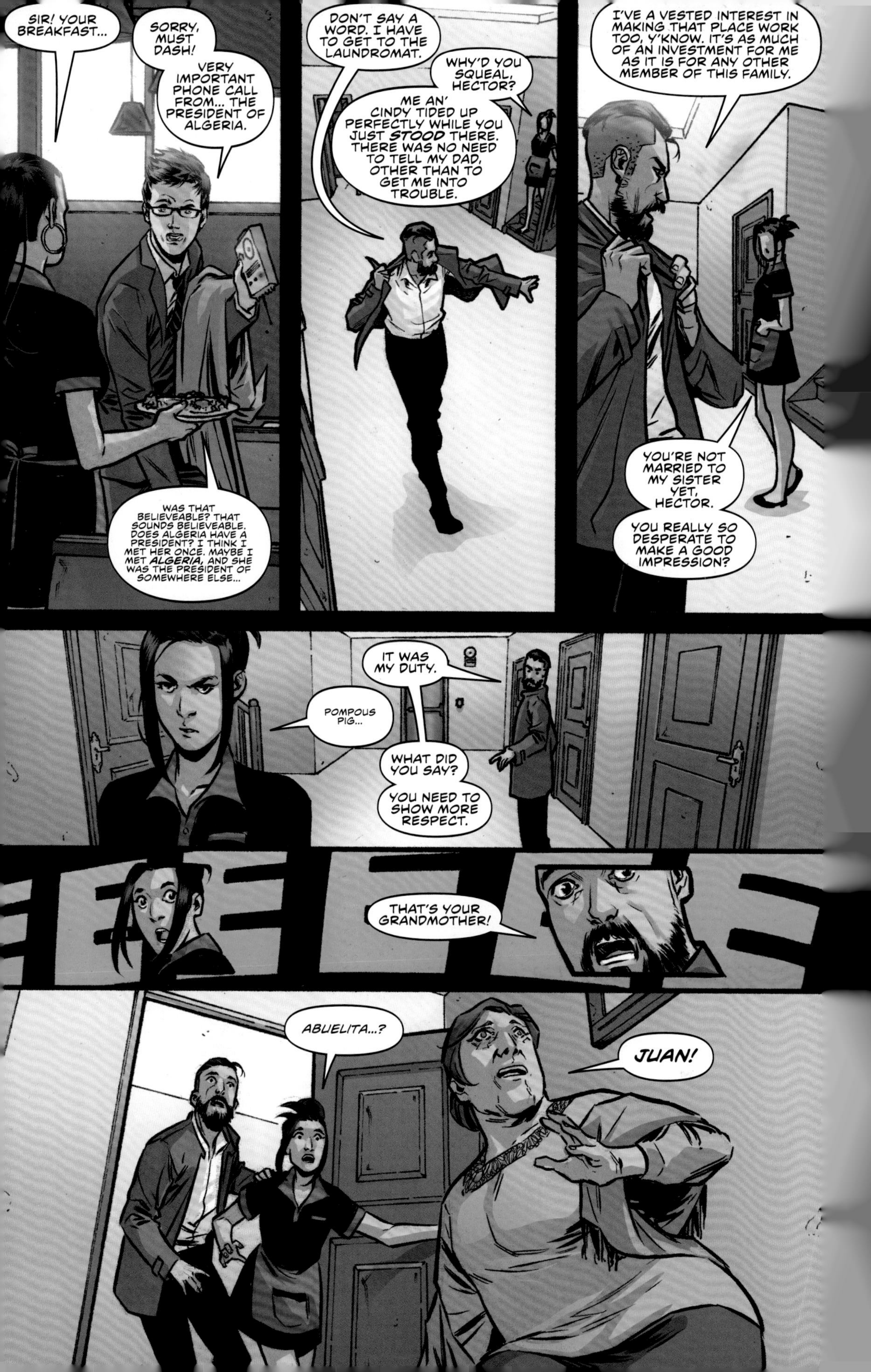
SIR! YOUR BREAKFAST...
SORRY, MUST DASH!
VERY IMPORTANT PHONE CALL FROM... THE PRESIDENT OF ALGERIA.
WAS THAT BELIEVEABLE? THAT SOUNDS BELIEVEABLE. DOES ALGERIA HAVE A PRESIDENT? I THINK I MET HER ONCE. MAYBE I MET ALGERIA, AND SHE WAS THE PRESIDENT OF SOMEWHERE ELSE...
DON'T SAY A WORD. I HAVE TO GET TO THE LAUNDROMAT.
WHY'D YOU SQUEAL, HECTOR?
ME AN' CINDY TIDED UP PERFECTLY WHILE YOU JUST STOOD THERE. THERE WAS NO NEED TO TELL MY DAD, OTHER THAN TO GET ME INTO TROUBLE.
I'VE A VESTED INTEREST IN MAKING THAT PLACE WORK TOO, Y'KNOW. IT'S AS MUCH OF AN INVESTMENT FOR ME AS IT IS FOR ANY OTHER MEMBER OF THIS FAMILY.
YOU'RE NOT MARRIED TO MY SISTER YET, HECTOR.
YOU REALLY SO DESPERATE TO MAKE A GOOD IMPRESSION?
IT WAS MY DUTY.
POMPOUS PIG...
WHAT DID YOU SAY?
YOU NEED TO SHOW MORE RESPECT.
THAT'S YOUR GRANDMOTHER!
ABUELITA...?
JUAN!

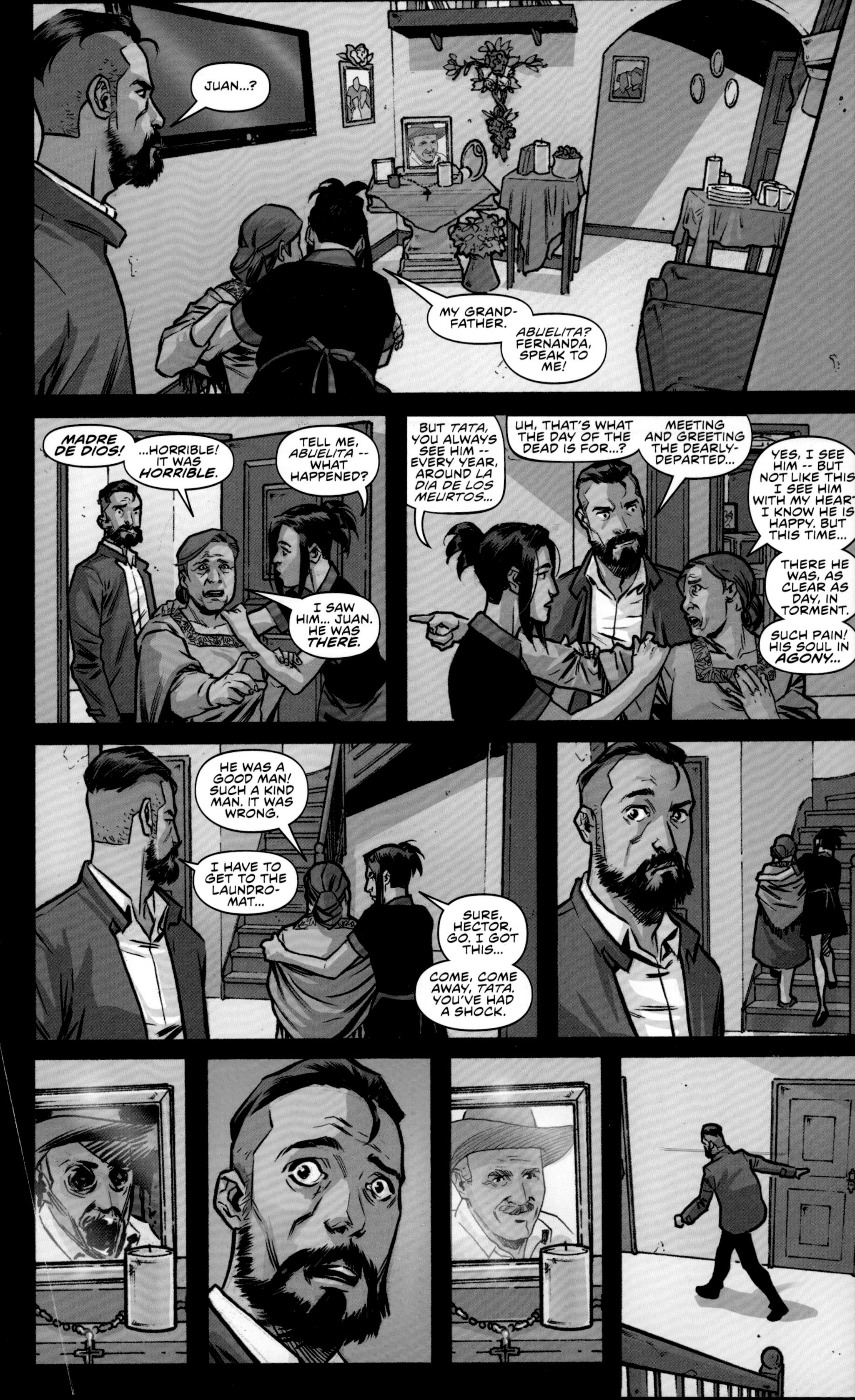
JUAN...?
MY GRAND-FATHER.
ABUELITA? FERNANDA, SPEAK TO ME!
MADRE DE DIOS!
...HORRIBLE! IT WAS HORRIBLE.
TELL ME, ABUELITA -- WHAT HAPPENED?
I SAW HIM... JUAN. HE WAS THERE.
BUT TATA, YOU ALWAYS SEE HIM -- EVERY YEAR, AROUND LA DIA DE LOS MEURTOS...
UH, THAT'S WHAT THE DAY OF THE DEAD IS FOR...?
MEETING AND GREETING THE DEARLY-DEPARTED...
YES, I SEE HIM -- BUT NOT LIKE THIS. I SEE HIM WITH MY HEART. I KNOW HE IS HAPPY. BUT THIS TIME...
THERE HE WAS, AS CLEAR AS DAY, IN TORMENT.
SUCH PAIN! HIS SOUL IN AGONY...
HE WAS A GOOD MAN! SUCH A KIND MAN. IT WAS WRONG.
I HAVE TO GET TO THE LAUNDRO-MAT...
SURE, HECTOR, GO. I GOT THIS...
COME, COME AWAY, TATA. YOU'VE HAD A SHOCK.

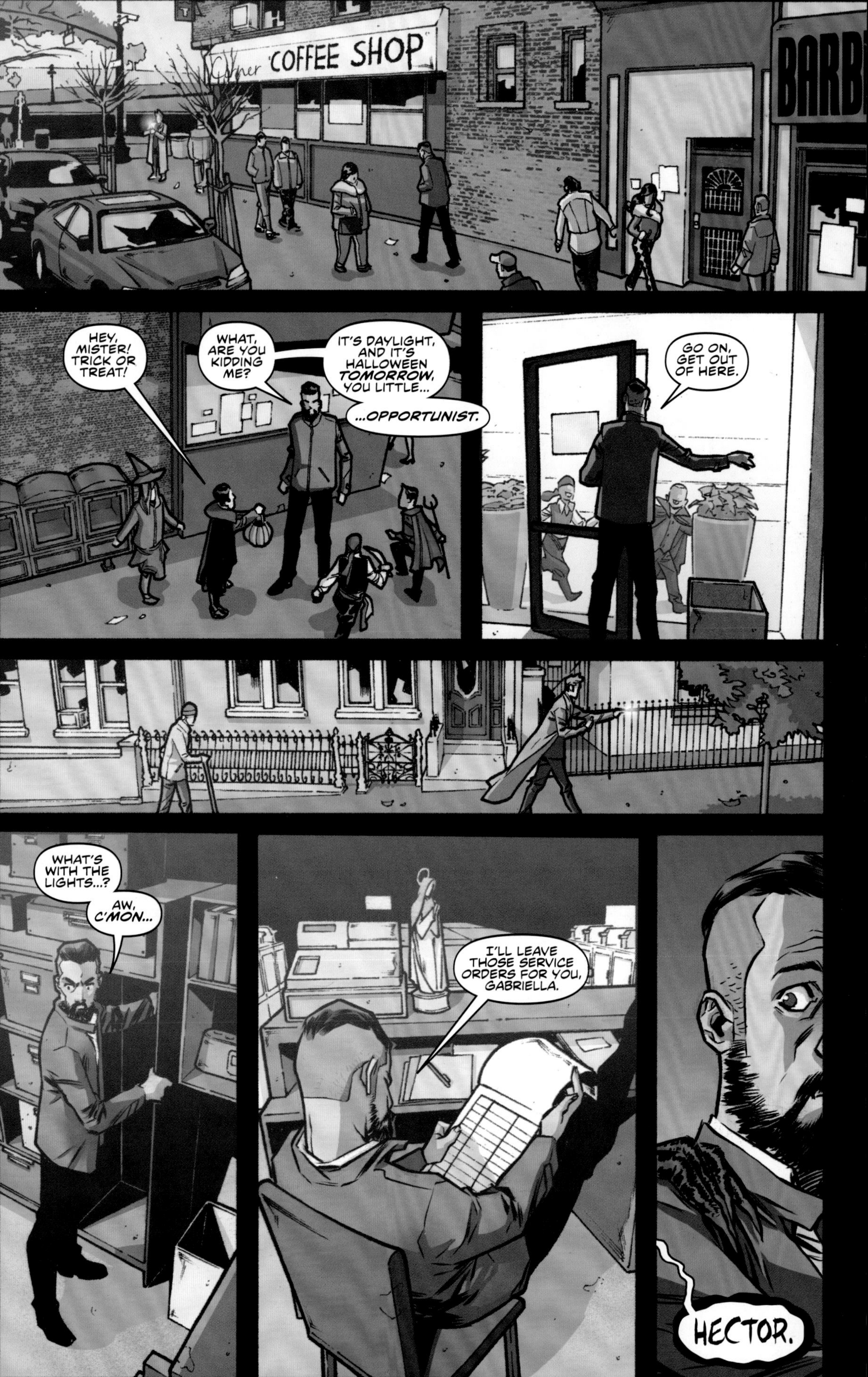

Corner COFFEE SHOP
BARB
HEY, MISTER! TRICK OR TREAT!
WHAT, ARE YOU KIDDING ME?
IT'S DAYLIGHT, AND IT'S HALLOWEEN *TOMORROW*, YOU LITTLE...
...OPPORTUNIST.
GO ON, GET OUT OF HERE.
WHAT'S WITH THE LIGHTS...?
AW, *C'MON*...
I'LL LEAVE THOSE SERVICE ORDERS FOR YOU, GABRIELLA.
HECTOR.

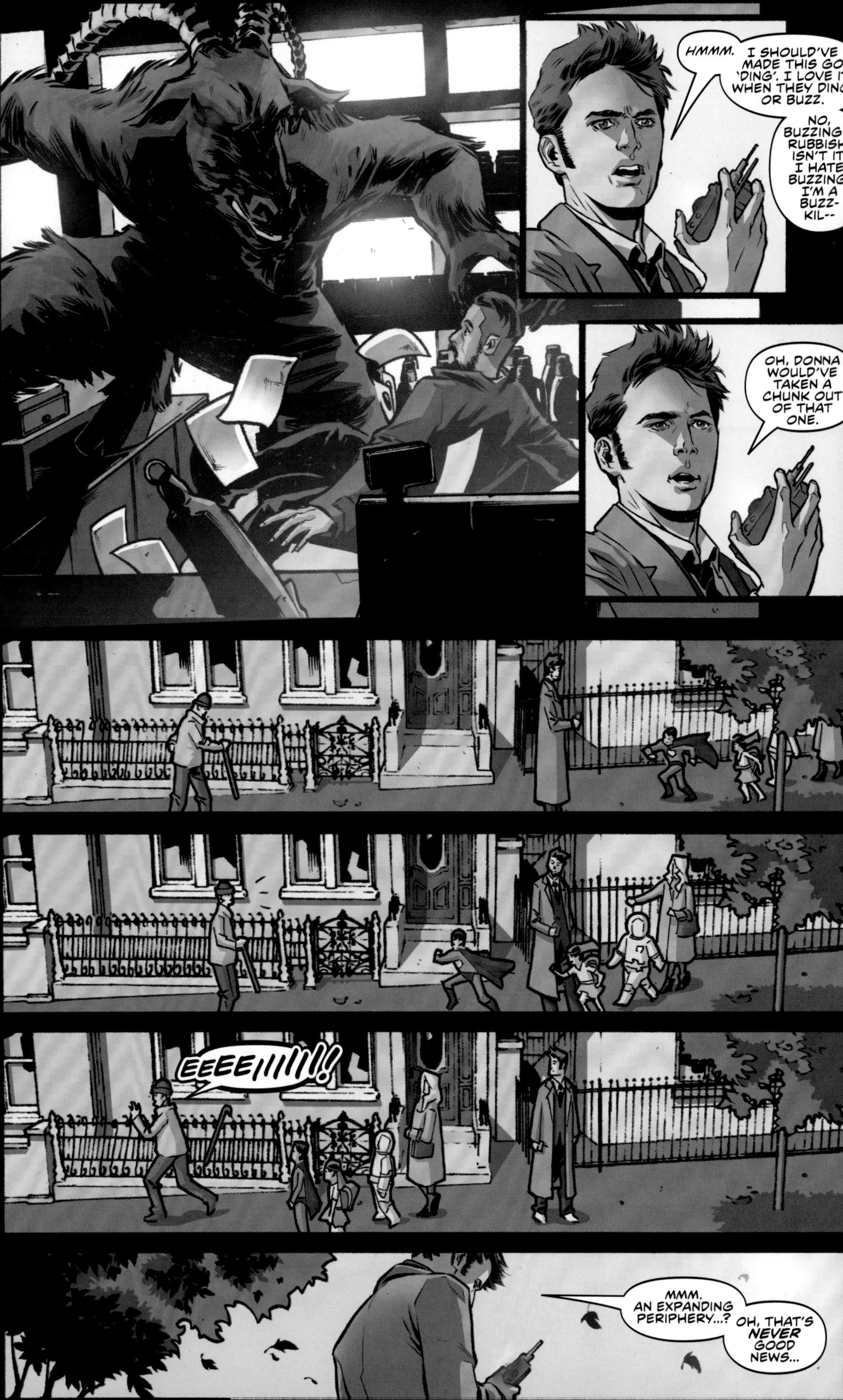

HMMM.
I SHOULD'VE MADE THIS GO 'DING'. I LOVE IT WHEN THEY DING OR BUZZ.
NO, BUZZING RUBBISH ISN'T IT I HATE BUZZING I'M A BUZZ-KIL--
OH, DONNA WOULD'VE TAKEN A CHUNK OUT OF THAT ONE.
EEEE!!!!!!!!
MMM. AN EXPANDING PERIPHERY...?
OH, THAT'S *NEVER* GOOD NEWS...

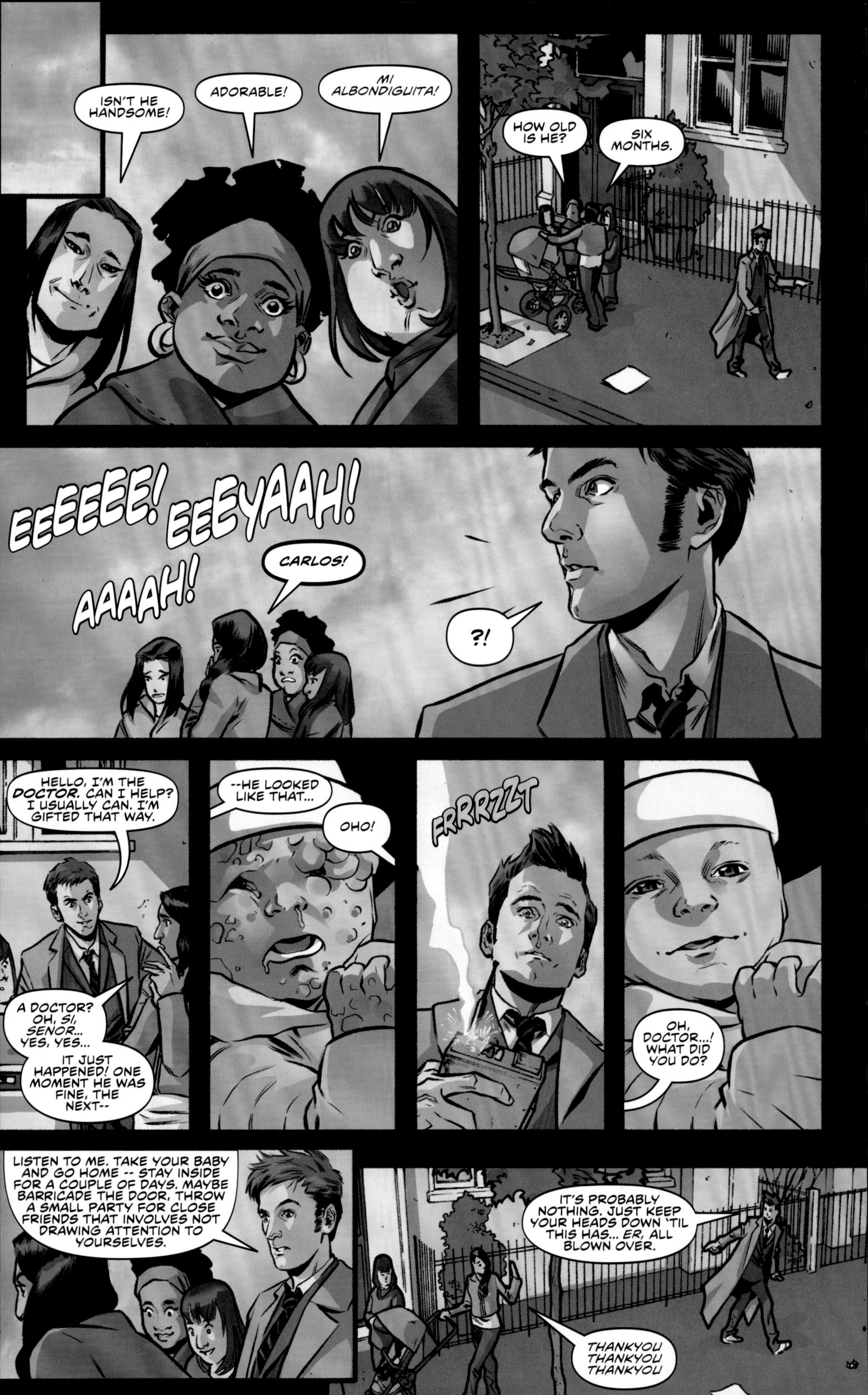
ISN'T HE HANDSOME!
ADORABLE!
MI ALBONDIGUITA!
HOW OLD IS HE?
SIX MONTHS.
EEEEEE!
EEEYAAH!
AAAAH!
CARLOS!
?!
HELLO, I'M THE DOCTOR. CAN I HELP? I USUALLY CAN. I'M GIFTED THAT WAY.
A DOCTOR? OH, SI, SENOR... YES, YES...
IT JUST HAPPENED! ONE MOMENT HE WAS FINE, THE NEXT--
--HE LOOKED LIKE THAT...
OHO!
FRRRZZT
OH, DOCTOR...! WHAT DID YOU DO?
LISTEN TO ME. TAKE YOUR BABY AND GO HOME -- STAY INSIDE FOR A COUPLE OF DAYS. MAYBE BARRICADE THE DOOR, THROW A SMALL PARTY FOR CLOSE FRIENDS THAT INVOLVES NOT DRAWING ATTENTION TO YOURSELVES.
IT'S PROBABLY NOTHING. JUST KEEP YOUR HEADS DOWN 'TIL THIS HAS... ER, ALL BLOWN OVER.
THANKYOU THANKYOU THANKYOU

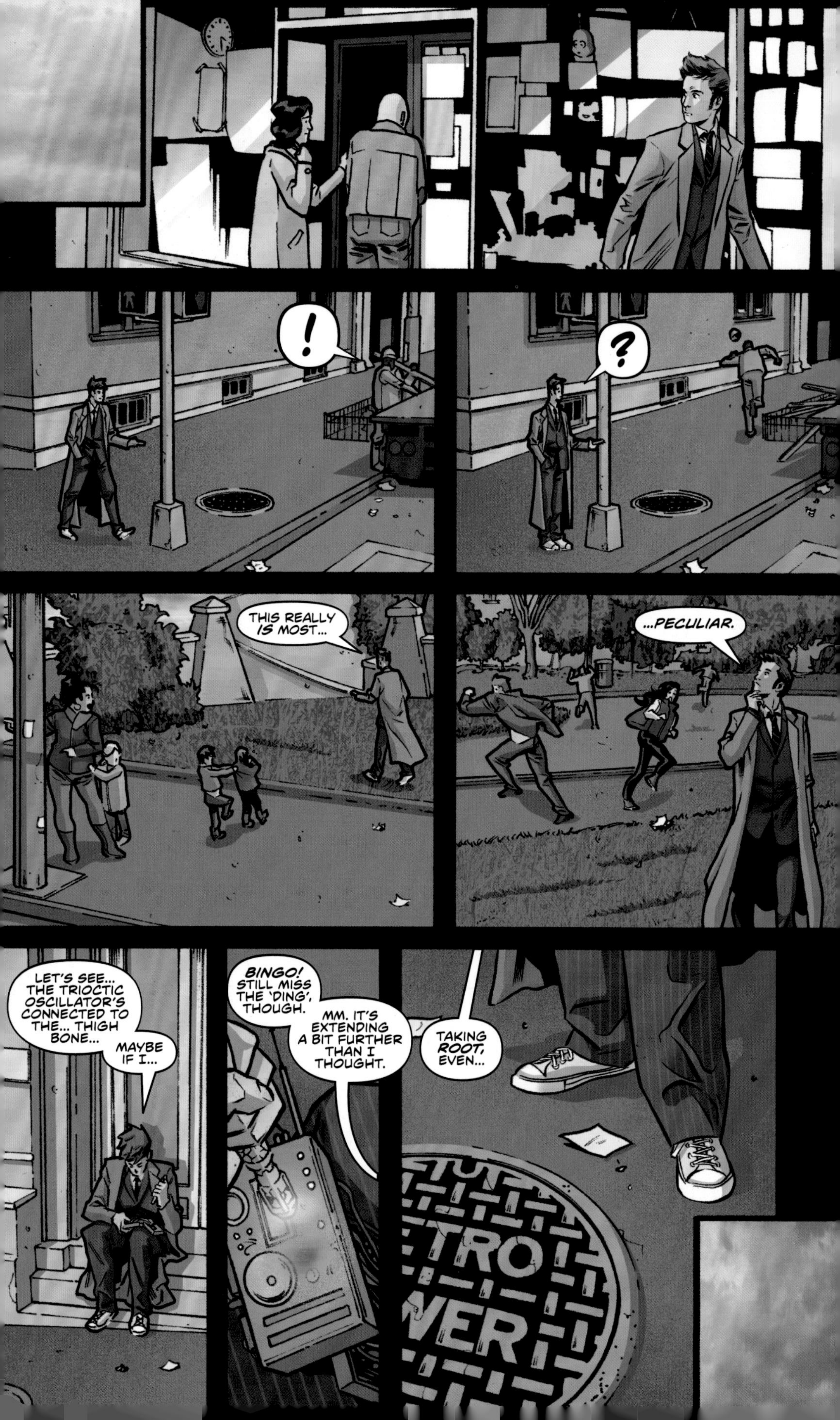
!
?
THIS REALLY IS MOST...
...PECULIAR.
LET'S SEE... THE TRIOCTIC OSCILLATOR'S CONNECTED TO THE... THIGH BONE...
MAYBE IF I...
BINGO! STILL MISS THE 'DING', THOUGH.
MM. IT'S EXTENDING A BIT FURTHER THAN I THOUGHT.
TAKING ROOT, EVEN...

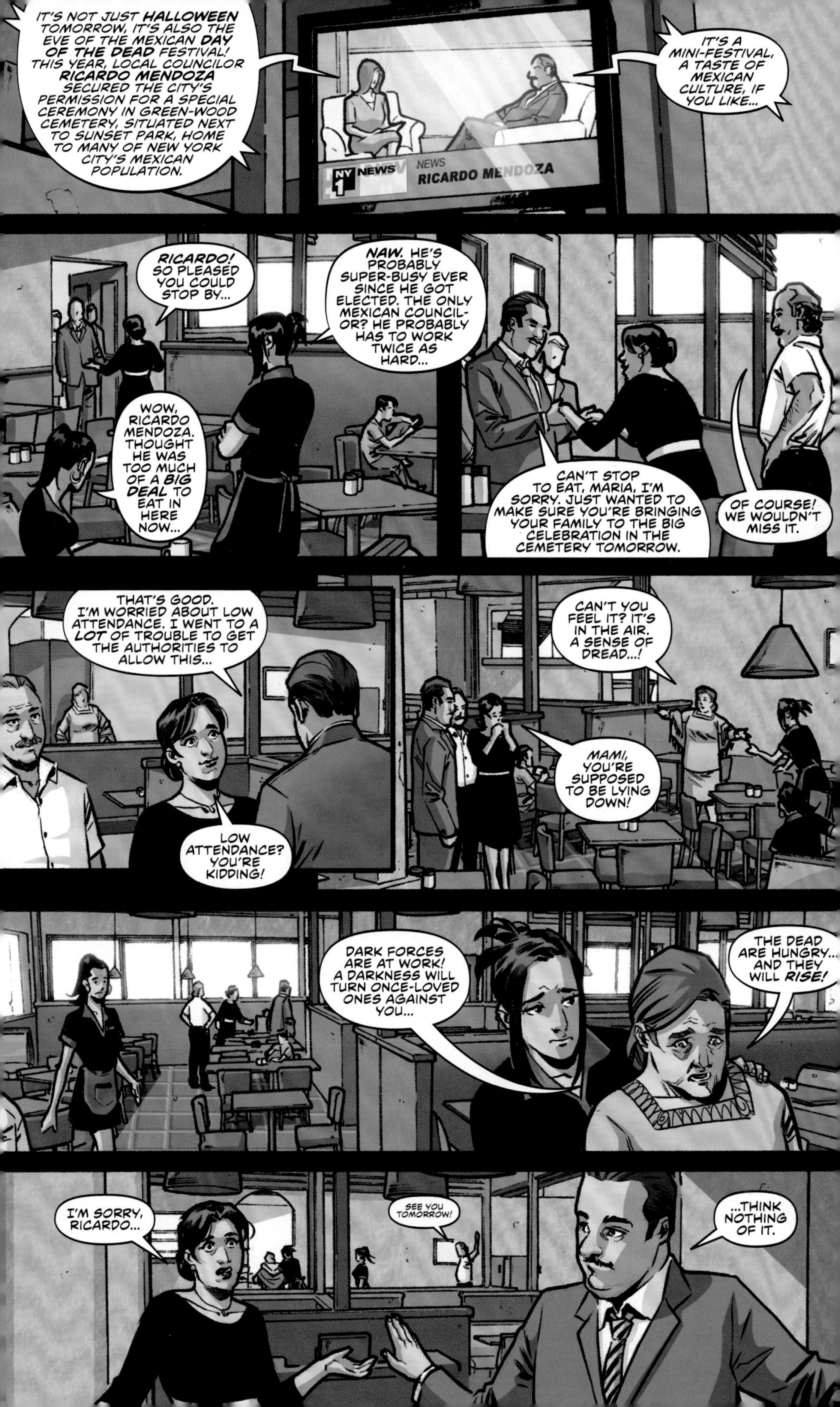
IT'S NOT JUST HALLOWEEN TOMORROW, IT'S ALSO THE EVE OF THE MEXICAN DAY OF THE DEAD FESTIVAL! THIS YEAR, LOCAL COUNCILOR RICARDO MENDOZA SECURED THE CITY'S PERMISSION FOR A SPECIAL CEREMONY IN GREEN-WOOD CEMETERY, SITUATED NEXT TO SUNSET PARK, HOME TO MANY OF NEW YORK CITY'S MEXICAN POPULATION.
NY 1 NEWS
NEWS
RICARDO MENDOZA
IT'S A MINI-FESTIVAL, A TASTE OF MEXICAN CULTURE, IF YOU LIKE...
RICARDO! SO PLEASED YOU COULD STOP BY...
WOW, RICARDO MENDOZA. THOUGHT HE WAS TOO MUCH OF A BIG DEAL TO EAT IN HERE NOW...
NAW. HE'S PROBABLY SUPER-BUSY EVER SINCE HE GOT ELECTED. THE ONLY MEXICAN COUNCIL-OR? HE PROBABLY HAS TO WORK TWICE AS HARD...
CAN'T STOP TO EAT, MARIA, I'M SORRY. JUST WANTED TO MAKE SURE YOU'RE BRINGING YOUR FAMILY TO THE BIG CELEBRATION IN THE CEMETERY TOMORROW.
OF COURSE! WE WOULDN'T MISS IT.
THAT'S GOOD. I'M WORRIED ABOUT LOW ATTENDANCE. I WENT TO A LOT OF TROUBLE TO GET THE AUTHORITIES TO ALLOW THIS...
LOW ATTENDANCE? YOU'RE KIDDING!
CAN'T YOU FEEL IT? IT'S IN THE AIR. A SENSE OF DREAD...!
MAMI, YOU'RE SUPPOSED TO BE LYING DOWN!
DARK FORCES ARE AT WORK! A DARKNESS WILL TURN ONCE-LOVED ONES AGAINST YOU...
THE DEAD ARE HUNGRY... AND THEY WILL RISE!
I'M SORRY, RICARDO...
SEE YOU TOMORROW!
...THINK NOTHING OF IT.

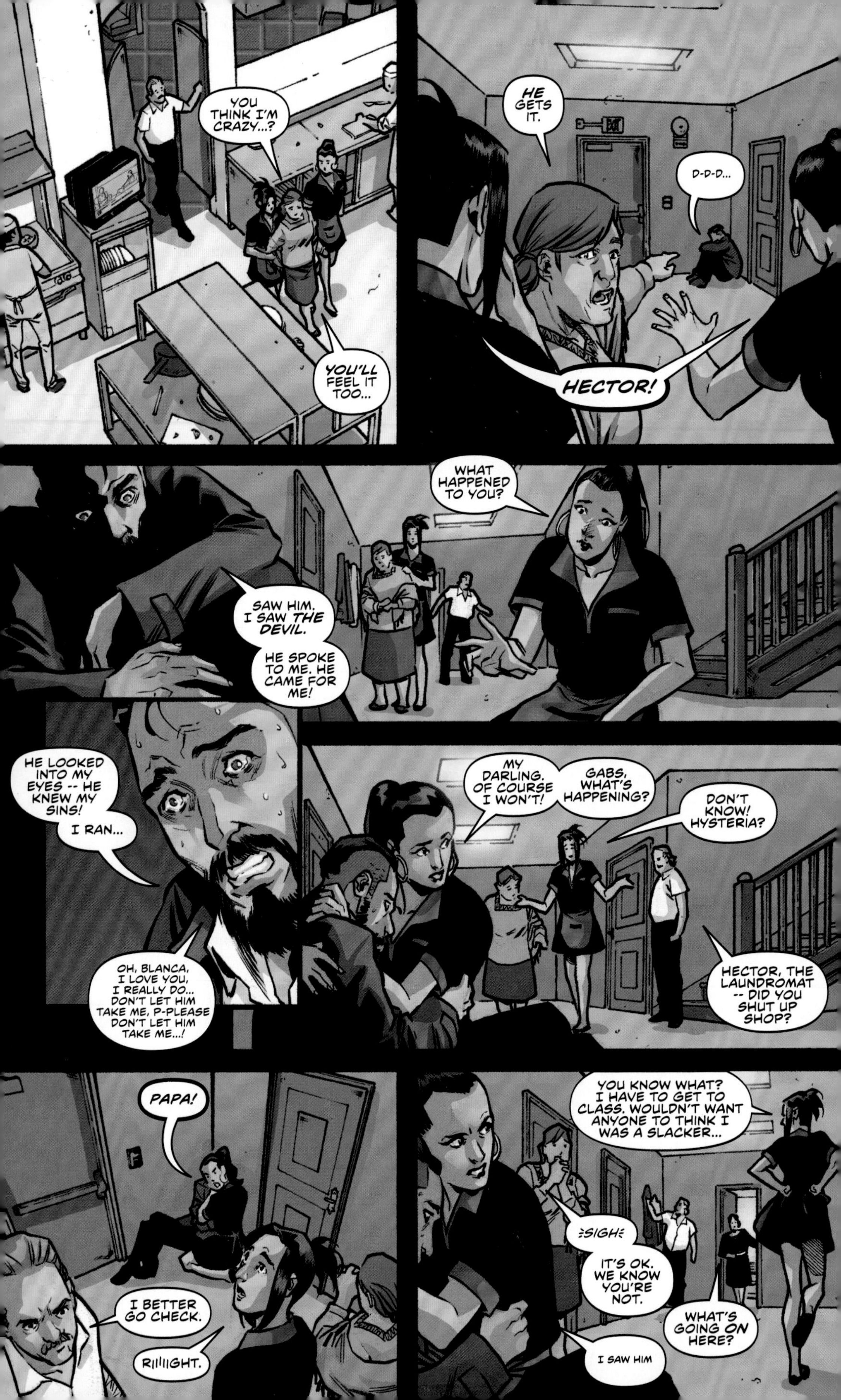

YOU THINK I'M CRAZY...?
YOU'LL FEEL IT TOO...
HE GETS IT.
D-D-D...
HECTOR!
WHAT HAPPENED TO YOU?
SAW HIM. I SAW THE DEVIL.
HE SPOKE TO ME. HE CAME FOR ME!
HE LOOKED INTO MY EYES -- HE KNEW MY SINS!
I RAN...
OH, BLANCA, I LOVE YOU, I REALLY DO... DON'T LET HIM TAKE ME, P-PLEASE DON'T LET HIM TAKE ME...!
MY DARLING. OF COURSE I WON'T!
GABS, WHAT'S HAPPENING?
DON'T KNOW! HYSTERIA?
HECTOR, THE LAUNDROMAT -- DID YOU SHUT UP SHOP?
PAPA!
I BETTER GO CHECK.
RIIIIGHT.
YOU KNOW WHAT? I HAVE TO GET TO CLASS. WOULDN'T WANT ANYONE TO THINK I WAS A SLACKER...
SIGH
IT'S OK. WE KNOW YOU'RE NOT.
I SAW HIM
WHAT'S GOING ON HERE?

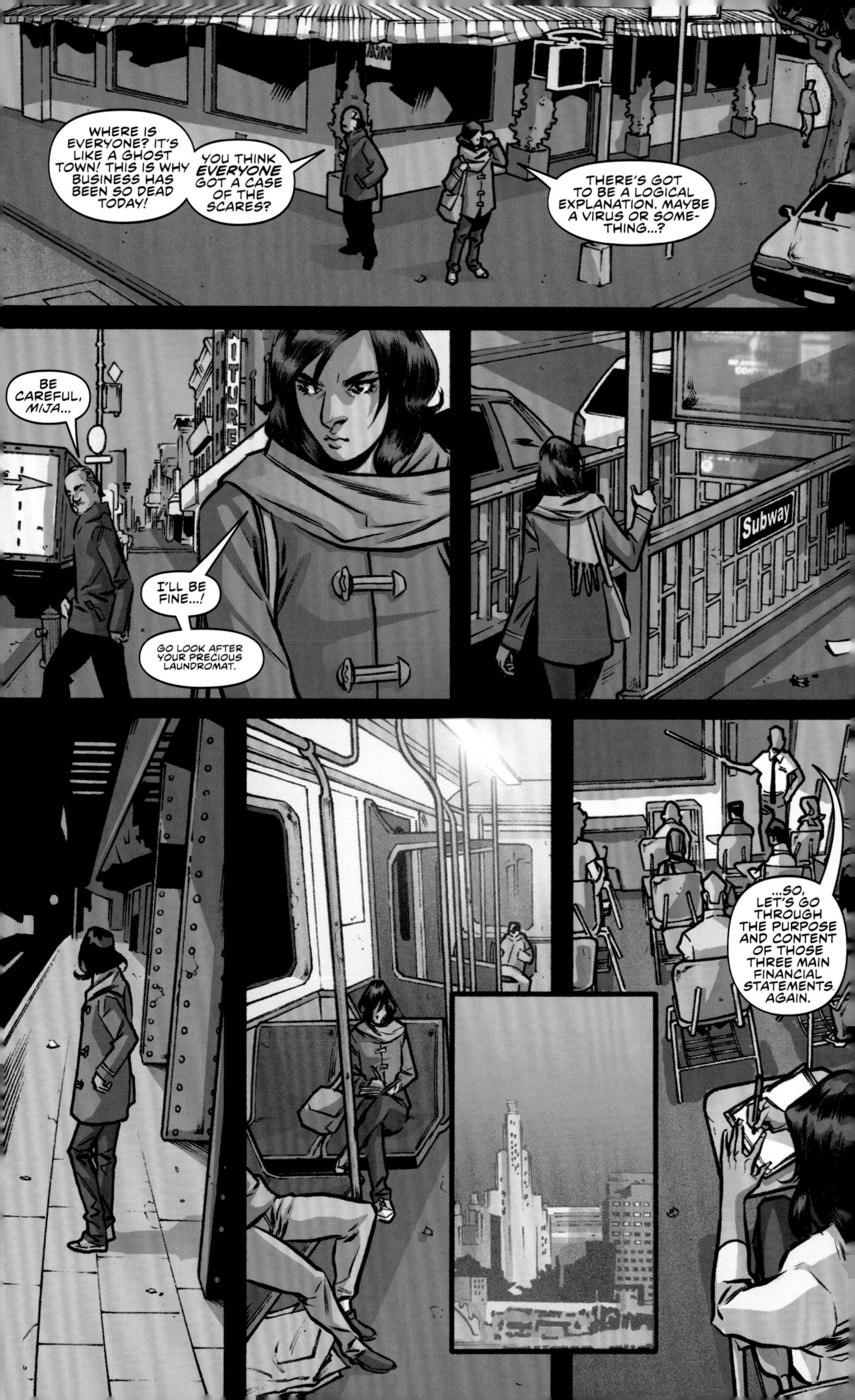
WHERE IS EVERYONE? IT'S LIKE A GHOST TOWN! THIS IS WHY BUSINESS HAS BEEN SO DEAD TODAY!
YOU THINK EVERYONE GOT A CASE OF THE SCARES?
THERE'S GOT TO BE A LOGICAL EXPLANATION. MAYBE A VIRUS OR SOME-THING...?
BE CAREFUL, MIJA...
I'LL BE FINE...!
GO LOOK AFTER YOUR PRECIOUS LAUNDROMAT.
Subway
...SO, LET'S GO THROUGH THE PURPOSE AND CONTENT OF THOSE THREE MAIN FINANCIAL STATEMENTS AGAIN.

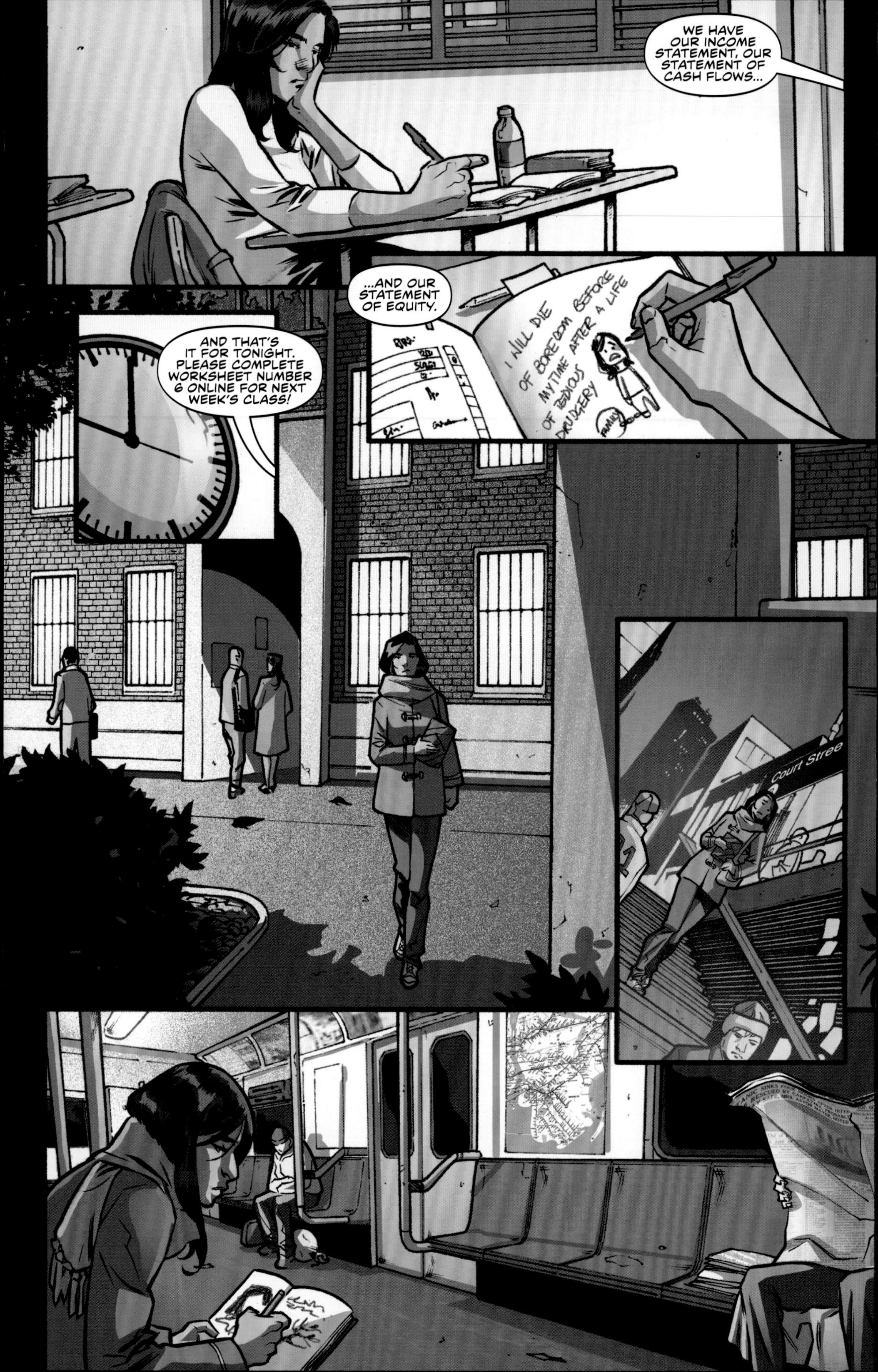
WE HAVE OUR INCOME STATEMENT, OUR STATEMENT OF CASH FLOWS...
...AND OUR STATEMENT OF EQUITY.
I WILL DIE OF BOREDOM BEFORE MY TIME AFTER A LIFE OF TEDIOUS DRUDGERY
AND THAT'S IT FOR TONIGHT. PLEASE COMPLETE WORKSHEET NUMBER 6 ONLINE FOR NEXT WEEK'S CLASS!
Court Stree

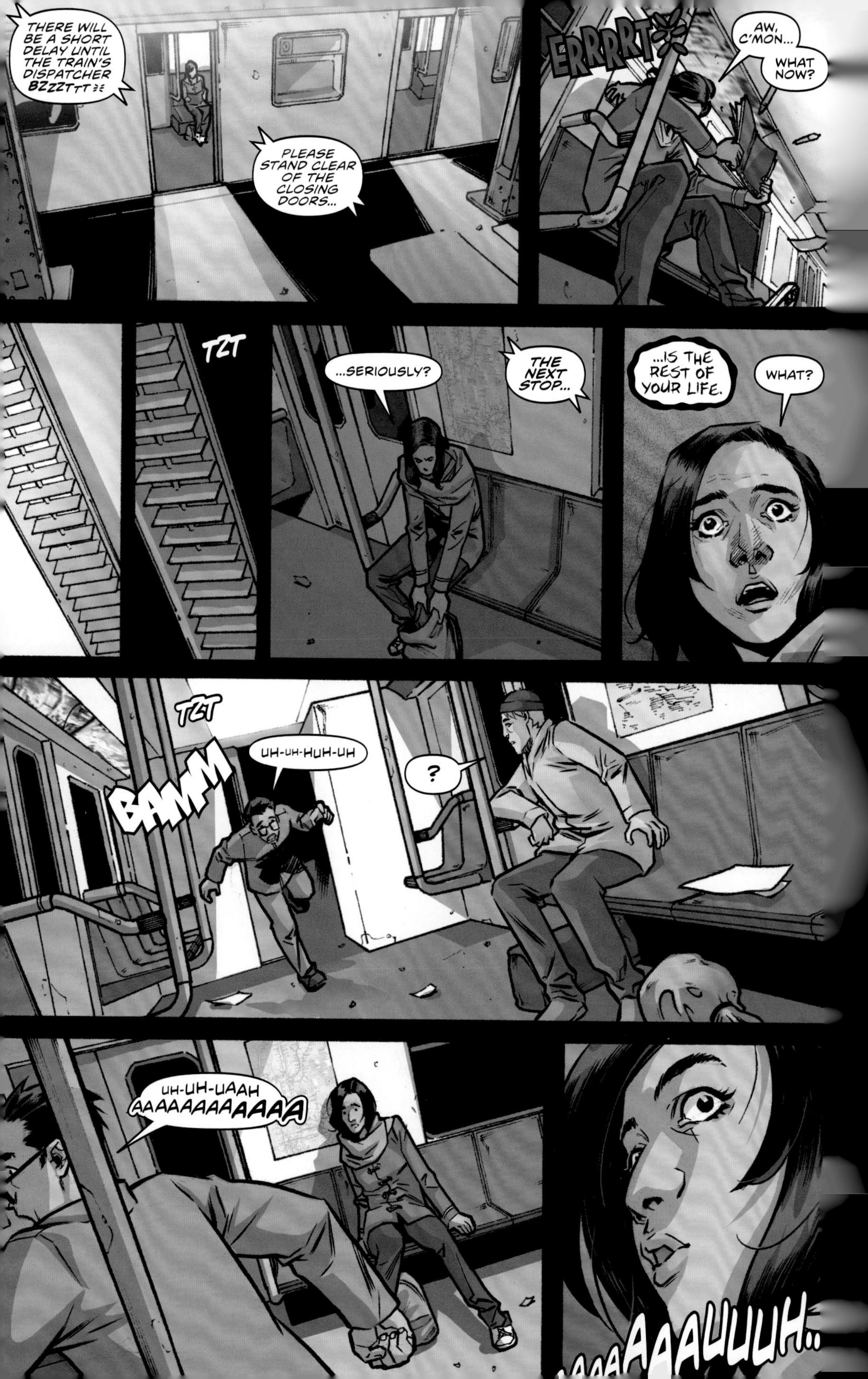
THERE WILL BE A SHORT DELAY UNTIL THE TRAIN'S DISPATCHER BZZZTTT
PLEASE STAND CLEAR OF THE CLOSING DOORS...
ERRRRT
AW, C'MON...
WHAT NOW?
TZT
...SERIOUSLY?
THE NEXT STOP...
...IS THE REST OF YOUR LIFE.
WHAT?
TZT
BAMM
UH-UH-HUH-UH
?
UH-UH-UAAH AAAAAAAAAAAA
AAAAAAAUUUH..

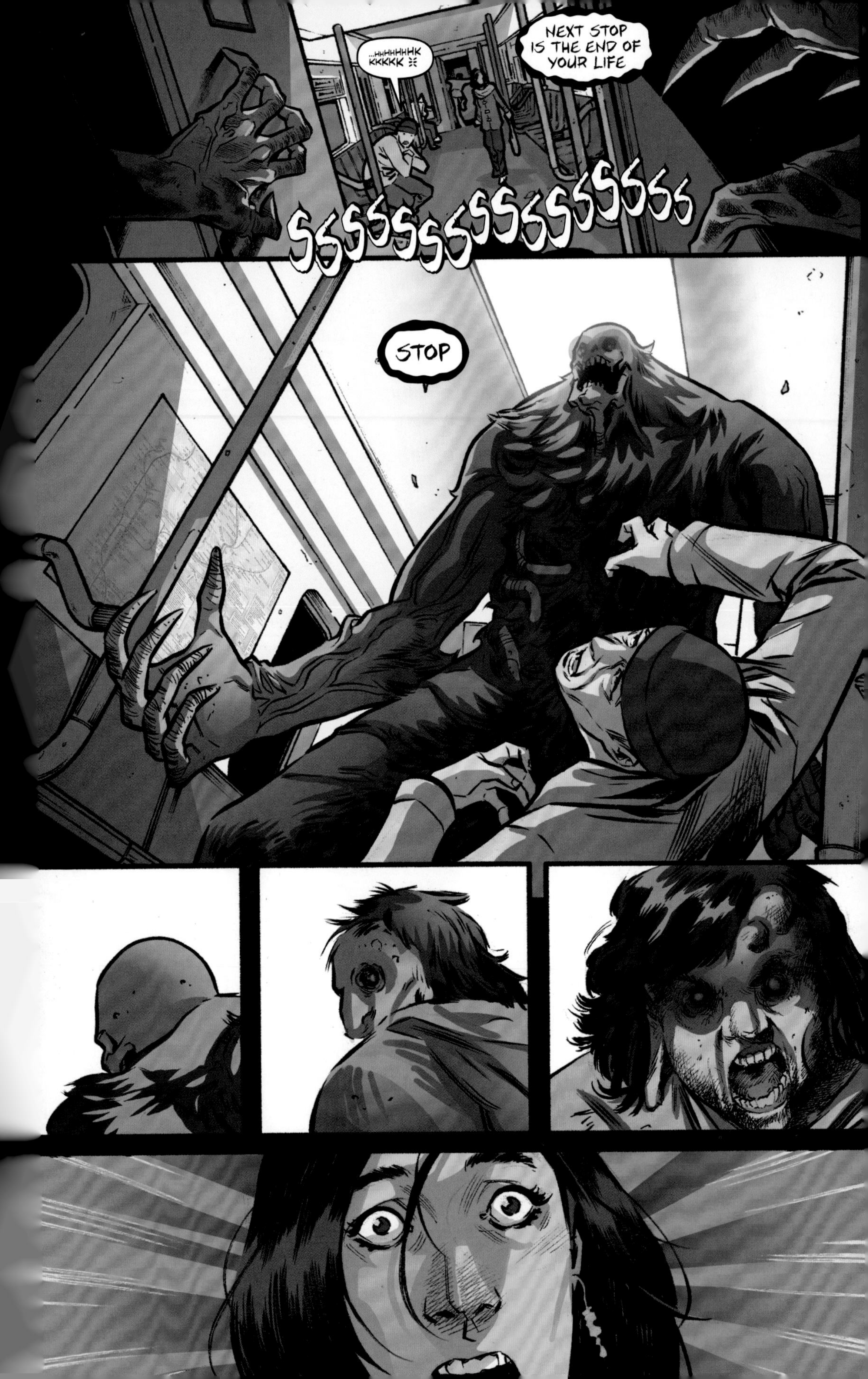

...HHHHHHHK KKKKK
NEXT STOP IS THE END OF YOUR LIFE
SSSSSSSSSSSSSSSSSSSS
STOP

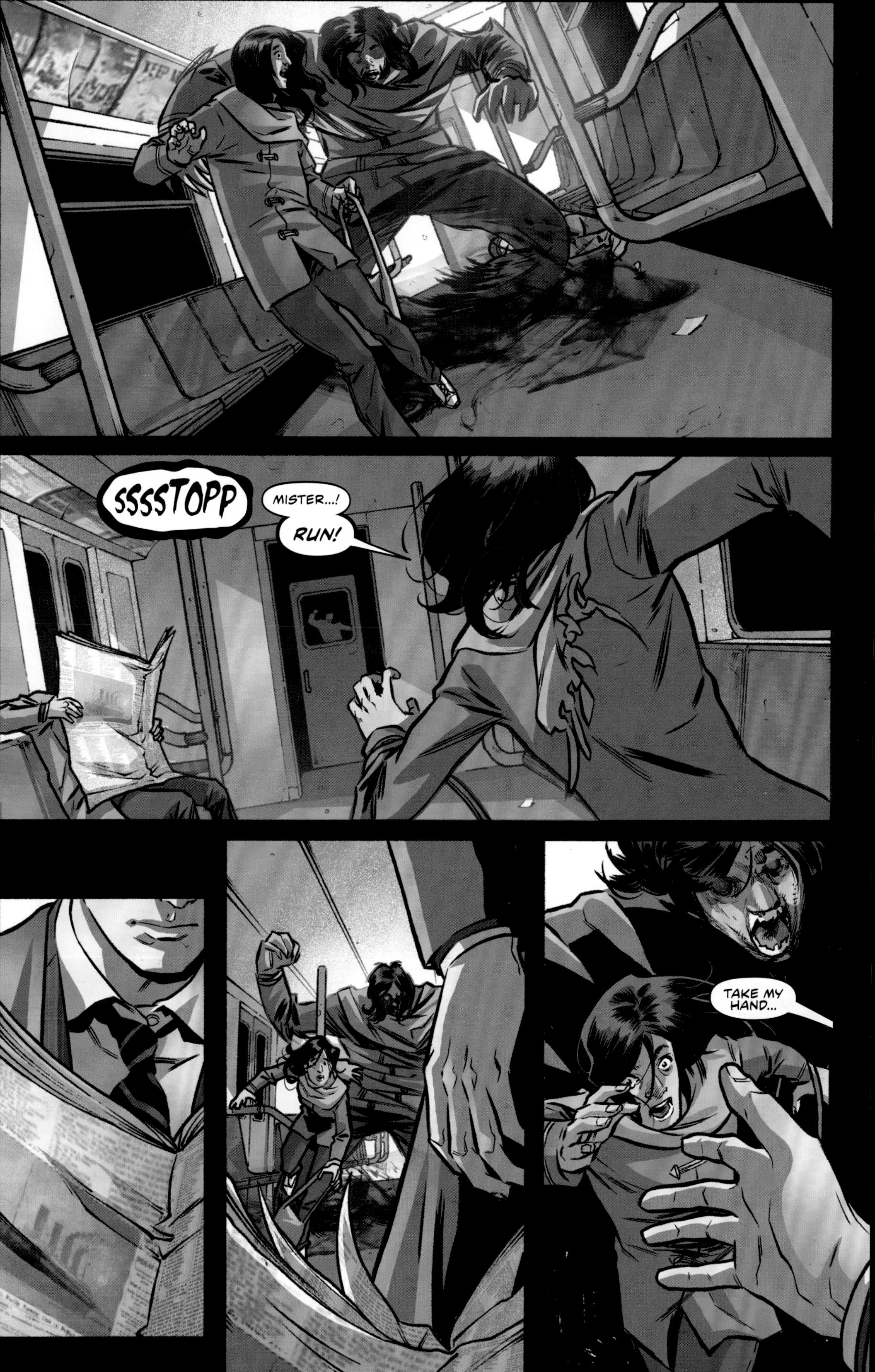
SSSSTOPP
MISTER...!
RUN!
TAKE MY HAND...

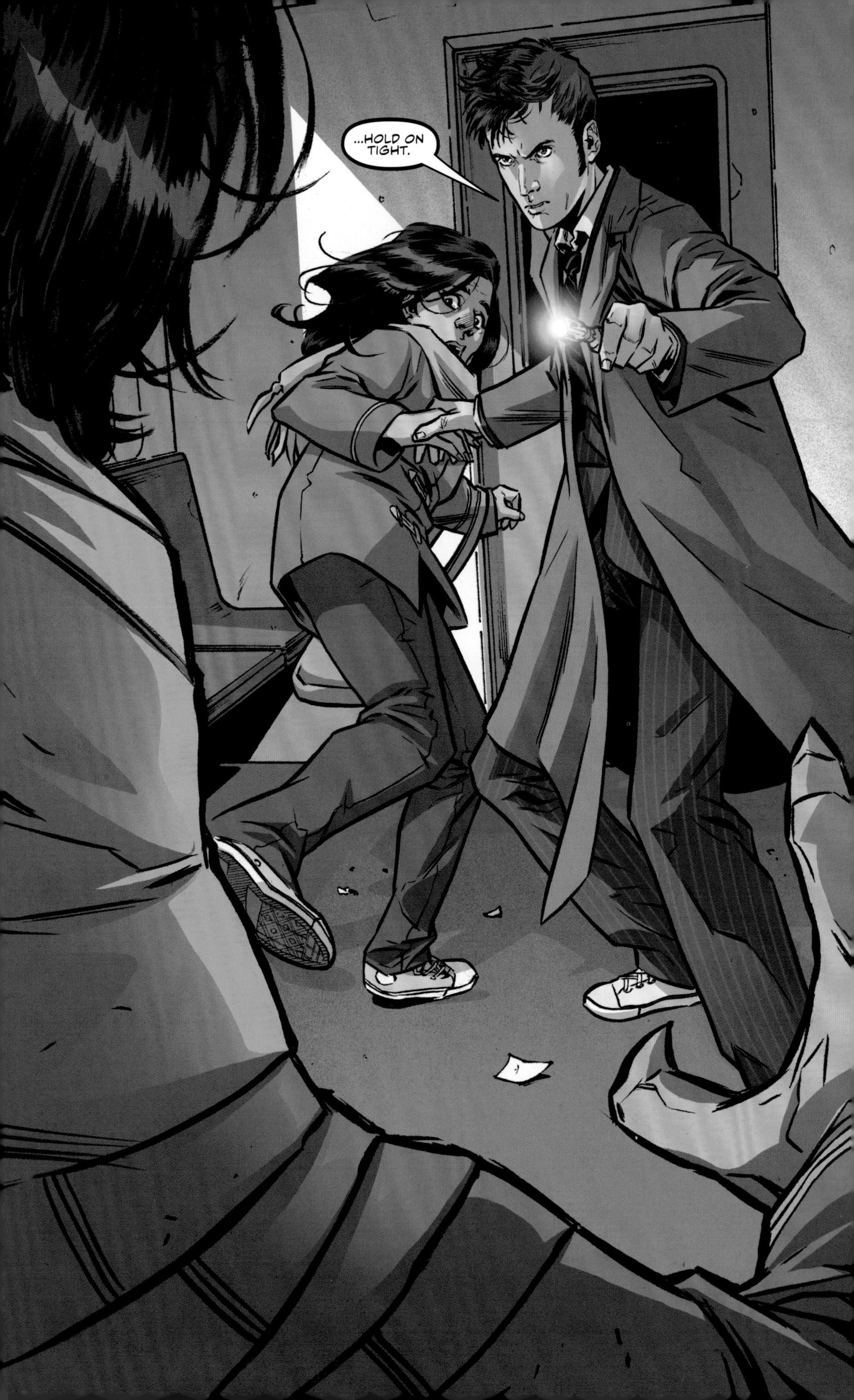
...HOLD ON TIGHT.

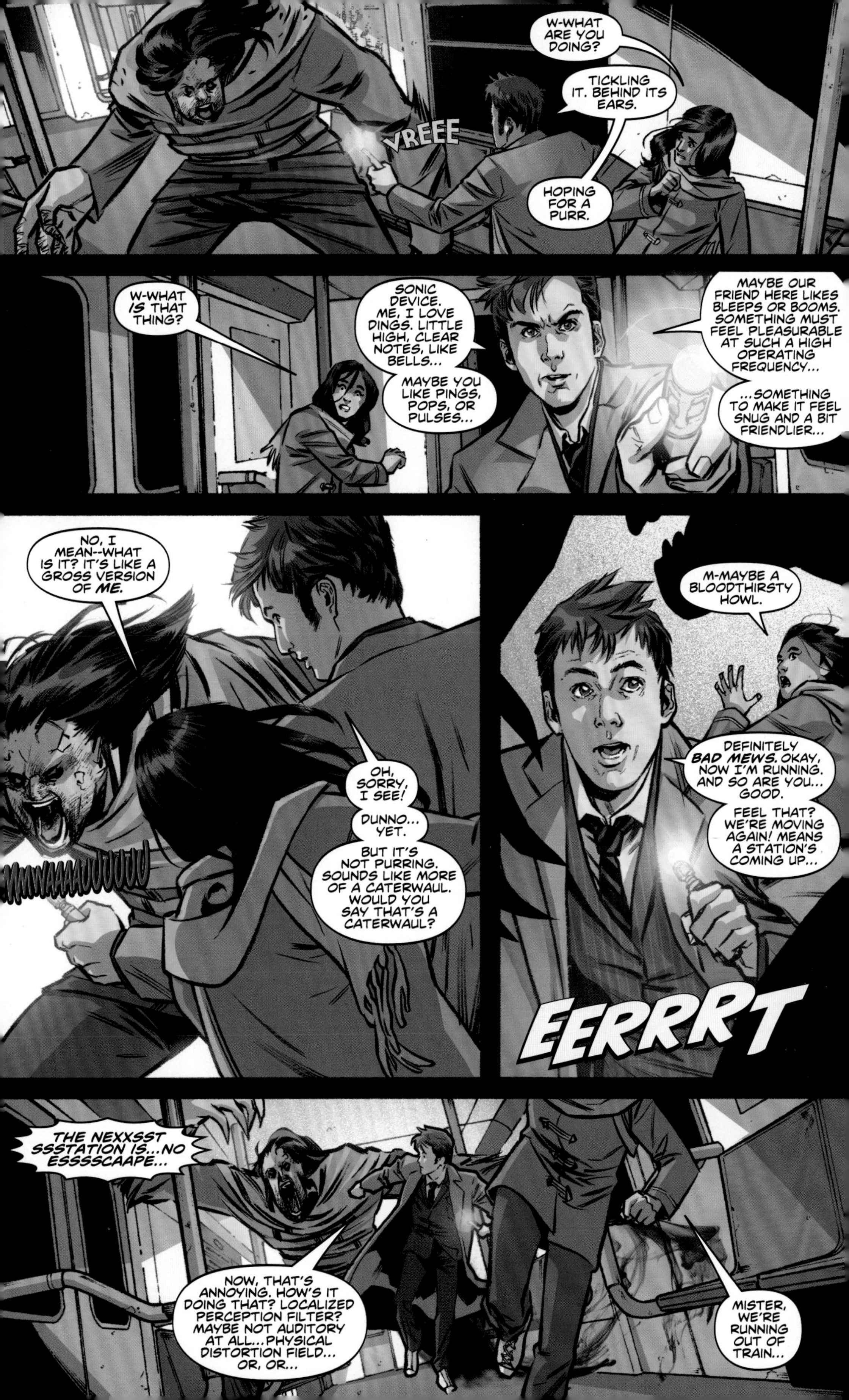
W-WHAT ARE YOU DOING?
TICKLING IT. BEHIND ITS EARS.
VREEE
HOPING FOR A PURR.
W-WHAT *IS* THAT THING?
SONIC DEVICE. ME, I LOVE DINGS. LITTLE HIGH, CLEAR NOTES, LIKE BELLS...
MAYBE YOU LIKE PINGS, POPS, OR PULSES...
MAYBE OUR FRIEND HERE LIKES BLEEPS OR BOOMS. SOMETHING MUST FEEL PLEASURABLE AT SUCH A HIGH OPERATING FREQUENCY...
...SOMETHING TO MAKE IT FEEL SNUG AND A BIT FRIENDLIER...
NO, I MEAN--WHAT IS IT? IT'S LIKE A GROSS VERSION OF **ME**.
OH, SORRY, I SEE!
DUNNO... YET.
BUT IT'S NOT PURRING. SOUNDS LIKE MORE OF A CATERWAUL. WOULD YOU SAY THAT'S A CATERWAUL?
MMWAAAAUUUUU
M-MAYBE A BLOODTHIRSTY HOWL.
DEFINITELY ***BAD MEWS.*** OKAY, NOW I'M RUNNING. AND SO ARE YOU... GOOD.
FEEL THAT? WE'RE MOVING AGAIN! MEANS A STATION'S COMING UP...
EERRRT
THE NEXXSST SSSTATION IS...NO ESSSSCAAPE...
NOW, THAT'S ANNOYING. HOW'S IT DOING THAT? LOCALIZED PERCEPTION FILTER? MAYBE NOT AUDITORY AT ALL...PHYSICAL DISTORTION FIELD... OR, OR...
MISTER, WE'RE RUNNING OUT OF TRAIN...

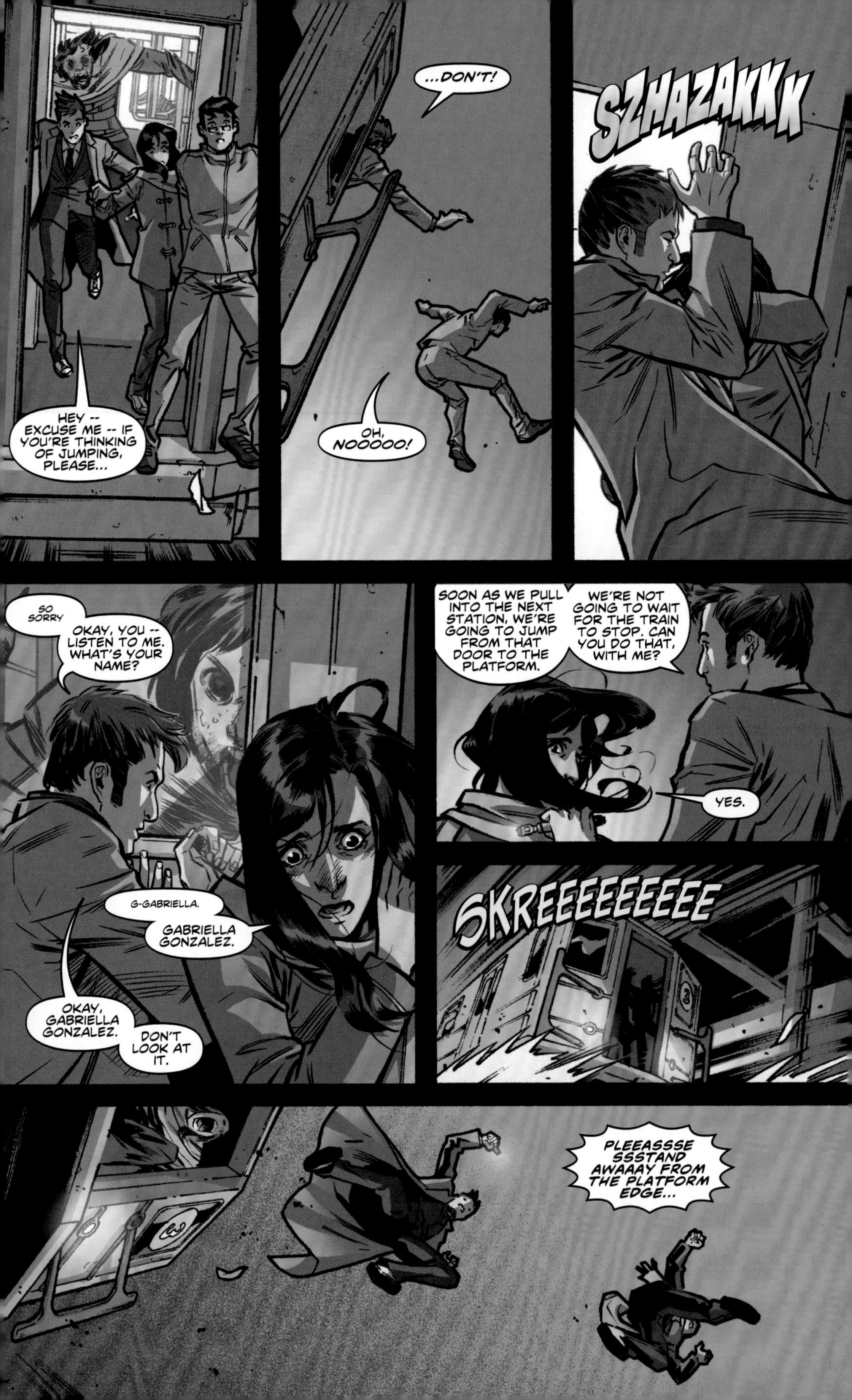
HEY -- EXCUSE ME -- IF YOU'RE THINKING OF JUMPING, PLEASE...
...DON'T!
OH, NOOOOO!
SZHAZAKKK
SO SORRY
OKAY, YOU -- LISTEN TO ME. WHAT'S YOUR NAME?
G-GABRIELLA.
GABRIELLA GONZALEZ.
OKAY, GABRIELLA GONZALEZ.
DON'T LOOK AT IT.
SOON AS WE PULL INTO THE NEXT STATION, WE'RE GOING TO JUMP FROM THAT DOOR TO THE PLATFORM.
WE'RE NOT GOING TO WAIT FOR THE TRAIN TO STOP. CAN YOU DO THAT, WITH ME?
YES.
SKREEEEEEEEE
PLEEASSSE SSSTAND AWAAAY FROM THE PLATFORM EDGE...

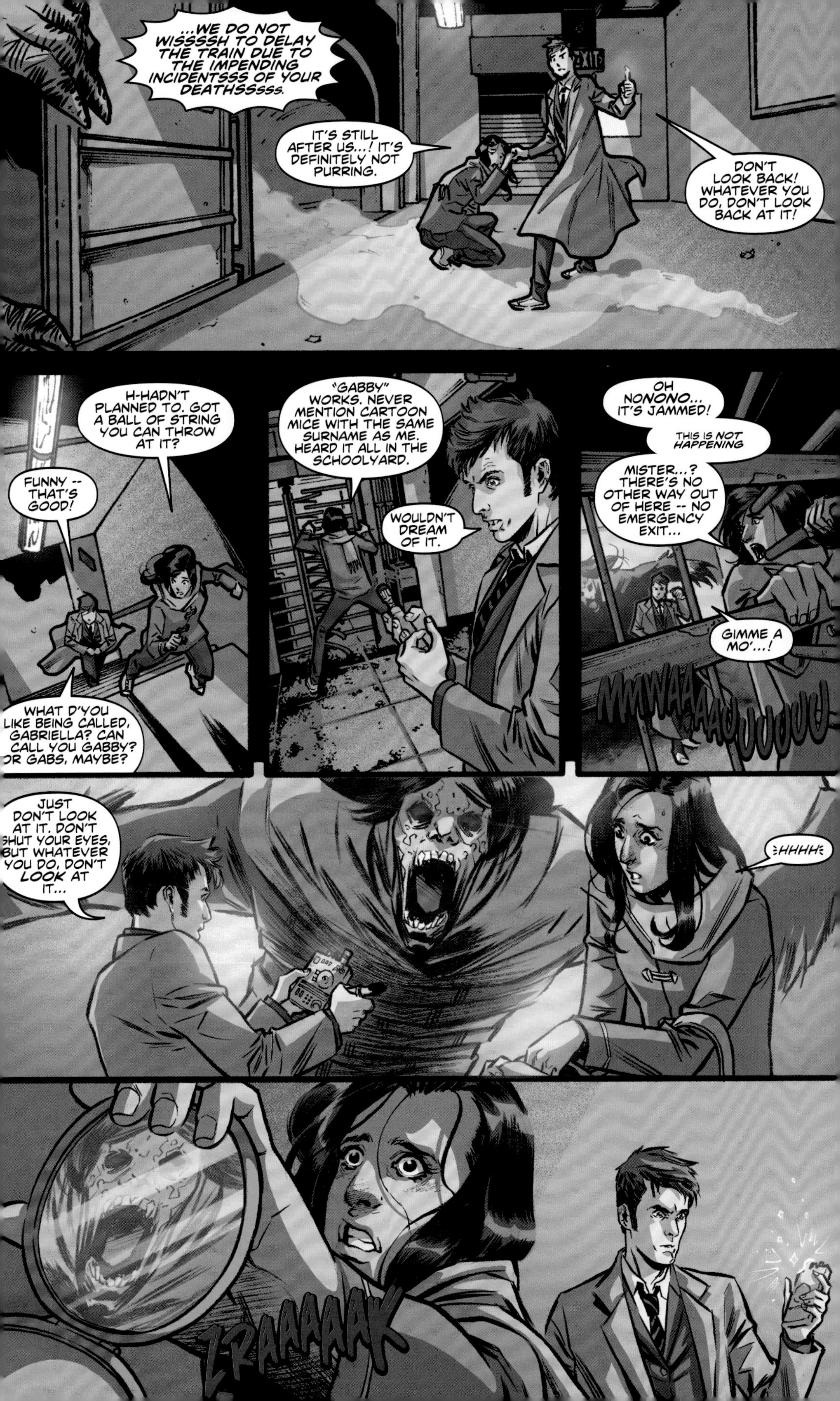
...WE DO NOT WISSSSH TO DELAY THE TRAIN DUE TO THE IMPENDING INCIDENTSSS OF YOUR DEATHSSSSS.
IT'S STILL AFTER US...! IT'S DEFINITELY NOT PURRING.
DON'T LOOK BACK! WHATEVER YOU DO, DON'T LOOK BACK AT IT!
WHAT D'YOU LIKE BEING CALLED, GABRIELLA? CAN I CALL YOU GABBY? OR GABS, MAYBE?
FUNNY -- THAT'S GOOD!
H-HADN'T PLANNED TO. GOT A BALL OF STRING YOU CAN THROW AT IT?
"GABBY" WORKS. NEVER MENTION CARTOON MICE WITH THE SAME SURNAME AS ME. HEARD IT ALL IN THE SCHOOLYARD.
WOULDN'T DREAM OF IT.
OH NONONO... IT'S JAMMED!
THIS IS NOT HAPPENING
MISTER...? THERE'S NO OTHER WAY OUT OF HERE -- NO EMERGENCY EXIT...
GIMME A MO'...!
MMWAAAAAUUUUUU
JUST DON'T LOOK AT IT. DON'T SHUT YOUR EYES, BUT WHATEVER YOU DO, DON'T LOOK AT IT...
HHHH
ZRAAAAAK

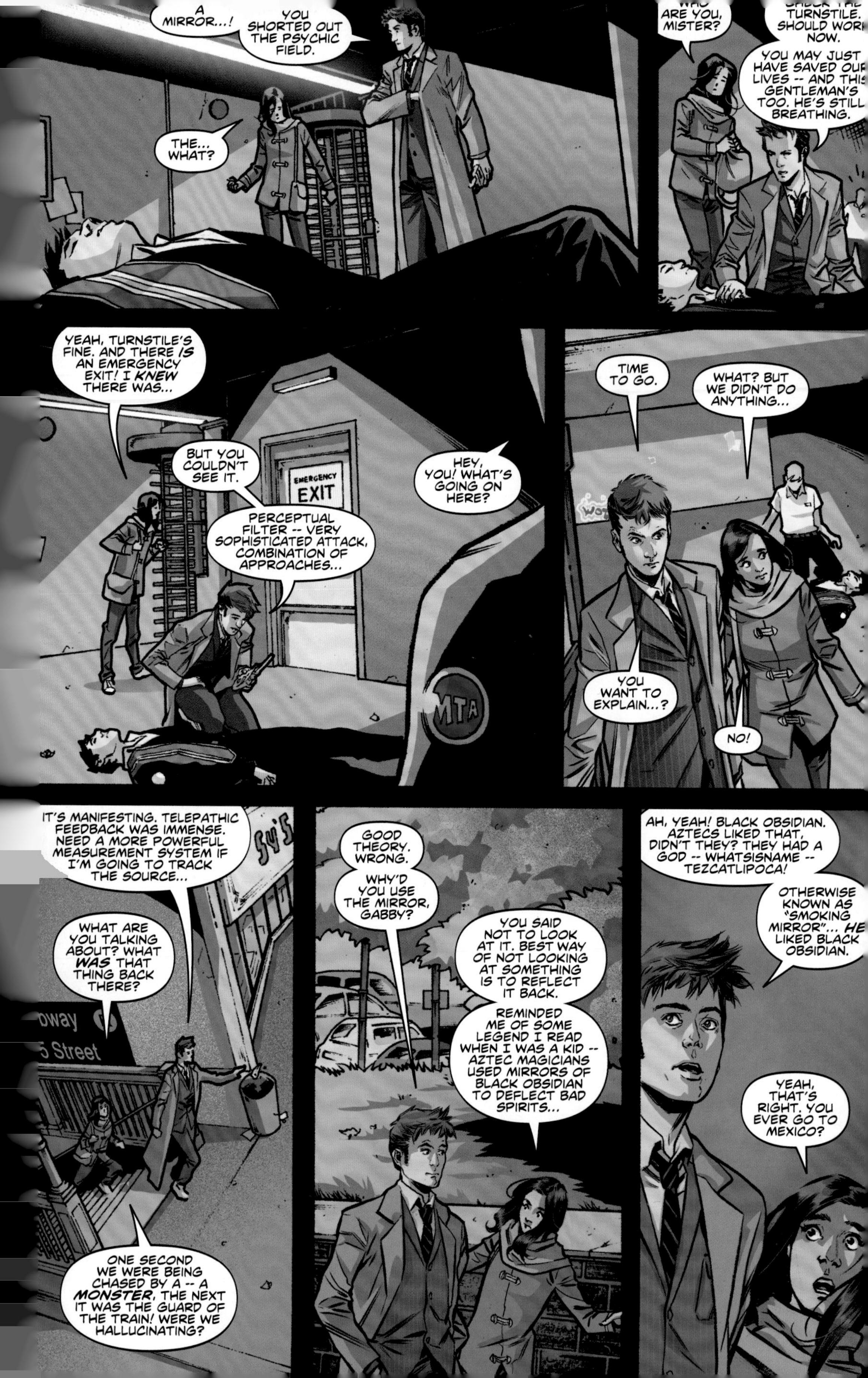
A MIRROR...!
YOU SHORTED OUT THE PSYCHIC FIELD.
THE... WHAT?
ARE YOU, MISTER?
TURNSTILE. SHOULD WOR NOW.
YOU MAY JUST HAVE SAVED OU LIVES -- AND THIS GENTLEMAN'S TOO. HE'S STILL BREATHING.
YEAH, TURNSTILE'S FINE. AND THERE *IS* AN EMERGENCY EXIT! I *KNEW* THERE WAS...
BUT YOU COULDN'T SEE IT.
EMERGENCY EXIT
PERCEPTUAL FILTER -- VERY SOPHISTICATED ATTACK, COMBINATION OF APPROACHES...
HEY, YOU! WHAT'S GOING ON HERE?
MTA
TIME TO GO.
WHAT? BUT WE DIDN'T DO ANYTHING...
YOU WANT TO EXPLAIN...?
NO!
IT'S MANIFESTING. TELEPATHIC FEEDBACK WAS IMMENSE. NEED A MORE POWERFUL MEASUREMENT SYSTEM IF I'M GOING TO TRACK THE SOURCE...
WHAT ARE YOU TALKING ABOUT? WHAT *WAS* THAT THING BACK THERE?
oway
5 Street
ONE SECOND WE WERE BEING CHASED BY A -- A *MONSTER*, THE NEXT IT WAS THE GUARD OF THE TRAIN! WERE WE HALLUCINATING?
GOOD THEORY. WRONG.
WHY'D YOU USE THE MIRROR, GABBY?
YOU SAID NOT TO LOOK AT IT. BEST WAY OF NOT LOOKING AT SOMETHING IS TO REFLECT IT BACK.
REMINDED ME OF SOME LEGEND I READ WHEN I WAS A KID -- AZTEC MAGICIANS USED MIRRORS OF BLACK OBSIDIAN TO DEFLECT BAD SPIRITS...
AH, YEAH! BLACK OBSIDIAN. AZTECS LIKED THAT, DIDN'T THEY? THEY HAD A GOD -- WHATSISNAME -- TEZCATLIPOCA!
OTHERWISE KNOWN AS "SMOKING MIRROR"... *HE* LIKED BLACK OBSIDIAN.
YEAH, THAT'S RIGHT. YOU EVER GO TO MEXICO?

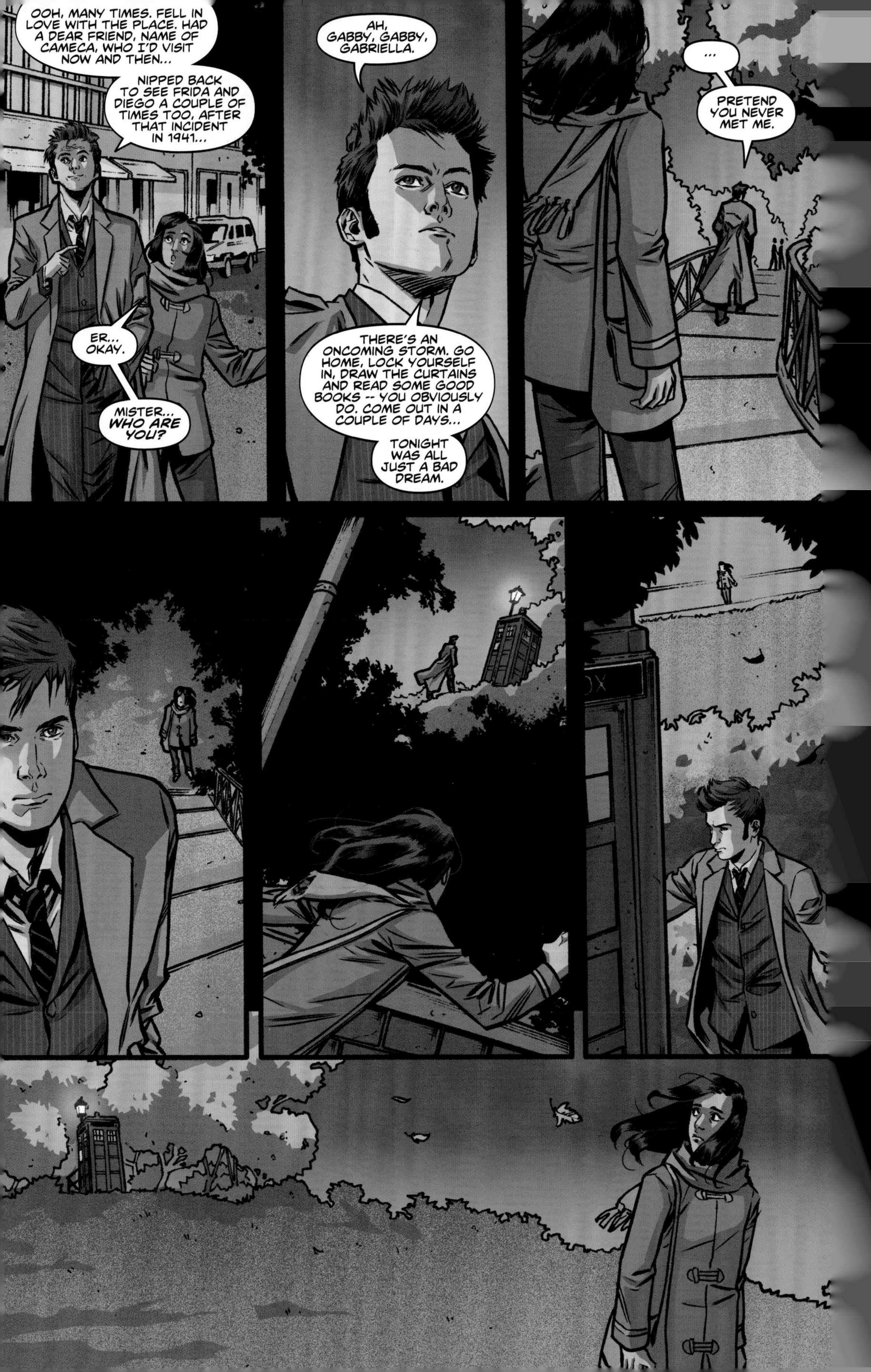
OOH, MANY TIMES. FELL IN LOVE WITH THE PLACE. HAD A DEAR FRIEND, NAME OF CAMECA, WHO I'D VISIT NOW AND THEN...
NIPPED BACK TO SEE FRIDA AND DIEGO A COUPLE OF TIMES TOO, AFTER THAT INCIDENT IN 1941...
ER... OKAY.
MISTER... *WHO ARE YOU?*
AH, GABBY, GABBY, GABRIELLA.
THERE'S AN ONCOMING STORM. GO HOME, LOCK YOURSELF IN, DRAW THE CURTAINS AND READ SOME GOOD BOOKS -- YOU OBVIOUSLY DO. COME OUT IN A COUPLE OF DAYS...
TONIGHT WAS ALL JUST A BAD DREAM.
...
PRETEND YOU NEVER MET ME.

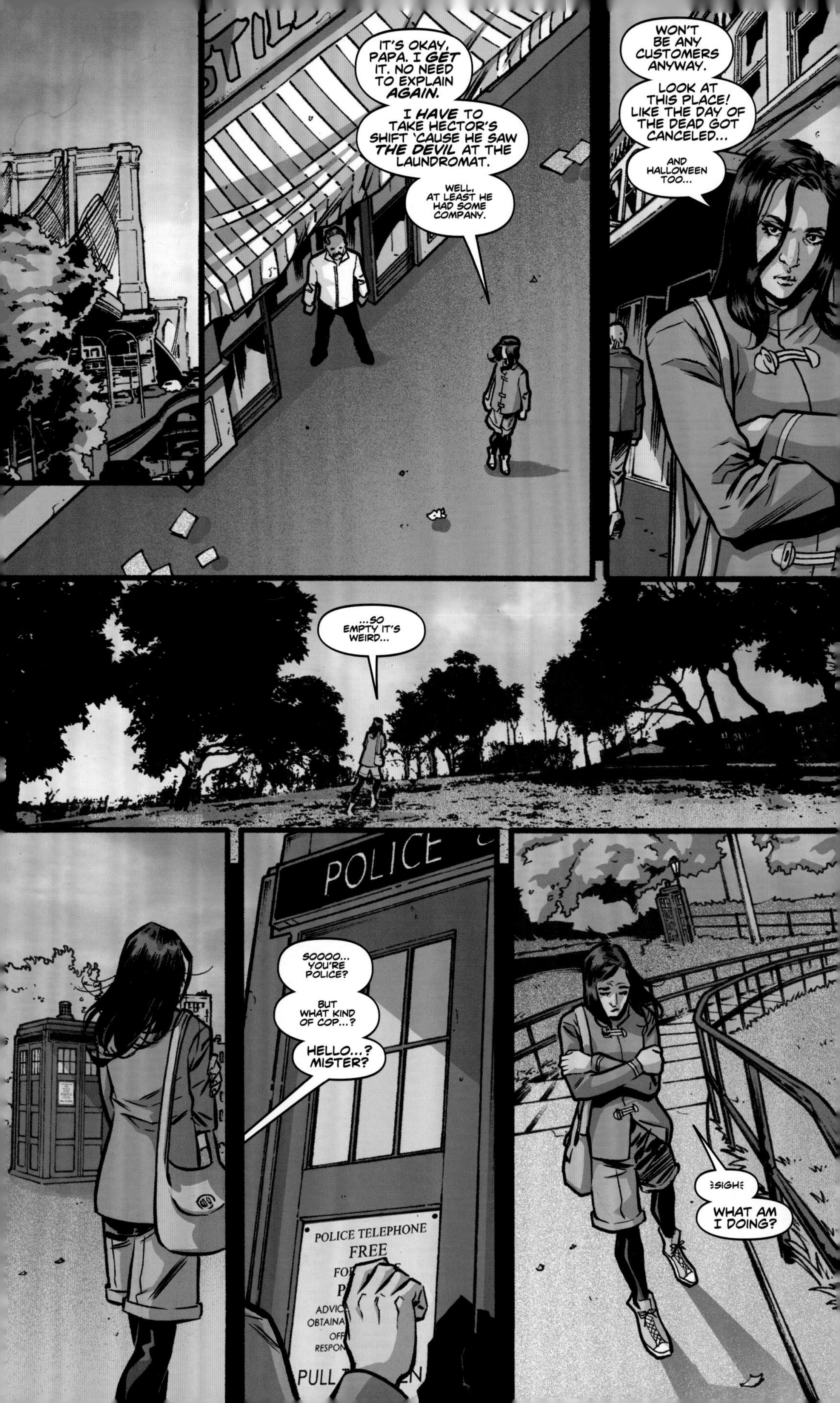
IT'S OKAY, PAPA. I GET IT. NO NEED TO EXPLAIN AGAIN.
I HAVE TO TAKE HECTOR'S SHIFT 'CAUSE HE SAW THE DEVIL AT THE LAUNDROMAT.
WELL, AT LEAST HE HAD SOME COMPANY.
WON'T BE ANY CUSTOMERS ANYWAY.
LOOK AT THIS PLACE! LIKE THE DAY OF THE DEAD GOT CANCELED...
AND HALLOWEEN TOO...
...SO EMPTY IT'S WEIRD...
SOOOO... YOU'RE POLICE?
BUT WHAT KIND OF COP...?
HELLO...? MISTER?
POLICE
POLICE TELEPHONE
FREE
SIGH
WHAT AM I DOING?

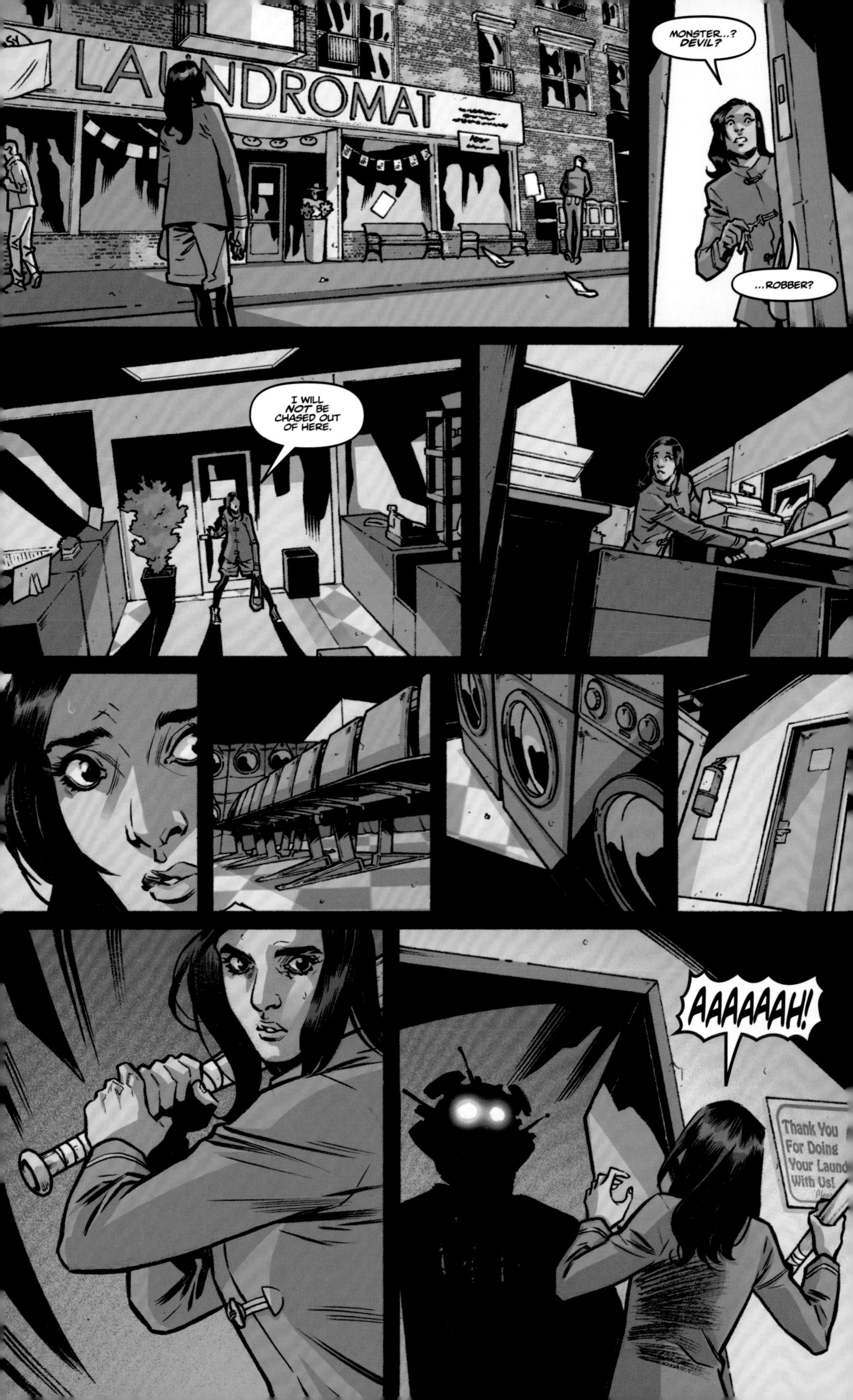

LAUNDROMAT
MONSTER...? DEVIL?
...ROBBER?
I WILL NOT BE CHASED OUT OF HERE.
AAAAAAH!
Thank You For Doing Your Laund With Us!

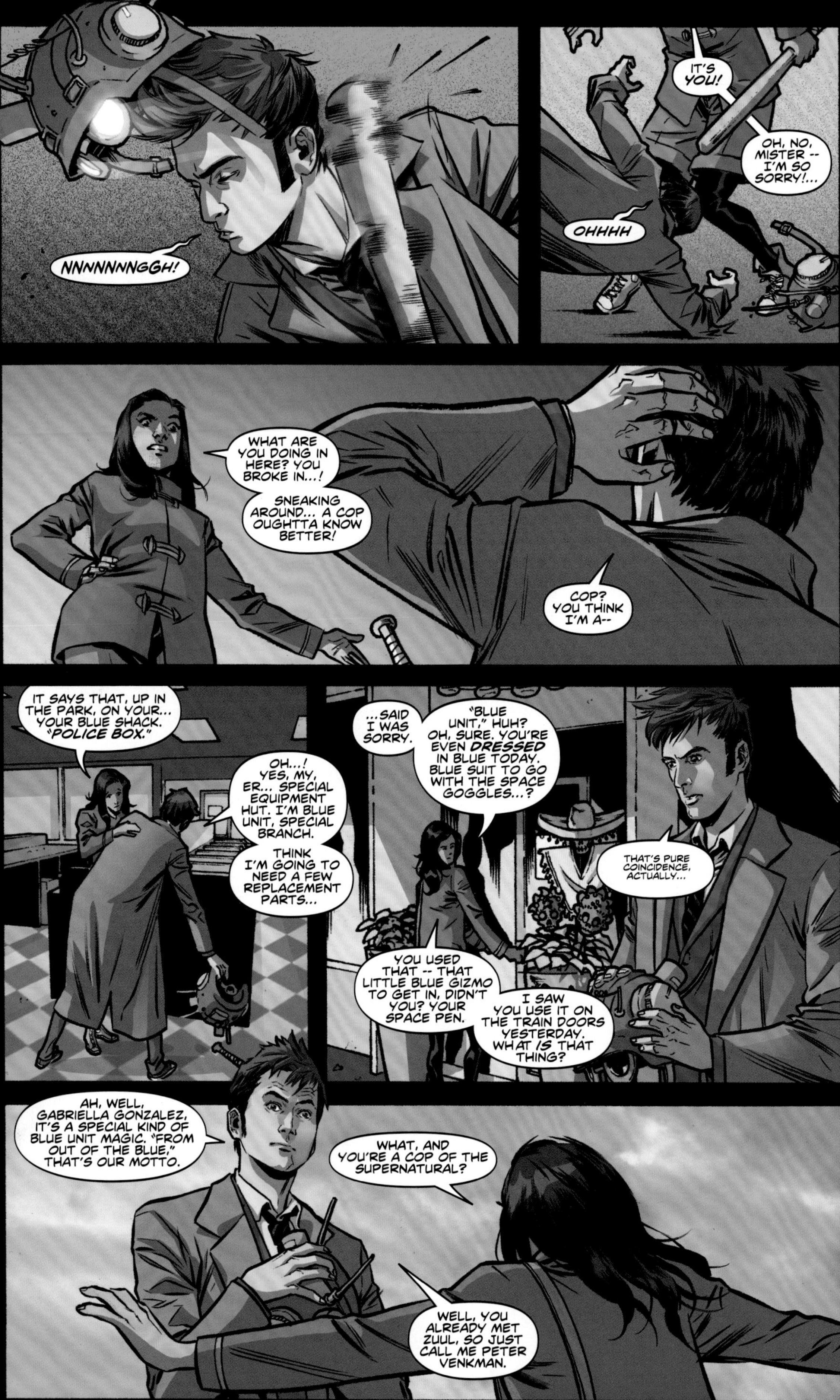
NNNNNNNGGH!
IT'S YOU!
OH, NO, MISTER -- I'M SO SORRY!...
OHHHH
WHAT ARE YOU DOING IN HERE? YOU BROKE IN...!
SNEAKING AROUND... A COP OUGHTTA KNOW BETTER!
COP? YOU THINK I'M A--
IT SAYS THAT, UP IN THE PARK, ON YOUR... YOUR BLUE SHACK. "POLICE BOX."
OH...! YES, MY, ER... SPECIAL EQUIPMENT HUT. I'M BLUE UNIT, SPECIAL BRANCH.
THINK I'M GOING TO NEED A FEW REPLACEMENT PARTS...
...SAID I WAS SORRY.
"BLUE UNIT," HUH? OH, SURE. YOU'RE EVEN DRESSED IN BLUE TODAY. BLUE SUIT TO GO WITH THE SPACE GOGGLES...?
THAT'S PURE COINCIDENCE, ACTUALLY...
YOU USED THAT -- THAT LITTLE BLUE GIZMO TO GET IN, DIDN'T YOU? YOUR SPACE PEN.
I SAW YOU USE IT ON THE TRAIN DOORS YESTERDAY. WHAT IS THAT THING?
AH, WELL, GABRIELLA GONZALEZ, IT'S A SPECIAL KIND OF BLUE UNIT MAGIC. "FROM OUT OF THE BLUE," THAT'S OUR MOTTO.
WHAT, AND YOU'RE A COP OF THE SUPERNATURAL?
WELL, YOU ALREADY MET ZUUL, SO JUST CALL ME PETER VENKMAN.

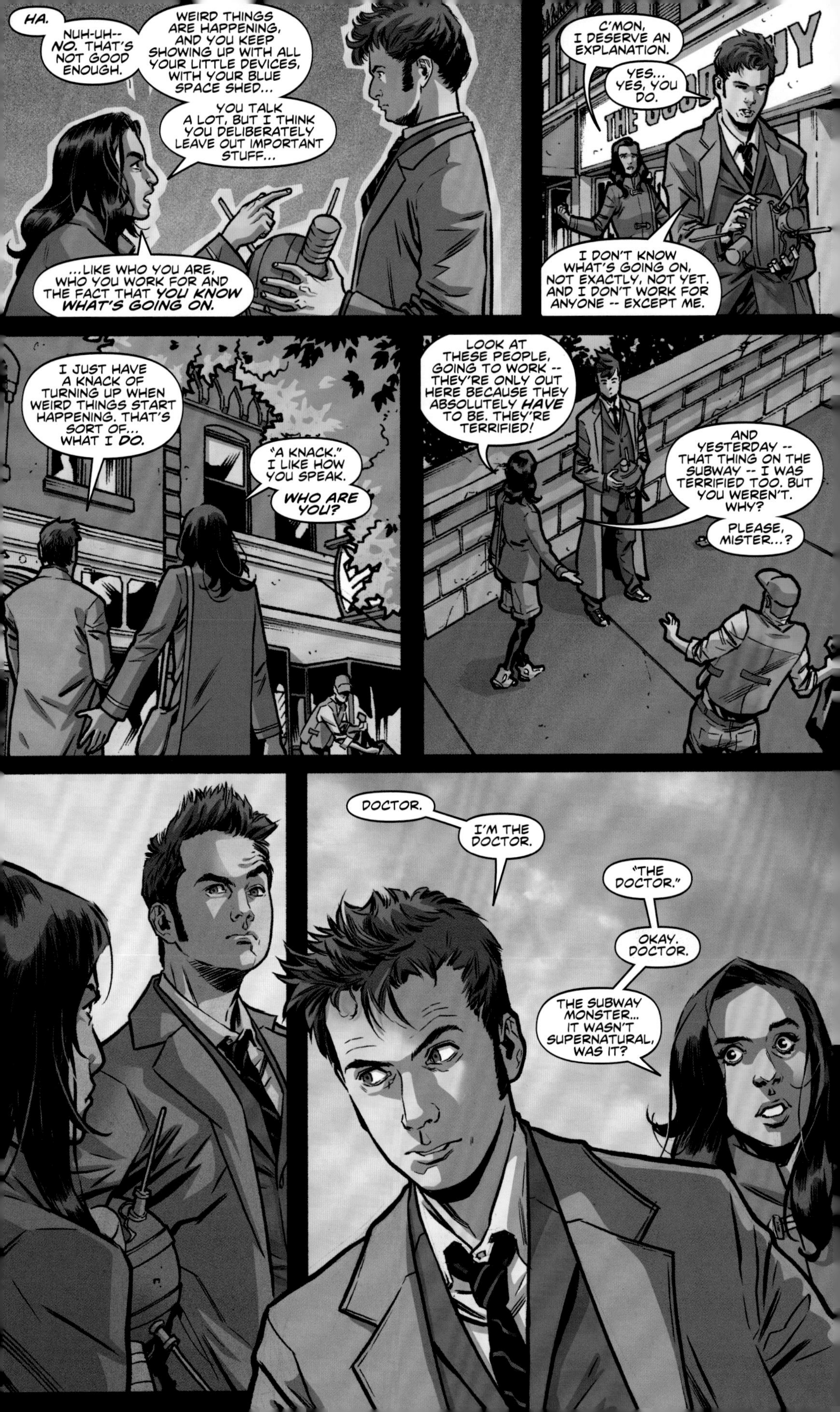
HA.
NUH-UH-- NO. THAT'S NOT GOOD ENOUGH.
WEIRD THINGS ARE HAPPENING, AND YOU KEEP SHOWING UP WITH ALL YOUR LITTLE DEVICES, WITH YOUR BLUE SPACE SHED...
YOU TALK A LOT, BUT I THINK YOU DELIBERATELY LEAVE OUT IMPORTANT STUFF...
...LIKE WHO YOU ARE, WHO YOU WORK FOR AND THE FACT THAT YOU KNOW WHAT'S GOING ON.
C'MON, I DESERVE AN EXPLANATION.
YES... YES, YOU DO.
I DON'T KNOW WHAT'S GOING ON, NOT EXACTLY, NOT YET. AND I DON'T WORK FOR ANYONE -- EXCEPT ME.
I JUST HAVE A KNACK OF TURNING UP WHEN WEIRD THINGS START HAPPENING. THAT'S SORT OF... WHAT I DO.
"A KNACK." I LIKE HOW YOU SPEAK.
WHO ARE YOU?
LOOK AT THESE PEOPLE, GOING TO WORK -- THEY'RE ONLY OUT HERE BECAUSE THEY ABSOLUTELY HAVE TO BE. THEY'RE TERRIFIED!
AND YESTERDAY -- THAT THING ON THE SUBWAY -- I WAS TERRIFIED TOO. BUT YOU WEREN'T. WHY?
PLEASE, MISTER...?
DOCTOR.
I'M THE DOCTOR.
"THE DOCTOR."
OKAY. DOCTOR.
THE SUBWAY MONSTER... IT WASN'T SUPERNATURAL, WAS IT?

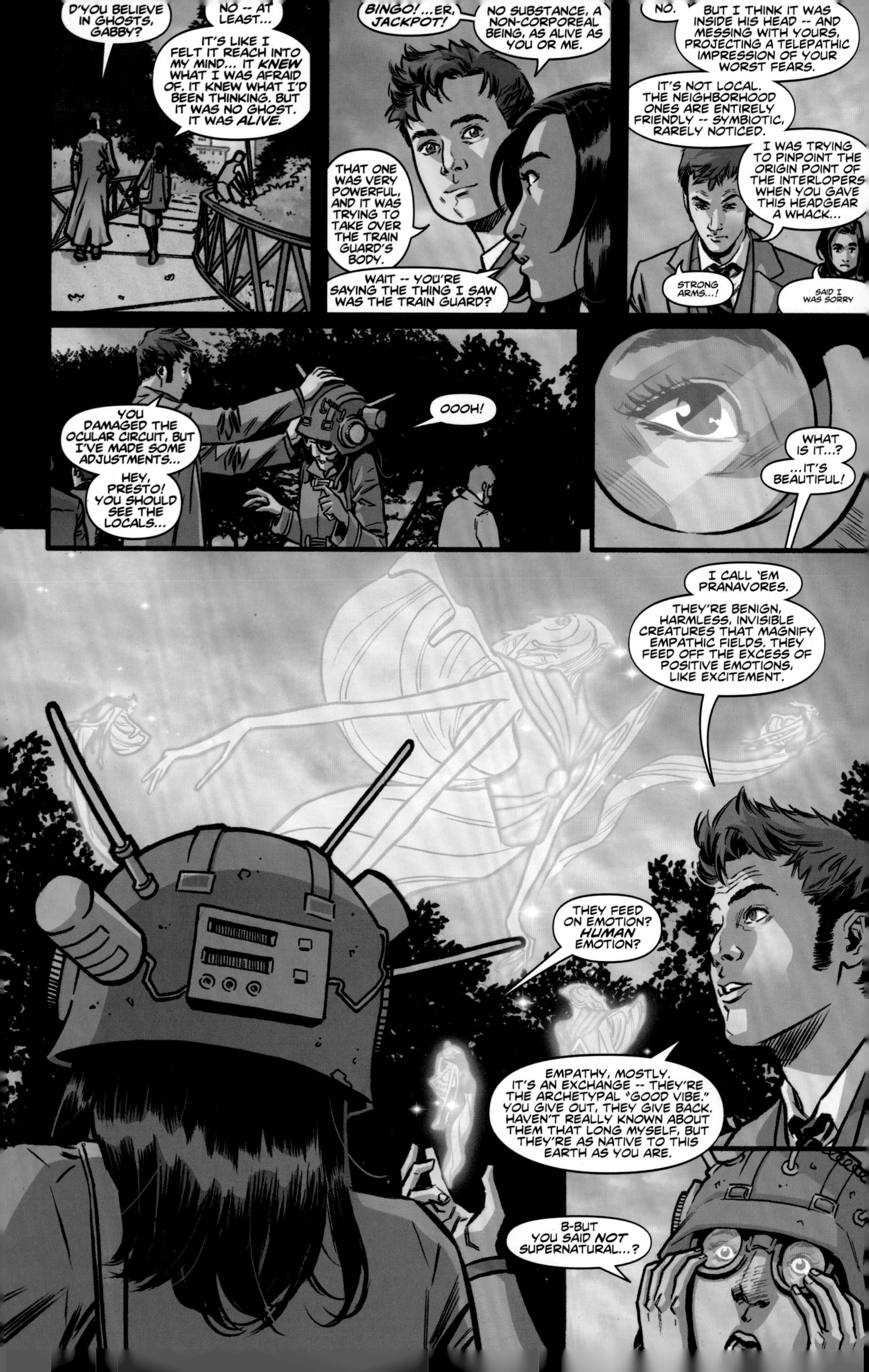

D'YOU BELIEVE IN GHOSTS, GABBY?
NO -- AT LEAST...
IT'S LIKE I FELT IT REACH INTO MY MIND... IT KNEW WHAT I WAS AFRAID OF. IT KNEW WHAT I'D BEEN THINKING. BUT IT WAS NO GHOST. IT WAS ALIVE.
BINGO! ...ER, JACKPOT!
NO SUBSTANCE, A NON-CORPOREAL BEING, AS ALIVE AS YOU OR ME.
THAT ONE WAS VERY POWERFUL, AND IT WAS TRYING TO TAKE OVER THE TRAIN GUARD'S BODY.
WAIT -- YOU'RE SAYING THE THING I SAW WAS THE TRAIN GUARD?
NO.
BUT I THINK IT WAS INSIDE HIS HEAD -- AND MESSING WITH YOURS, PROJECTING A TELEPATHIC IMPRESSION OF YOUR WORST FEARS.
IT'S NOT LOCAL. THE NEIGHBORHOOD ONES ARE ENTIRELY FRIENDLY -- SYMBIOTIC, RARELY NOTICED.
I WAS TRYING TO PINPOINT THE ORIGIN POINT OF THE INTERLOPERS WHEN YOU GAVE THIS HEADGEAR A WHACK...
STRONG ARMS...!
SAID I WAS SORRY
YOU DAMAGED THE OCULAR CIRCUIT, BUT I'VE MADE SOME ADJUSTMENTS...
HEY, PRESTO! YOU SHOULD SEE THE LOCALS...
OOOH!
WHAT IS IT...?
...IT'S BEAUTIFUL!
I CALL 'EM PRANAVORES.
THEY'RE BENIGN, HARMLESS, INVISIBLE CREATURES THAT MAGNIFY EMPATHIC FIELDS. THEY FEED OFF THE EXCESS OF POSITIVE EMOTIONS, LIKE EXCITEMENT.
THEY FEED ON EMOTION? HUMAN EMOTION?
EMPATHY, MOSTLY. IT'S AN EXCHANGE -- THEY'RE THE ARCHETYPAL "GOOD VIBE." YOU GIVE OUT, THEY GIVE BACK. HAVEN'T REALLY KNOWN ABOUT THEM THAT LONG MYSELF, BUT THEY'RE AS NATIVE TO THIS EARTH AS YOU ARE.
B-BUT YOU SAID NOT SUPERNATURAL...?

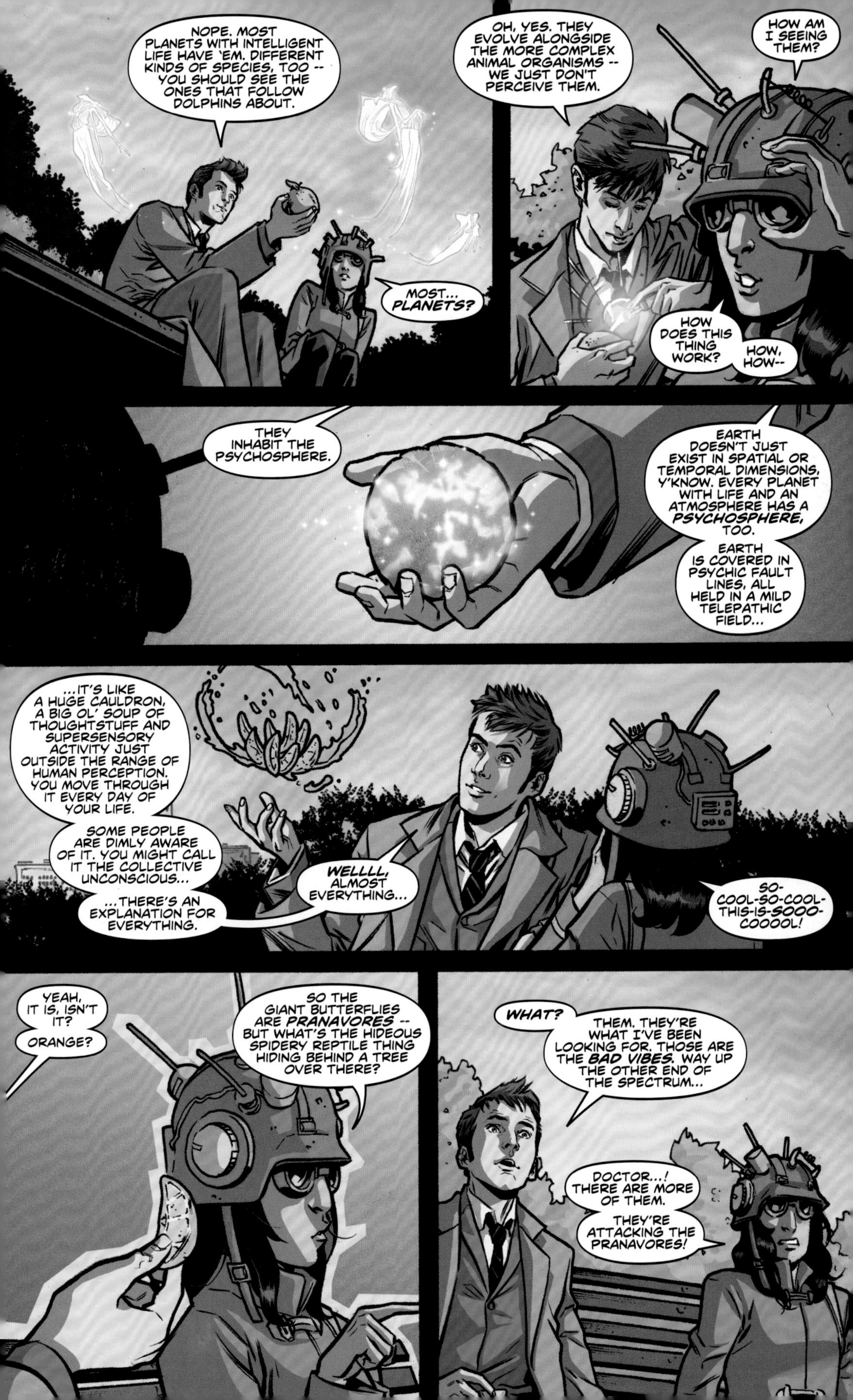
NOPE. MOST PLANETS WITH INTELLIGENT LIFE HAVE 'EM. DIFFERENT KINDS OF SPECIES, TOO -- YOU SHOULD SEE THE ONES THAT FOLLOW DOLPHINS ABOUT.
MOST... PLANETS?
OH, YES. THEY EVOLVE ALONGSIDE THE MORE COMPLEX ANIMAL ORGANISMS -- WE JUST DON'T PERCEIVE THEM.
HOW AM I SEEING THEM?
HOW DOES THIS THING WORK?
HOW, HOW--
THEY INHABIT THE PSYCHOSPHERE.
EARTH DOESN'T JUST EXIST IN SPATIAL OR TEMPORAL DIMENSIONS, Y'KNOW. EVERY PLANET WITH LIFE AND AN ATMOSPHERE HAS A PSYCHOSPHERE, TOO.
EARTH IS COVERED IN PSYCHIC FAULT LINES, ALL HELD IN A MILD TELEPATHIC FIELD...
...IT'S LIKE A HUGE CAULDRON, A BIG OL' SOUP OF THOUGHTSTUFF AND SUPERSENSORY ACTIVITY JUST OUTSIDE THE RANGE OF HUMAN PERCEPTION. YOU MOVE THROUGH IT EVERY DAY OF YOUR LIFE.
SOME PEOPLE ARE DIMLY AWARE OF IT. YOU MIGHT CALL IT THE COLLECTIVE UNCONSCIOUS...
...THERE'S AN EXPLANATION FOR EVERYTHING.
WELLLL, ALMOST EVERYTHING...
SO-COOL-SO-COOL-THIS-IS-SOOO-COOOOL!
YEAH, IT IS, ISN'T IT?
ORANGE?
SO THE GIANT BUTTERFLIES ARE PRANAVORES -- BUT WHAT'S THE HIDEOUS SPIDERY REPTILE THING HIDING BEHIND A TREE OVER THERE?
WHAT?
THEM. THEY'RE WHAT I'VE BEEN LOOKING FOR. THOSE ARE THE BAD VIBES. WAY UP THE OTHER END OF THE SPECTRUM...
DOCTOR...! THERE ARE MORE OF THEM.
THEY'RE ATTACKING THE PRANAVORES!

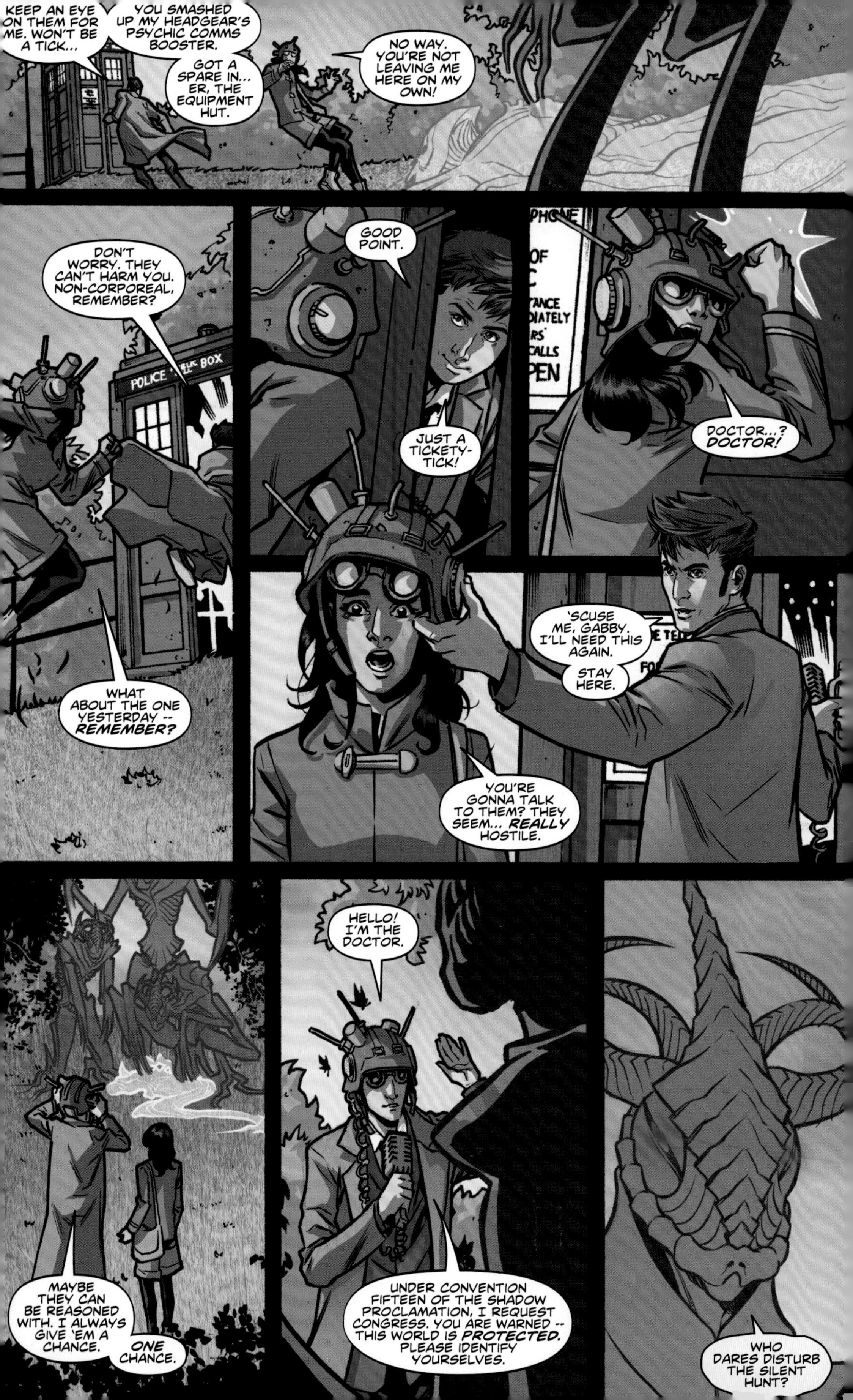
KEEP AN EYE ON THEM FOR ME. WON'T BE A TICK...
YOU SMASHED UP MY HEADGEAR'S PSYCHIC COMMS BOOSTER.
GOT A SPARE IN... ER, THE EQUIPMENT HUT.
NO WAY. YOU'RE NOT LEAVING ME HERE ON MY OWN!
DON'T WORRY. THEY CAN'T HARM YOU. NON-CORPOREAL, REMEMBER?
POLICE BOX
WHAT ABOUT THE ONE YESTERDAY -- REMEMBER?
GOOD POINT.
JUST A TICKETY-TICK!
DOCTOR...? DOCTOR!
'SCUSE ME, GABBY. I'LL NEED THIS AGAIN.
STAY HERE.
YOU'RE GONNA TALK TO THEM? THEY SEEM... REALLY HOSTILE.
MAYBE THEY CAN BE REASONED WITH. I ALWAYS GIVE 'EM A CHANCE.
ONE CHANCE.
HELLO! I'M THE DOCTOR.
UNDER CONVENTION FIFTEEN OF THE SHADOW PROCLAMATION, I REQUEST CONGRESS. YOU ARE WARNED -- THIS WORLD IS PROTECTED. PLEASE IDENTIFY YOURSELVES.
WHO DARES DISTURB THE SILENT HUNT?

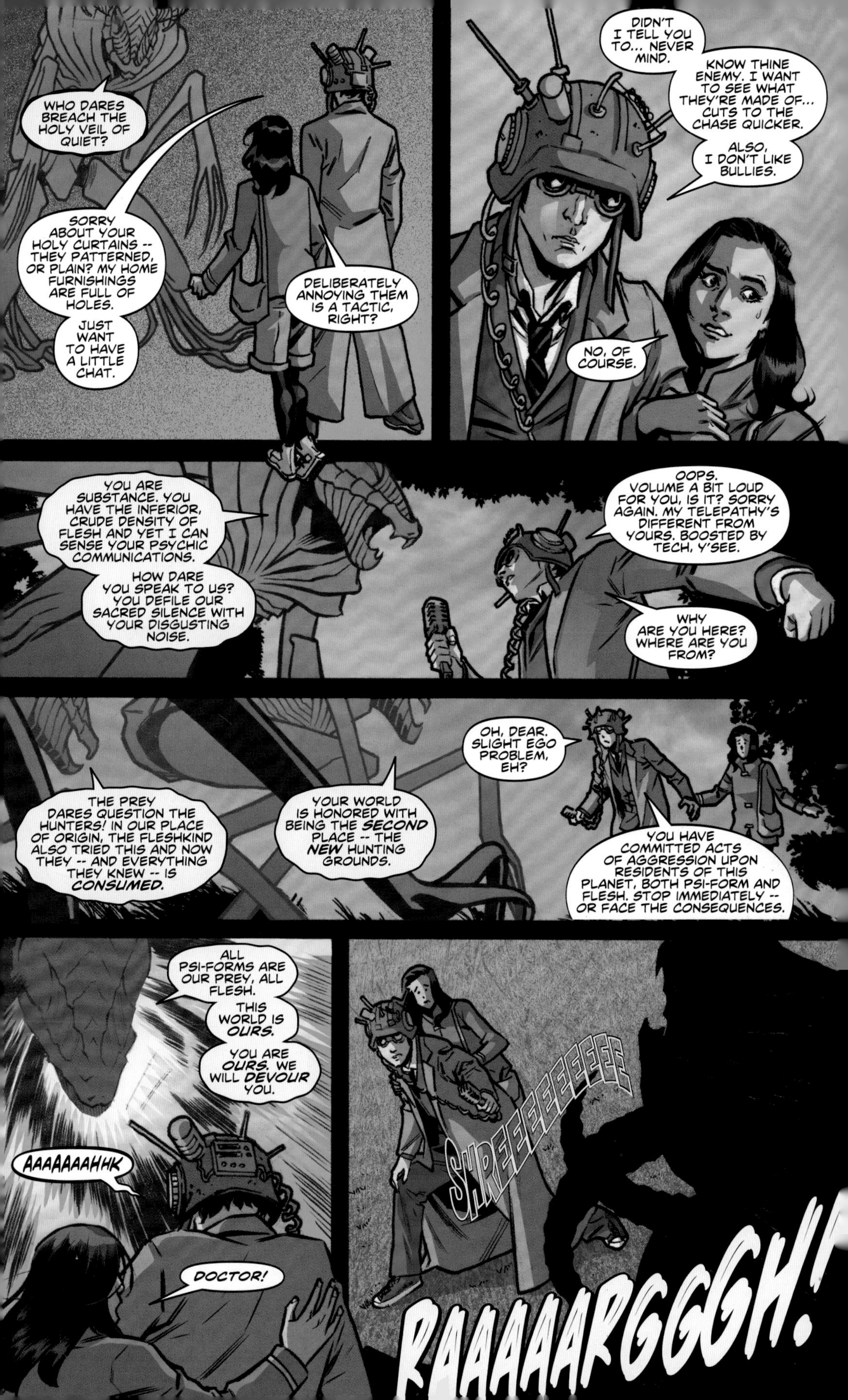
WHO DARES BREACH THE HOLY VEIL OF QUIET?
SORRY ABOUT YOUR HOLY CURTAINS -- THEY PATTERNED, OR PLAIN? MY HOME FURNISHINGS ARE FULL OF HOLES.
JUST WANT TO HAVE A LITTLE CHAT.
DELIBERATELY ANNOYING THEM IS A TACTIC, RIGHT?
DIDN'T I TELL YOU TO... NEVER MIND.
KNOW THINE ENEMY. I WANT TO SEE WHAT THEY'RE MADE OF... CUTS TO THE CHASE QUICKER.
ALSO, I DON'T LIKE BULLIES.
NO, OF COURSE.
YOU ARE SUBSTANCE. YOU HAVE THE INFERIOR, CRUDE DENSITY OF FLESH AND YET I CAN SENSE YOUR PSYCHIC COMMUNICATIONS.
HOW DARE YOU SPEAK TO US? YOU DEFILE OUR SACRED SILENCE WITH YOUR DISGUSTING NOISE.
OOPS. VOLUME A BIT LOUD FOR YOU, IS IT? SORRY AGAIN. MY TELEPATHY'S DIFFERENT FROM YOURS. BOOSTED BY TECH, Y'SEE.
WHY ARE YOU HERE? WHERE ARE YOU FROM?
THE PREY DARES QUESTION THE HUNTERS! IN OUR PLACE OF ORIGIN, THE FLESHKIND ALSO TRIED THIS AND NOW THEY -- AND EVERYTHING THEY KNEW -- IS CONSUMED.
YOUR WORLD IS HONORED WITH BEING THE SECOND PLACE -- THE NEW HUNTING GROUNDS.
OH, DEAR. SLIGHT EGO PROBLEM, EH?
YOU HAVE COMMITTED ACTS OF AGGRESSION UPON RESIDENTS OF THIS PLANET, BOTH PSI-FORM AND FLESH. STOP IMMEDIATELY -- OR FACE THE CONSEQUENCES.
ALL PSI-FORMS ARE OUR PREY, ALL FLESH.
THIS WORLD IS OURS.
YOU ARE OURS. WE WILL DEVOUR YOU.
AAAAAAAHHK
DOCTOR!
SHREEEEEEEEEEE
RAAAAARGGGH!

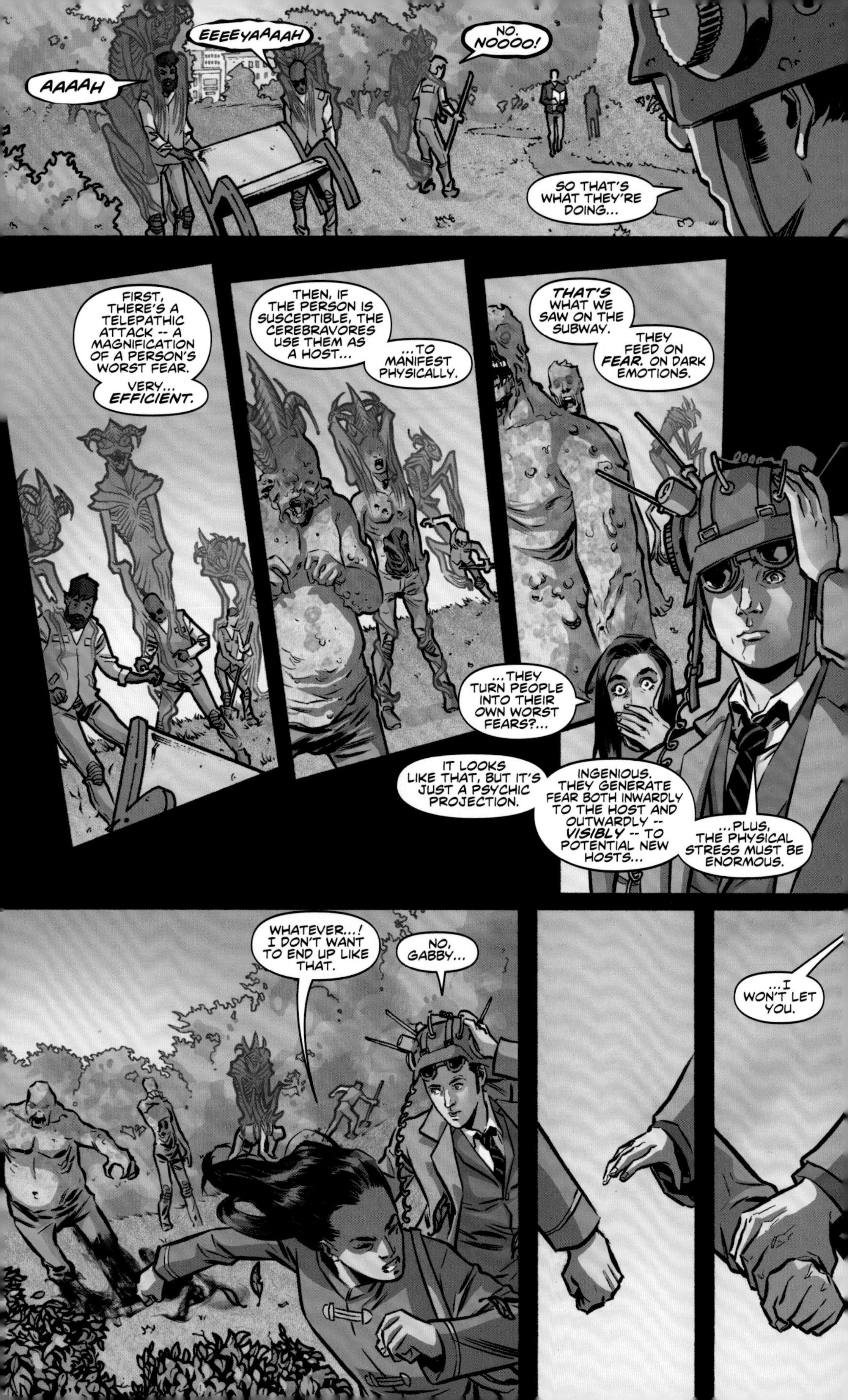
EEEEYAAAAH
AAAAH
NO. NOOOO!
SO THAT'S WHAT THEY'RE DOING...
FIRST, THERE'S A TELEPATHIC ATTACK -- A MAGNIFICATION OF A PERSON'S WORST FEAR.
VERY... EFFICIENT.
THEN, IF THE PERSON IS SUSCEPTIBLE, THE CEREBRAVORES USE THEM AS A HOST...
...TO MANIFEST PHYSICALLY.
THAT'S WHAT WE SAW ON THE SUBWAY.
THEY FEED ON FEAR. ON DARK EMOTIONS.
...THEY TURN PEOPLE INTO THEIR OWN WORST FEARS?...
IT LOOKS LIKE THAT, BUT IT'S JUST A PSYCHIC PROJECTION.
INGENIOUS. THEY GENERATE FEAR BOTH INWARDLY TO THE HOST AND OUTWARDLY -- VISIBLY -- TO POTENTIAL NEW HOSTS...
...PLUS, THE PHYSICAL STRESS MUST BE ENORMOUS.
WHATEVER...! I DON'T WANT TO END UP LIKE THAT.
NO, GABBY...
...I WON'T LET YOU.

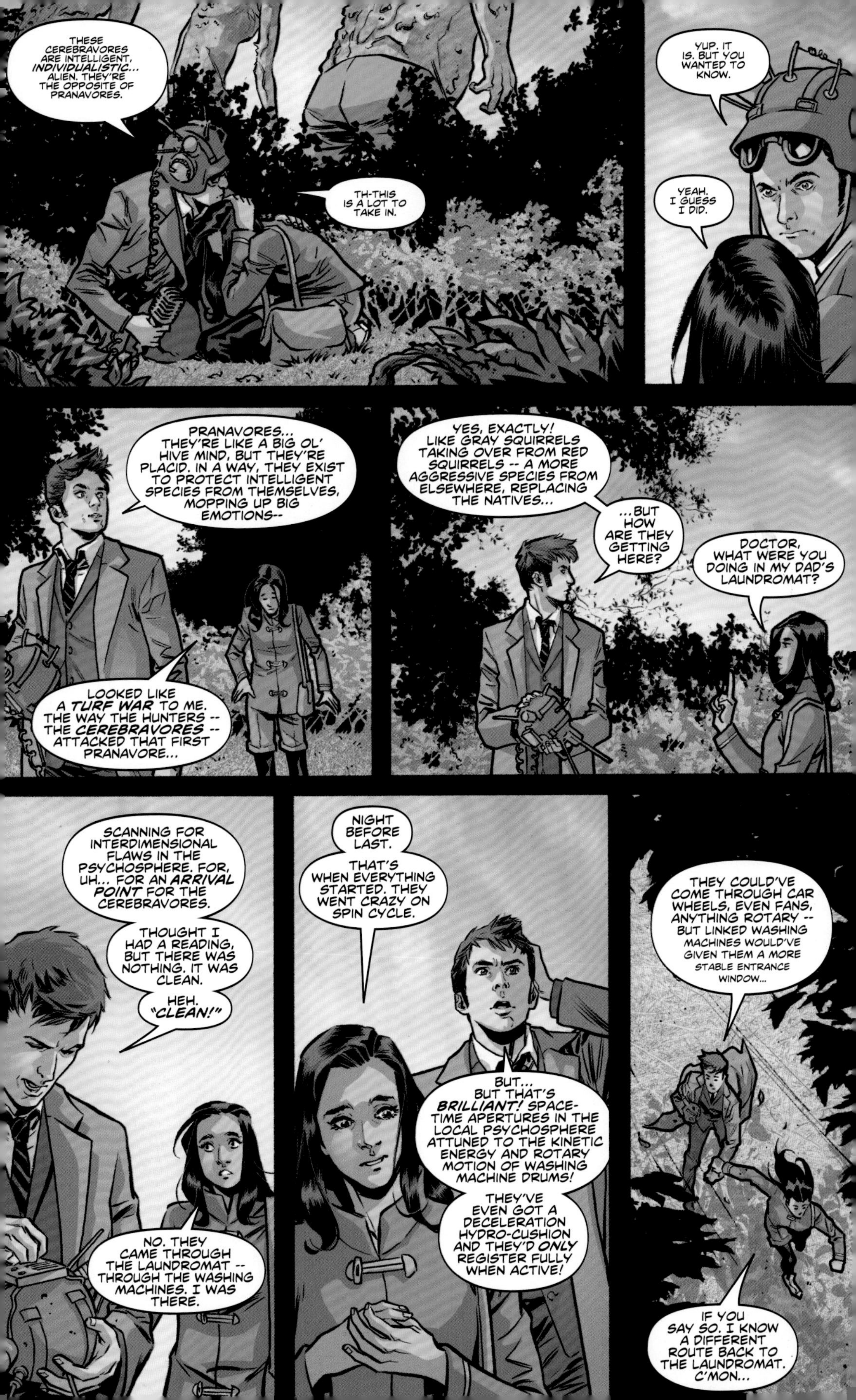

THESE CEREBRAVORES ARE INTELLIGENT, INDIVIDUALISTIC... ALIEN. THEY'RE THE OPPOSITE OF PRANAVORES.
TH-THIS IS A LOT TO TAKE IN.
YUP. IT IS. BUT YOU WANTED TO KNOW.
YEAH. I GUESS I DID.
PRANAVORES... THEY'RE LIKE A BIG OL' HIVE MIND, BUT THEY'RE PLACID. IN A WAY, THEY EXIST TO PROTECT INTELLIGENT SPECIES FROM THEMSELVES, MOPPING UP BIG EMOTIONS--
LOOKED LIKE A TURF WAR TO ME. THE WAY THE HUNTERS -- THE CEREBRAVORES -- ATTACKED THAT FIRST PRANAVORE...
YES, EXACTLY! LIKE GRAY SQUIRRELS TAKING OVER FROM RED SQUIRRELS -- A MORE AGGRESSIVE SPECIES FROM ELSEWHERE, REPLACING THE NATIVES...
...BUT HOW ARE THEY GETTING HERE?
DOCTOR, WHAT WERE YOU DOING IN MY DAD'S LAUNDROMAT?
SCANNING FOR INTERDIMENSIONAL FLAWS IN THE PSYCHOSPHERE. FOR, UH... FOR AN ARRIVAL POINT FOR THE CEREBRAVORES.
THOUGHT I HAD A READING, BUT THERE WAS NOTHING. IT WAS CLEAN.
HEH. "CLEAN!"
NO. THEY CAME THROUGH THE LAUNDROMAT -- THROUGH THE WASHING MACHINES. I WAS THERE.
NIGHT BEFORE LAST.
THAT'S WHEN EVERYTHING STARTED. THEY WENT CRAZY ON SPIN CYCLE.
BUT... BUT THAT'S BRILLIANT! SPACE-TIME APERTURES IN THE LOCAL PSYCHOSPHERE ATTUNED TO THE KINETIC ENERGY AND ROTARY MOTION OF WASHING MACHINE DRUMS!
THEY'VE EVEN GOT A DECELERATION HYDRO-CUSHION AND THEY'D ONLY REGISTER FULLY WHEN ACTIVE!
THEY COULD'VE COME THROUGH CAR WHEELS, EVEN FANS, ANYTHING ROTARY -- BUT LINKED WASHING MACHINES WOULD'VE GIVEN THEM A MORE STABLE ENTRANCE WINDOW...
IF YOU SAY SO. I KNOW A DIFFERENT ROUTE BACK TO THE LAUNDROMAT. C'MON...

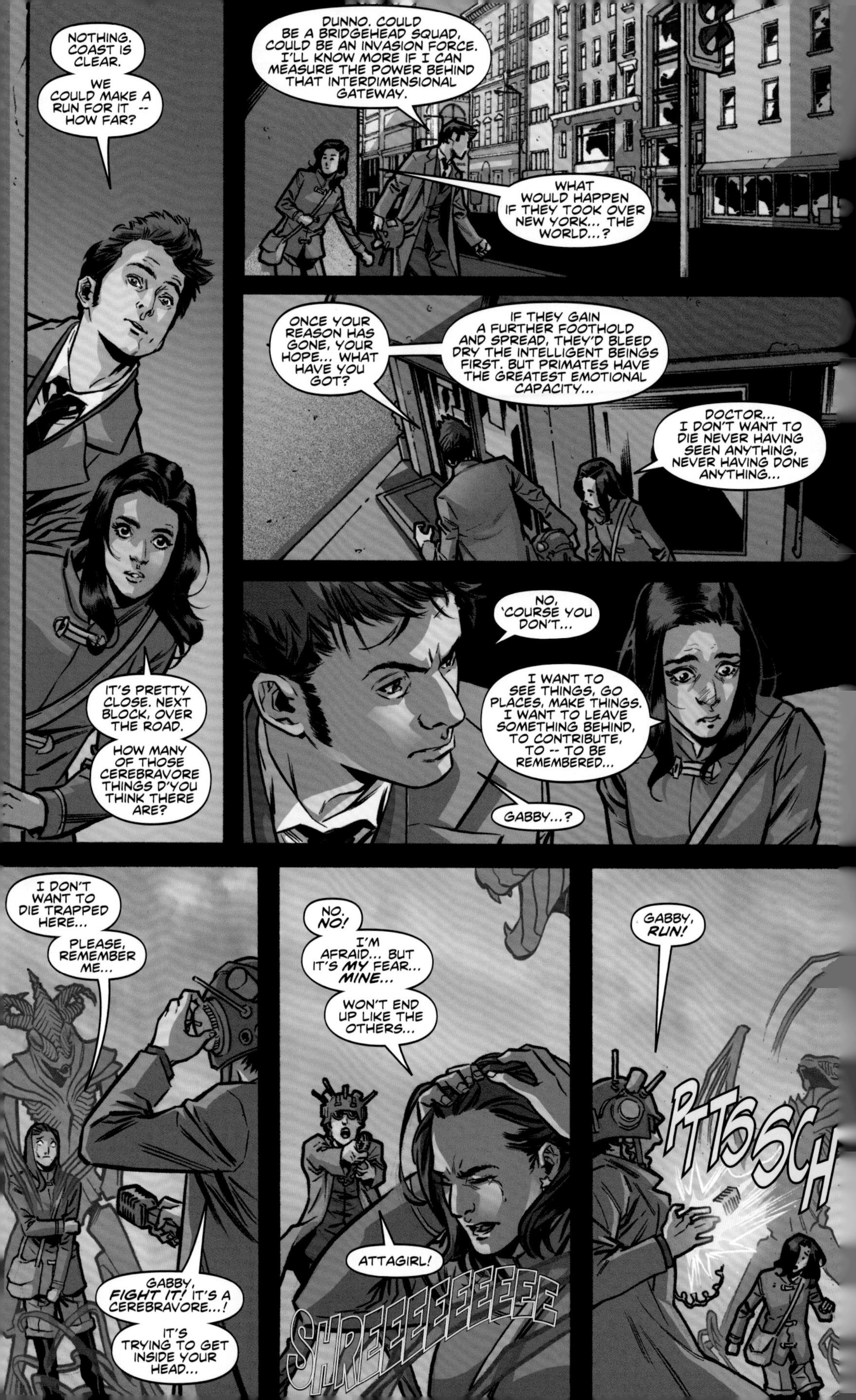
NOTHING. COAST IS CLEAR.
WE COULD MAKE A RUN FOR IT -- HOW FAR?
IT'S PRETTY CLOSE. NEXT BLOCK, OVER THE ROAD.
HOW MANY OF THOSE CEREBRAVORE THINGS D'YOU THINK THERE ARE?
DUNNO. COULD BE A BRIDGEHEAD SQUAD, COULD BE AN INVASION FORCE. I'LL KNOW MORE IF I CAN MEASURE THE POWER BEHIND THAT INTERDIMENSIONAL GATEWAY.
WHAT WOULD HAPPEN IF THEY TOOK OVER NEW YORK... THE WORLD...?
IF THEY GAIN A FURTHER FOOTHOLD AND SPREAD, THEY'D BLEED DRY THE INTELLIGENT BEINGS FIRST. BUT PRIMATES HAVE THE GREATEST EMOTIONAL CAPACITY...
ONCE YOUR REASON HAS GONE, YOUR HOPE... WHAT HAVE YOU GOT?
DOCTOR... I DON'T WANT TO DIE NEVER HAVING SEEN ANYTHING, NEVER HAVING DONE ANYTHING...
NO, 'COURSE YOU DON'T...
I WANT TO SEE THINGS, GO PLACES, MAKE THINGS. I WANT TO LEAVE SOMETHING BEHIND, TO CONTRIBUTE, TO -- TO BE REMEMBERED...
GABBY...?
I DON'T WANT TO DIE TRAPPED HERE...
PLEASE, REMEMBER ME...
GABBY, FIGHT IT! IT'S A CEREBRAVORE...!
IT'S TRYING TO GET INSIDE YOUR HEAD...
NO. NO!
I'M AFRAID... BUT IT'S MY FEAR... MINE...
WON'T END UP LIKE THE OTHERS...
ATTAGIRL!
SHREEEEEEEEEE
GABBY, RUN!
PTTSSCH

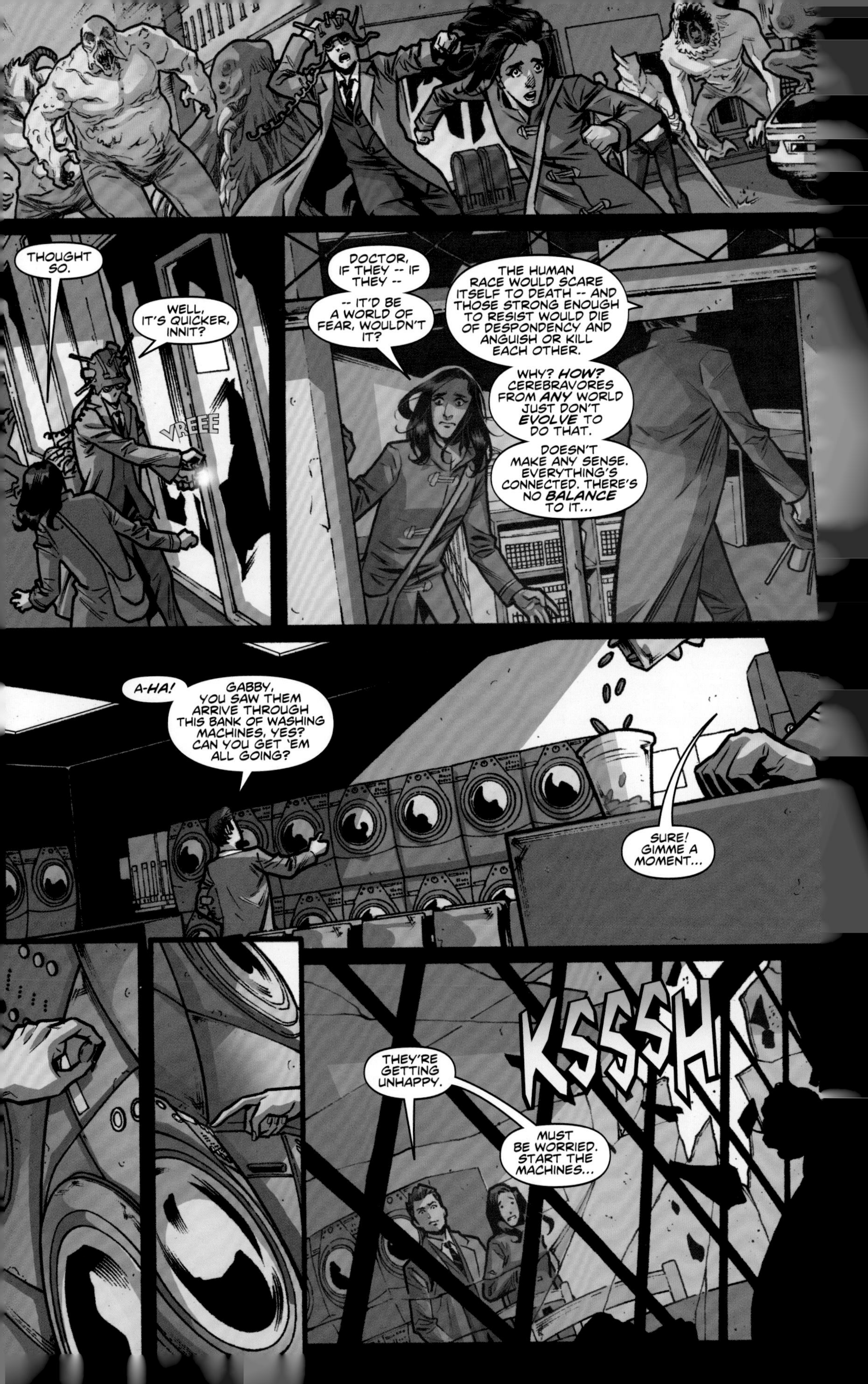
THOUGHT SO.
WELL, IT'S QUICKER, INNIT?
VREEE
DOCTOR, IF THEY -- IF THEY --
-- IT'D BE A WORLD OF FEAR, WOULDN'T IT?
THE HUMAN RACE WOULD SCARE ITSELF TO DEATH -- AND THOSE STRONG ENOUGH TO RESIST WOULD DIE OF DESPONDENCY AND ANGUISH OR KILL EACH OTHER.
WHY? HOW? CEREBRAVORES FROM ANY WORLD JUST DON'T EVOLVE TO DO THAT.
DOESN'T MAKE ANY SENSE. EVERYTHING'S CONNECTED. THERE'S NO BALANCE TO IT...
A-HA!
GABBY, YOU SAW THEM ARRIVE THROUGH THIS BANK OF WASHING MACHINES, YES? CAN YOU GET 'EM ALL GOING?
SURE! GIMME A MOMENT...
KSSSH
THEY'RE GETTING UNHAPPY.
MUST BE WORRIED. START THE MACHINES...

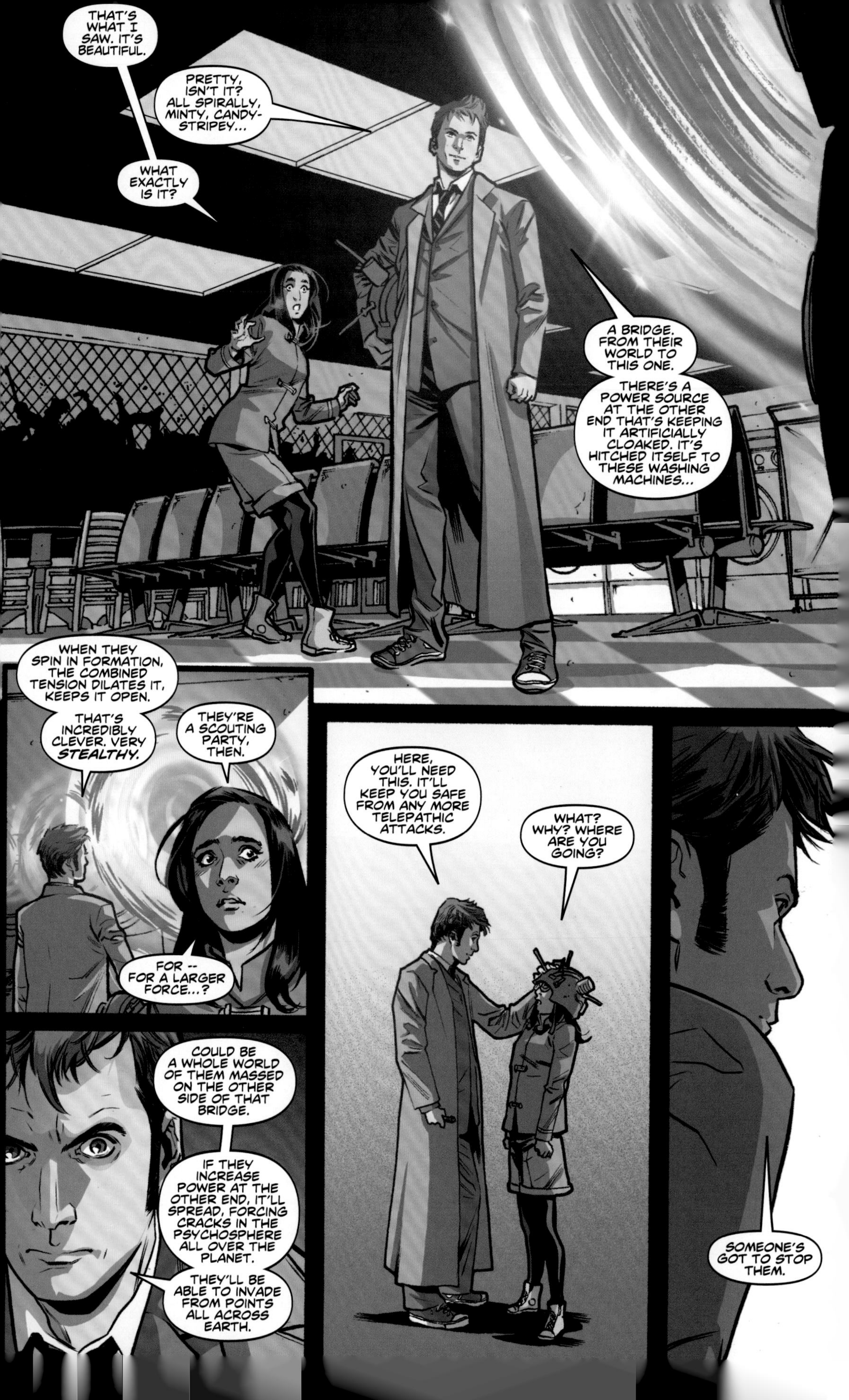
THAT'S WHAT I SAW. IT'S BEAUTIFUL.
PRETTY, ISN'T IT? ALL SPIRALLY, MINTY, CANDY-STRIPEY...
WHAT EXACTLY IS IT?
A BRIDGE. FROM THEIR WORLD TO THIS ONE.
THERE'S A POWER SOURCE AT THE OTHER END THAT'S KEEPING IT ARTIFICIALLY CLOAKED. IT'S HITCHED ITSELF TO THESE WASHING MACHINES...
WHEN THEY SPIN IN FORMATION, THE COMBINED TENSION DILATES IT, KEEPS IT OPEN.
THAT'S INCREDIBLY CLEVER. VERY *STEALTHY.*
THEY'RE A SCOUTING PARTY, THEN.
FOR -- FOR A LARGER FORCE...?
COULD BE A WHOLE WORLD OF THEM MASSED ON THE OTHER SIDE OF THAT BRIDGE.
IF THEY INCREASE POWER AT THE OTHER END, IT'LL SPREAD, FORCING CRACKS IN THE PSYCHOSPHERE ALL OVER THE PLANET.
THEY'LL BE ABLE TO INVADE FROM POINTS ALL ACROSS EARTH.
HERE, YOU'LL NEED THIS. IT'LL KEEP YOU SAFE FROM ANY MORE TELEPATHIC ATTACKS.
WHAT? WHY? WHERE ARE YOU GOING?
SOMEONE'S GOT TO STOP THEM.

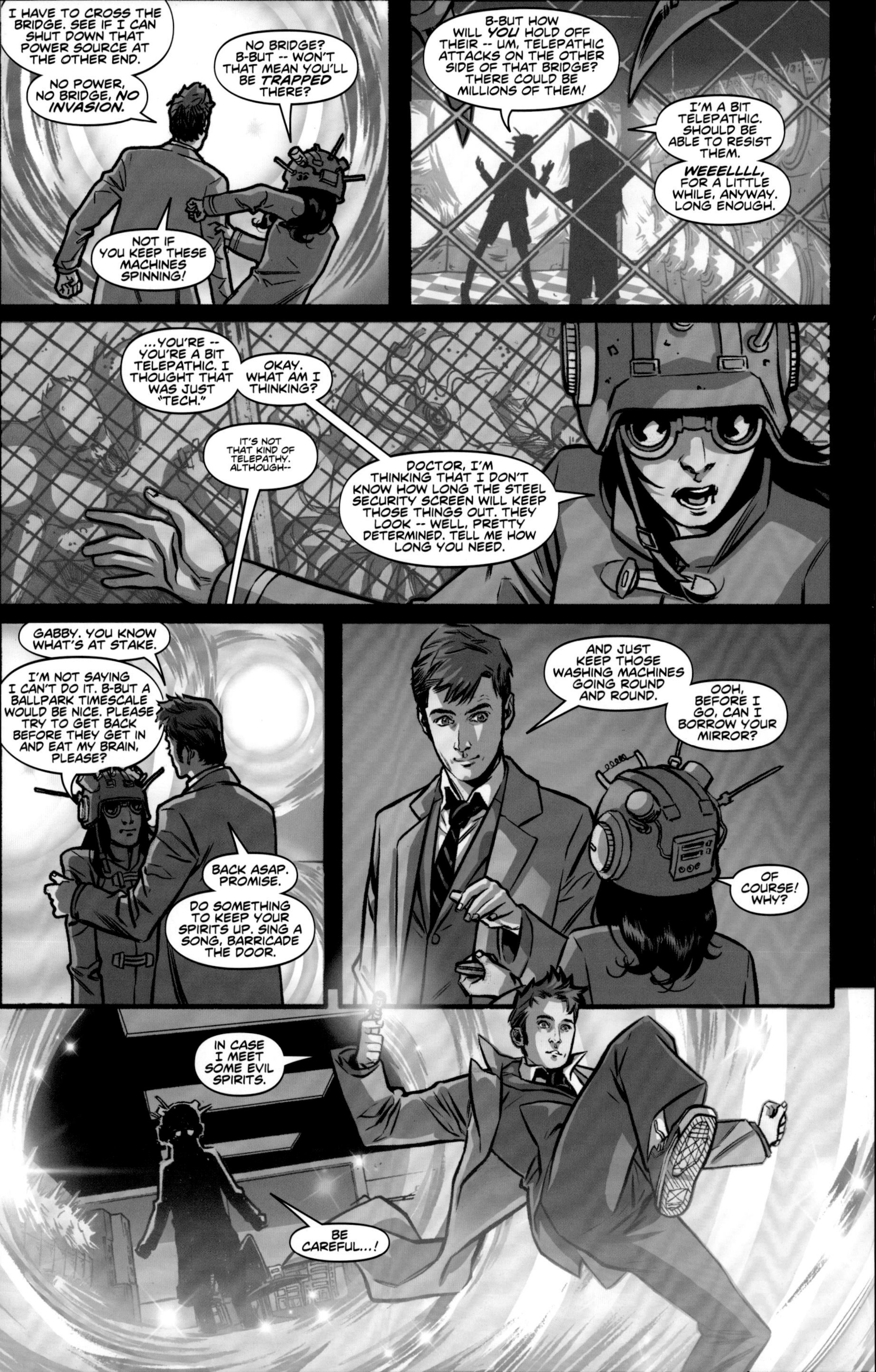
I HAVE TO CROSS THE BRIDGE. SEE IF I CAN SHUT DOWN THAT POWER SOURCE AT THE OTHER END.
NO POWER, NO BRIDGE, *NO INVASION.*
NO BRIDGE? B-BUT -- WON'T THAT MEAN YOU'LL BE *TRAPPED* THERE?
NOT IF YOU KEEP THESE MACHINES SPINNING!
B-BUT HOW WILL *YOU* HOLD OFF THEIR -- UM, TELEPATHIC ATTACKS ON THE OTHER SIDE OF THAT BRIDGE? THERE COULD BE MILLIONS OF THEM!
I'M A BIT TELEPATHIC. SHOULD BE ABLE TO RESIST THEM.
WEEELLLL, FOR A LITTLE WHILE, ANYWAY. LONG ENOUGH.
...YOU'RE -- YOU'RE A BIT TELEPATHIC. I THOUGHT THAT WAS JUST "TECH."
OKAY. WHAT AM I THINKING?
IT'S NOT THAT KIND OF TELEPATHY. ALTHOUGH--
DOCTOR, I'M THINKING THAT I DON'T KNOW HOW LONG THE STEEL SECURITY SCREEN WILL KEEP THOSE THINGS OUT. THEY LOOK -- WELL, PRETTY DETERMINED. TELL ME HOW LONG YOU NEED.
GABBY. YOU KNOW WHAT'S AT STAKE.
I'M NOT SAYING I CAN'T DO IT. B-BUT A BALLPARK TIMESCALE WOULD BE NICE. PLEASE TRY TO GET BACK BEFORE THEY GET IN AND EAT MY BRAIN, PLEASE?
BACK ASAP. PROMISE.
DO SOMETHING TO KEEP YOUR SPIRITS UP. SING A SONG, BARRICADE THE DOOR.
AND JUST KEEP THOSE WASHING MACHINES GOING ROUND AND ROUND.
OOH, BEFORE I GO, CAN I BORROW YOUR MIRROR?
OF COURSE! WHY?
IN CASE I MEET SOME EVIL SPIRITS.
BE CAREFUL...!

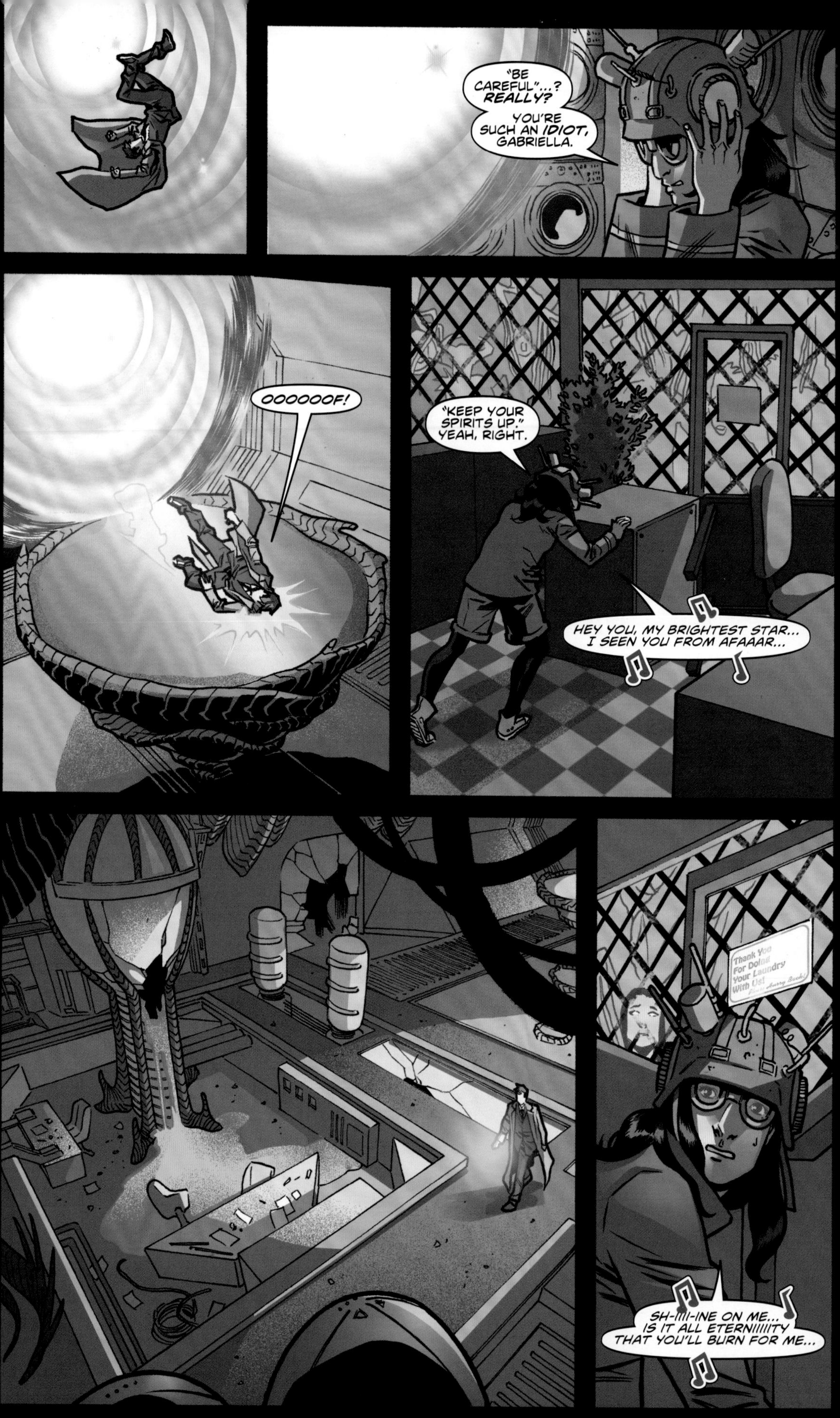

"BE CAREFUL"...? REALLY?
YOU'RE SUCH AN IDIOT, GABRIELLA.
OOOOOOF!
"KEEP YOUR SPIRITS UP." YEAH, RIGHT.
HEY YOU, MY BRIGHTEST STAR... I SEEN YOU FROM AFAAAR...
Thank You For Doing Your Laundry With Us!
SH-IIII-INE ON ME... IS IT ALL ETERNIIIIITY THAT YOU'LL BURN FOR ME...

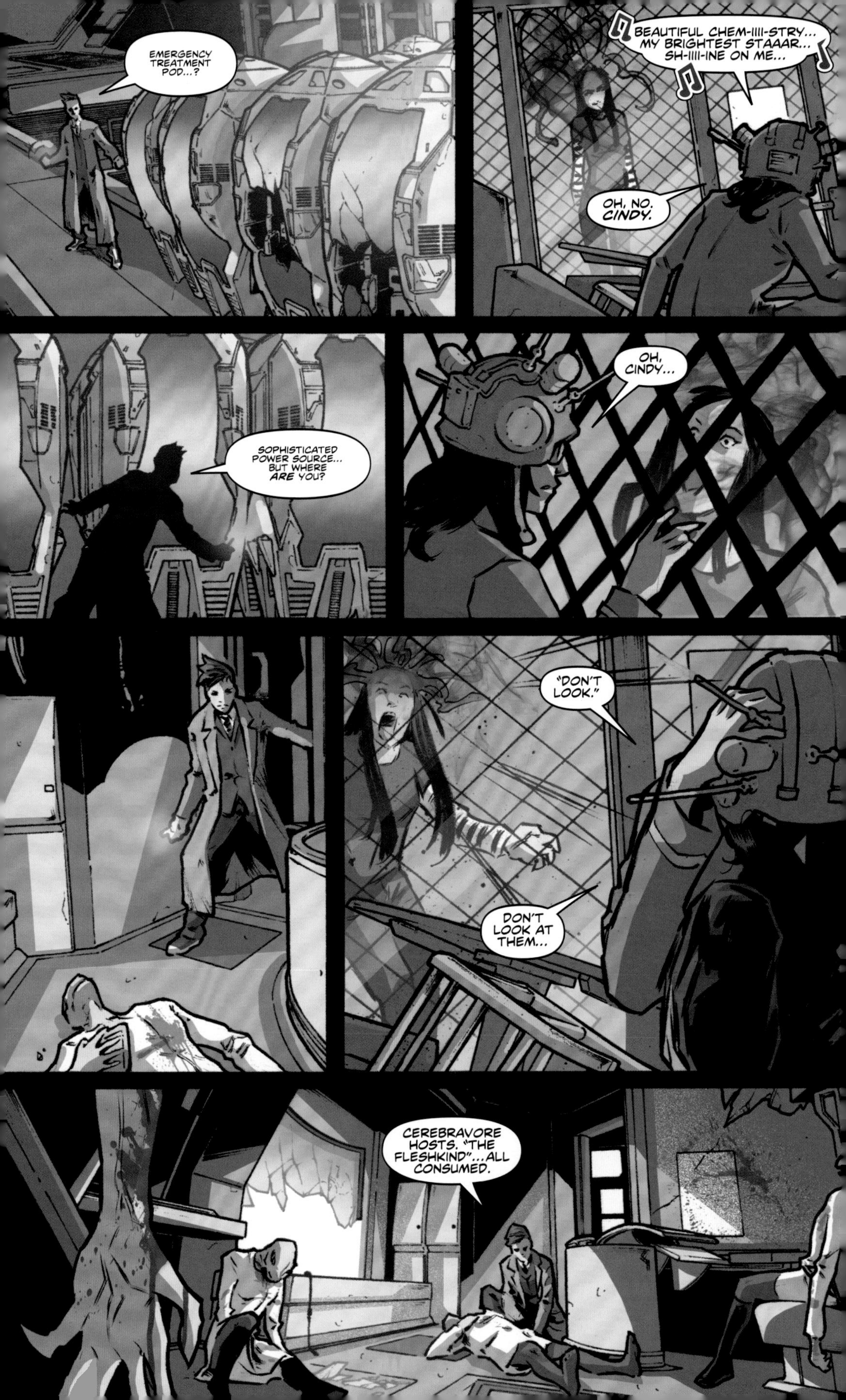
EMERGENCY TREATMENT POD...?
BEAUTIFUL CHEM-IIII-STRY... MY BRIGHTEST STAAAR... SH-IIII-INE ON ME...
OH, NO. CINDY.
SOPHISTICATED POWER SOURCE... BUT WHERE ARE YOU?
OH, CINDY...
"DON'T LOOK."
DON'T LOOK AT THEM...
CEREBRAVORE HOSTS. "THE FLESHKIND"...ALL CONSUMED.

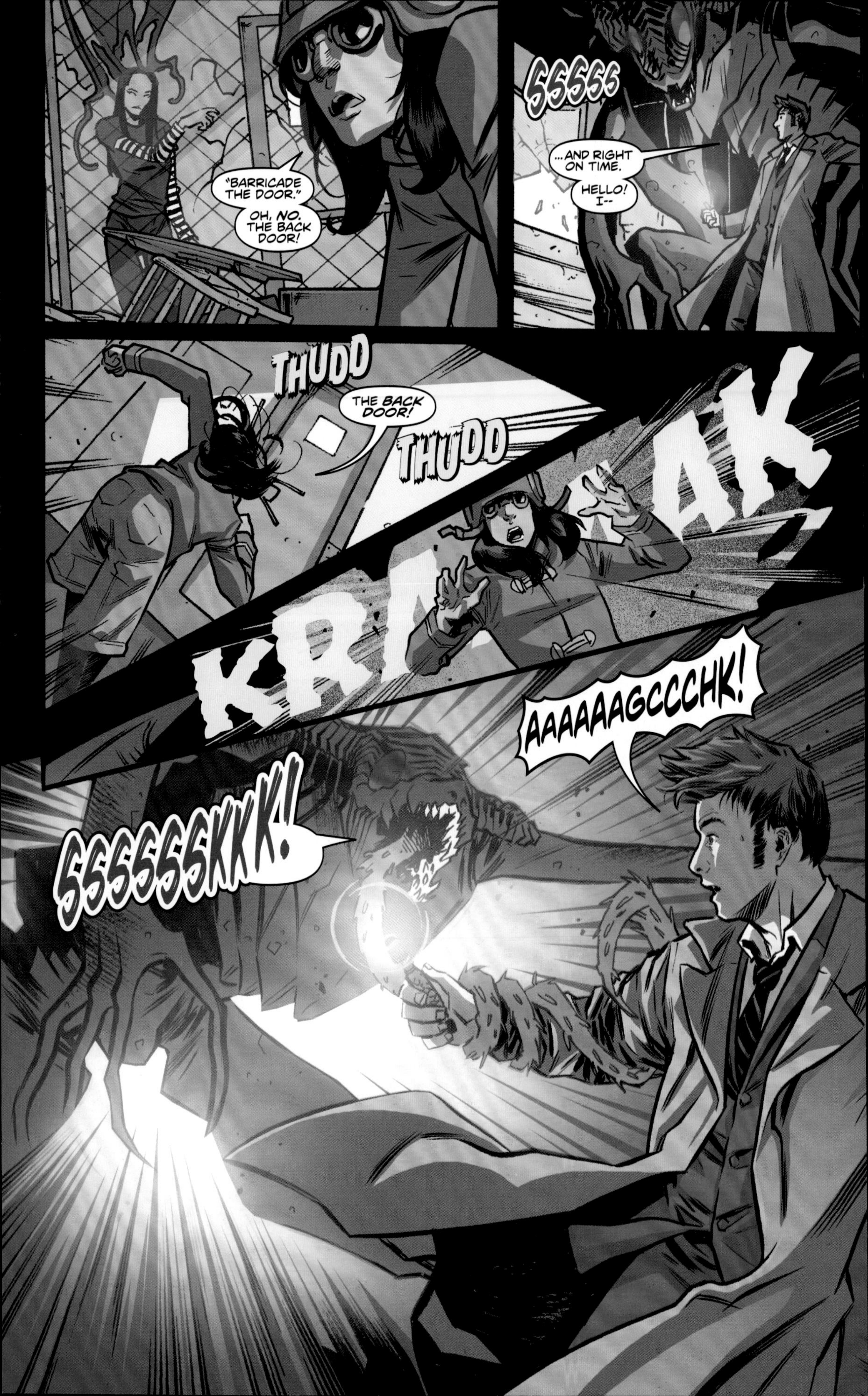
"BARRICADE THE DOOR."
OH, NO. THE BACK DOOR!
SSSSS
...AND RIGHT ON TIME.
HELLO! I--
THUDD
THE BACK DOOR!
THUDD
KRAKAK
AAAAAAGCCCHK!
SSSSSSKKK!

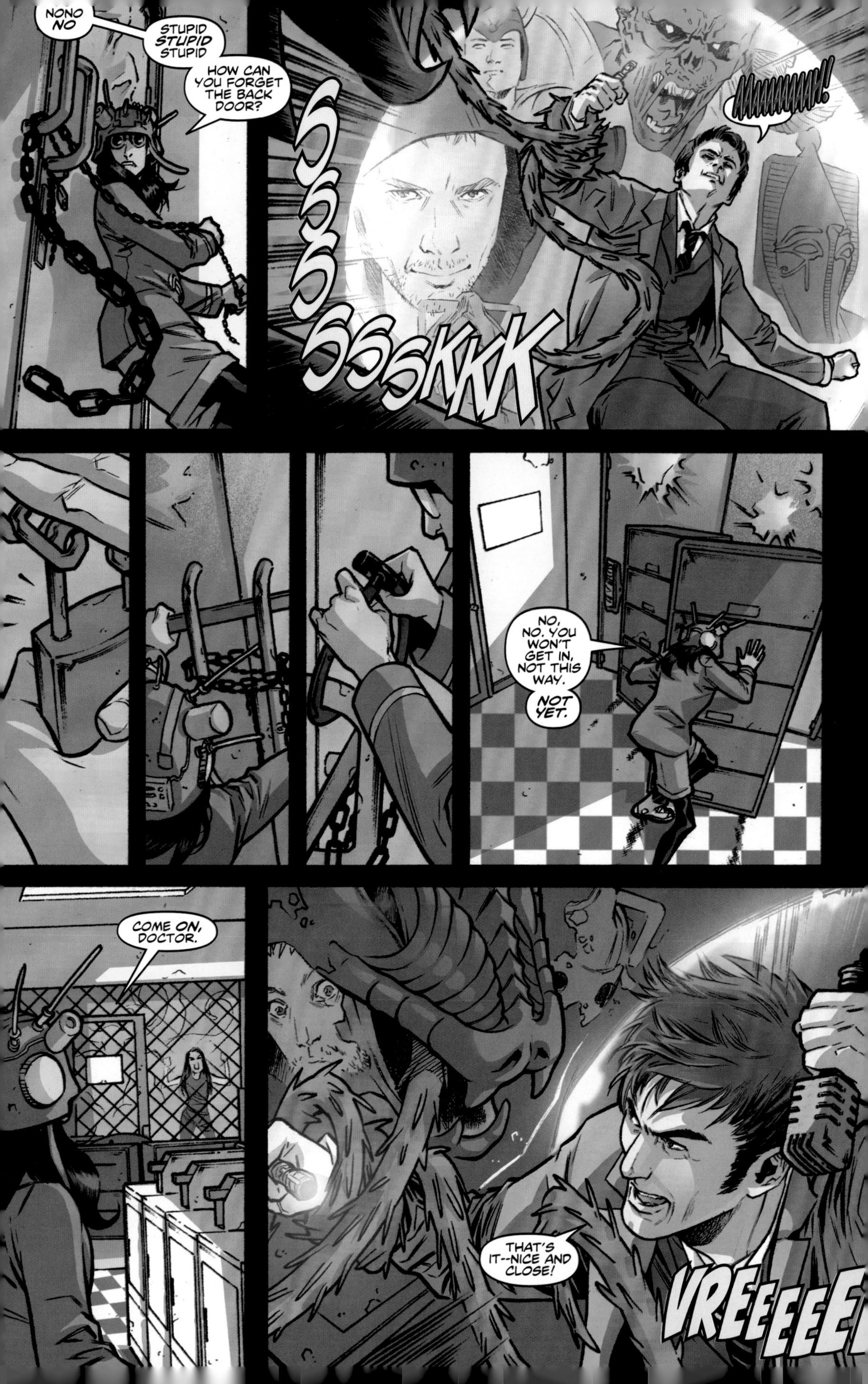
NONO NO
STUPID STUPID STUPID
HOW CAN YOU FORGET THE BACK DOOR?
SSSSSSSKKK
AAAAAAAAAH!
NO, NO. YOU WON'T GET IN, NOT THIS WAY.
NOT YET.
COME ON, DOCTOR.
THAT'S IT--NICE AND CLOSE!
VREEEEEE

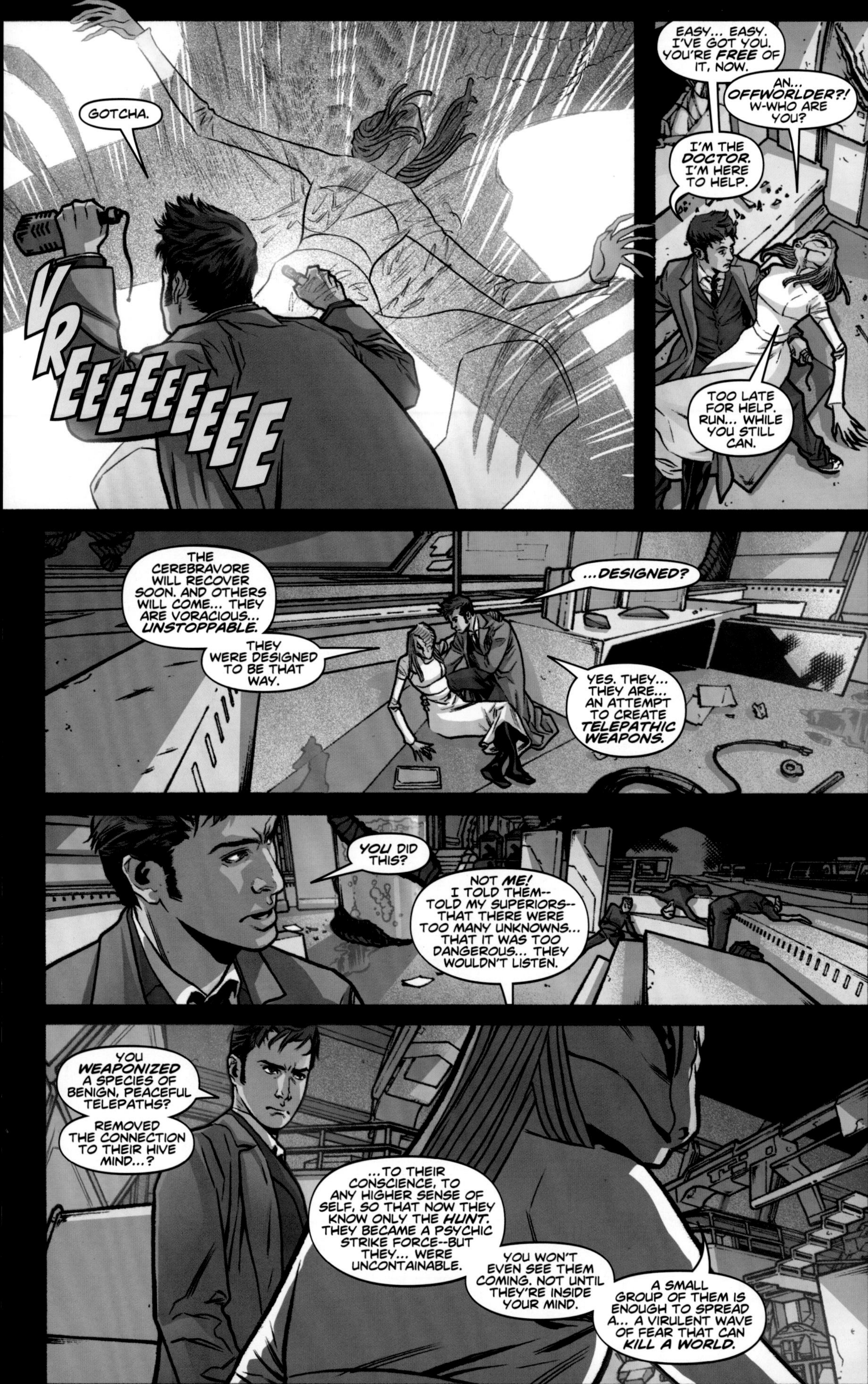
GOTCHA.
VREEEEEEEEEE
EASY... EASY. I'VE GOT YOU. YOU'RE FREE OF IT, NOW.
AN... OFFWORLDER?! W-WHO ARE YOU?
I'M THE DOCTOR. I'M HERE TO HELP.
TOO LATE FOR HELP. RUN... WHILE YOU STILL CAN.
THE CEREBRAVORE WILL RECOVER SOON. AND OTHERS WILL COME... THEY ARE VORACIOUS... UNSTOPPABLE.
THEY WERE DESIGNED TO BE THAT WAY.
...DESIGNED?
YES. THEY... THEY ARE... AN ATTEMPT TO CREATE TELEPATHIC WEAPONS.
YOU DID THIS?
NOT ME! I TOLD THEM-- TOLD MY SUPERIORS-- THAT THERE WERE TOO MANY UNKNOWNS... THAT IT WAS TOO DANGEROUS... THEY WOULDN'T LISTEN.
YOU WEAPONIZED A SPECIES OF BENIGN, PEACEFUL TELEPATHS?
REMOVED THE CONNECTION TO THEIR HIVE MIND...?
...TO THEIR CONSCIENCE, TO ANY HIGHER SENSE OF SELF, SO THAT NOW THEY KNOW ONLY THE HUNT. THEY BECAME A PSYCHIC STRIKE FORCE--BUT THEY... WERE UNCONTAINABLE.
YOU WON'T EVEN SEE THEM COMING. NOT UNTIL THEY'RE INSIDE YOUR MIND.
A SMALL GROUP OF THEM IS ENOUGH TO SPREAD A... A VIRULENT WAVE OF FEAR THAT CAN KILL A WORLD.

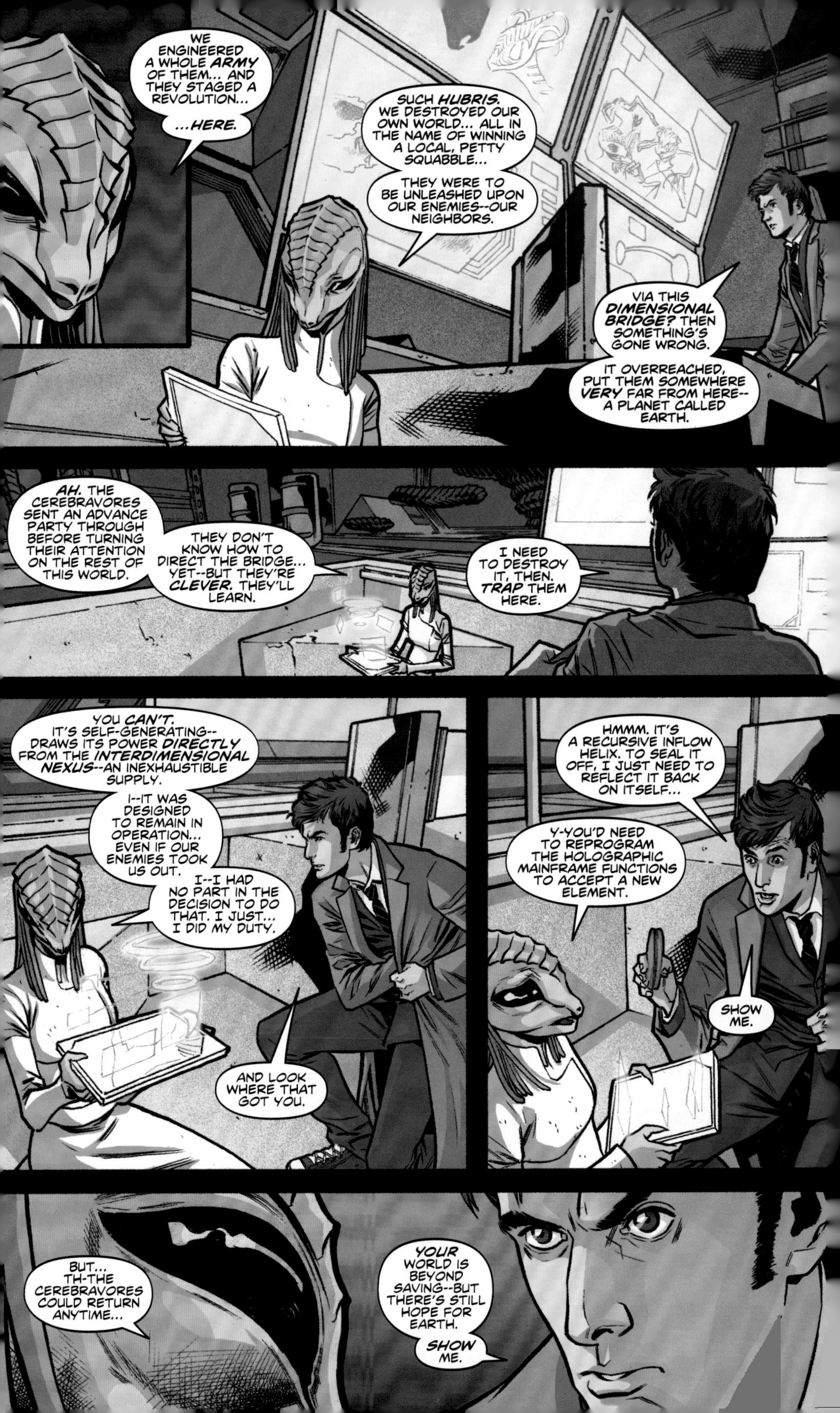
WE ENGINEERED A WHOLE ARMY OF THEM... AND THEY STAGED A REVOLUTION...
...HERE.
SUCH HUBRIS. WE DESTROYED OUR OWN WORLD... ALL IN THE NAME OF WINNING A LOCAL, PETTY SQUABBLE...
THEY WERE TO BE UNLEASHED UPON OUR ENEMIES--OUR NEIGHBORS.
VIA THIS DIMENSIONAL BRIDGE? THEN SOMETHING'S GONE WRONG.
IT OVERREACHED, PUT THEM SOMEWHERE VERY FAR FROM HERE-- A PLANET CALLED EARTH.
AH. THE CEREBRAVORES SENT AN ADVANCE PARTY THROUGH BEFORE TURNING THEIR ATTENTION ON THE REST OF THIS WORLD.
THEY DON'T KNOW HOW TO DIRECT THE BRIDGE... YET--BUT THEY'RE CLEVER. THEY'LL LEARN.
I NEED TO DESTROY IT, THEN. TRAP THEM HERE.
YOU CAN'T. IT'S SELF-GENERATING-- DRAWS ITS POWER DIRECTLY FROM THE INTERDIMENSIONAL NEXUS--AN INEXHAUSTIBLE SUPPLY.
I--IT WAS DESIGNED TO REMAIN IN OPERATION... EVEN IF OUR ENEMIES TOOK US OUT.
I--I HAD NO PART IN THE DECISION TO DO THAT. I JUST... I DID MY DUTY.
AND LOOK WHERE THAT GOT YOU.
HMMM. IT'S A RECURSIVE INFLOW HELIX. TO SEAL IT OFF, I JUST NEED TO REFLECT IT BACK ON ITSELF...
Y-YOU'D NEED TO REPROGRAM THE HOLOGRAPHIC MAINFRAME FUNCTIONS TO ACCEPT A NEW ELEMENT.
SHOW ME.
BUT... TH-THE CEREBRAVORES COULD RETURN ANYTIME...
YOUR WORLD IS BEYOND SAVING--BUT THERE'S STILL HOPE FOR EARTH.
SHOW ME.

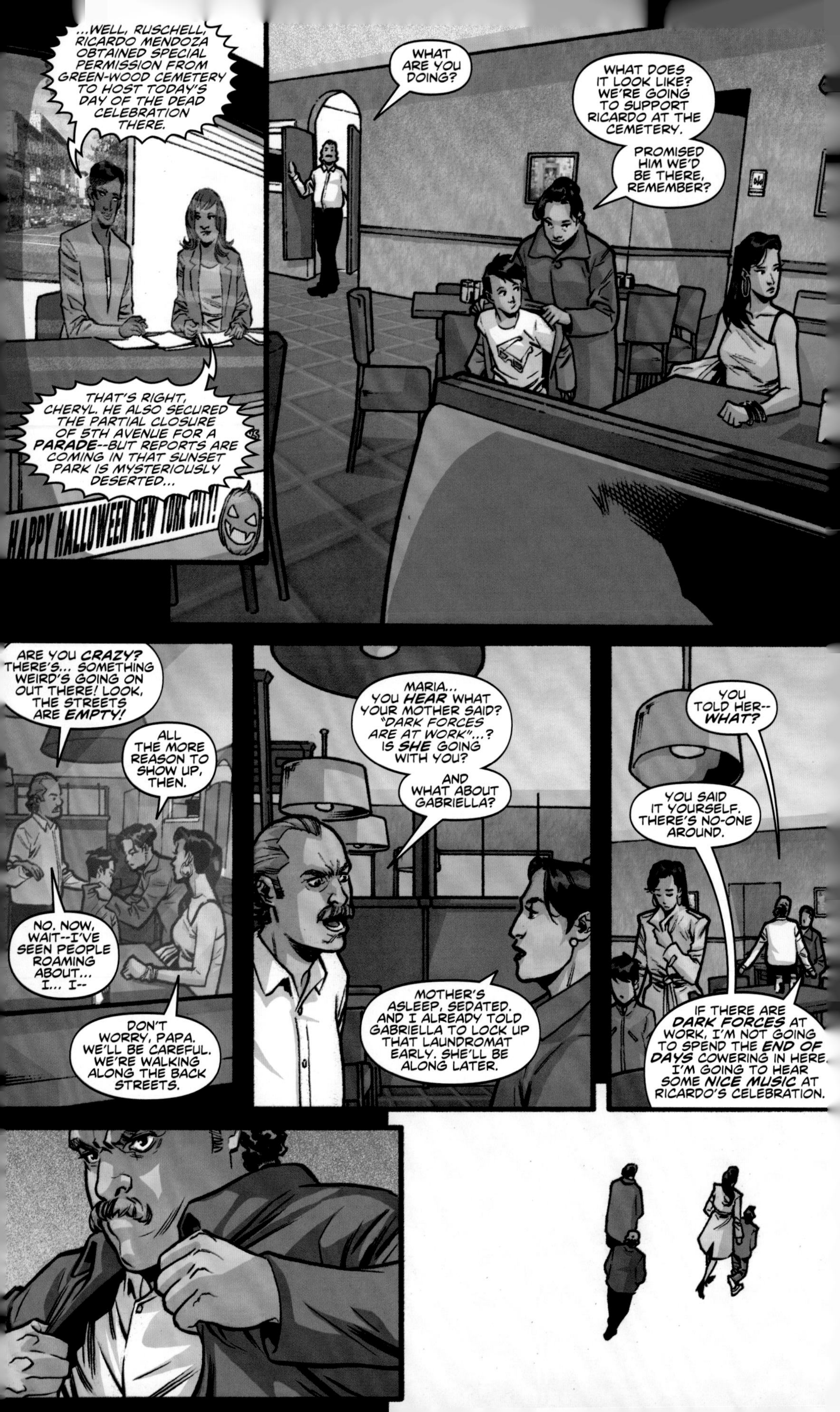
...WELL, RUSCHELL, RICARDO MENDOZA OBTAINED SPECIAL PERMISSION FROM GREEN-WOOD CEMETERY TO HOST TODAY'S DAY OF THE DEAD CELEBRATION THERE.
THAT'S RIGHT, CHERYL. HE ALSO SECURED THE PARTIAL CLOSURE OF 5TH AVENUE FOR A PARADE--BUT REPORTS ARE COMING IN THAT SUNSET PARK IS MYSTERIOUSLY DESERTED...
HAPPY HALLOWEEN NEW YORK CITY!
WHAT ARE YOU DOING?
WHAT DOES IT LOOK LIKE? WE'RE GOING TO SUPPORT RICARDO AT THE CEMETERY.
PROMISED HIM WE'D BE THERE, REMEMBER?
ARE YOU CRAZY? THERE'S... SOMETHING WEIRD'S GOING ON OUT THERE! LOOK, THE STREETS ARE EMPTY!
ALL THE MORE REASON TO SHOW UP, THEN.
NO. NOW, WAIT--I'VE SEEN PEOPLE ROAMING ABOUT... I... I--
DON'T WORRY, PAPA. WE'LL BE CAREFUL. WE'RE WALKING ALONG THE BACK STREETS.
MARIA... YOU HEAR WHAT YOUR MOTHER SAID? "DARK FORCES ARE AT WORK"...? IS SHE GOING WITH YOU?
AND WHAT ABOUT GABRIELLA?
MOTHER'S ASLEEP, SEDATED. AND I ALREADY TOLD GABRIELLA TO LOCK UP THAT LAUNDROMAT EARLY. SHE'LL BE ALONG LATER.
YOU TOLD HER-- WHAT?
YOU SAID IT YOURSELF. THERE'S NO-ONE AROUND.
IF THERE ARE DARK FORCES AT WORK, I'M NOT GOING TO SPEND THE END OF DAYS COWERING IN HERE. I'M GOING TO HEAR SOME NICE MUSIC AT RICARDO'S CELEBRATION.

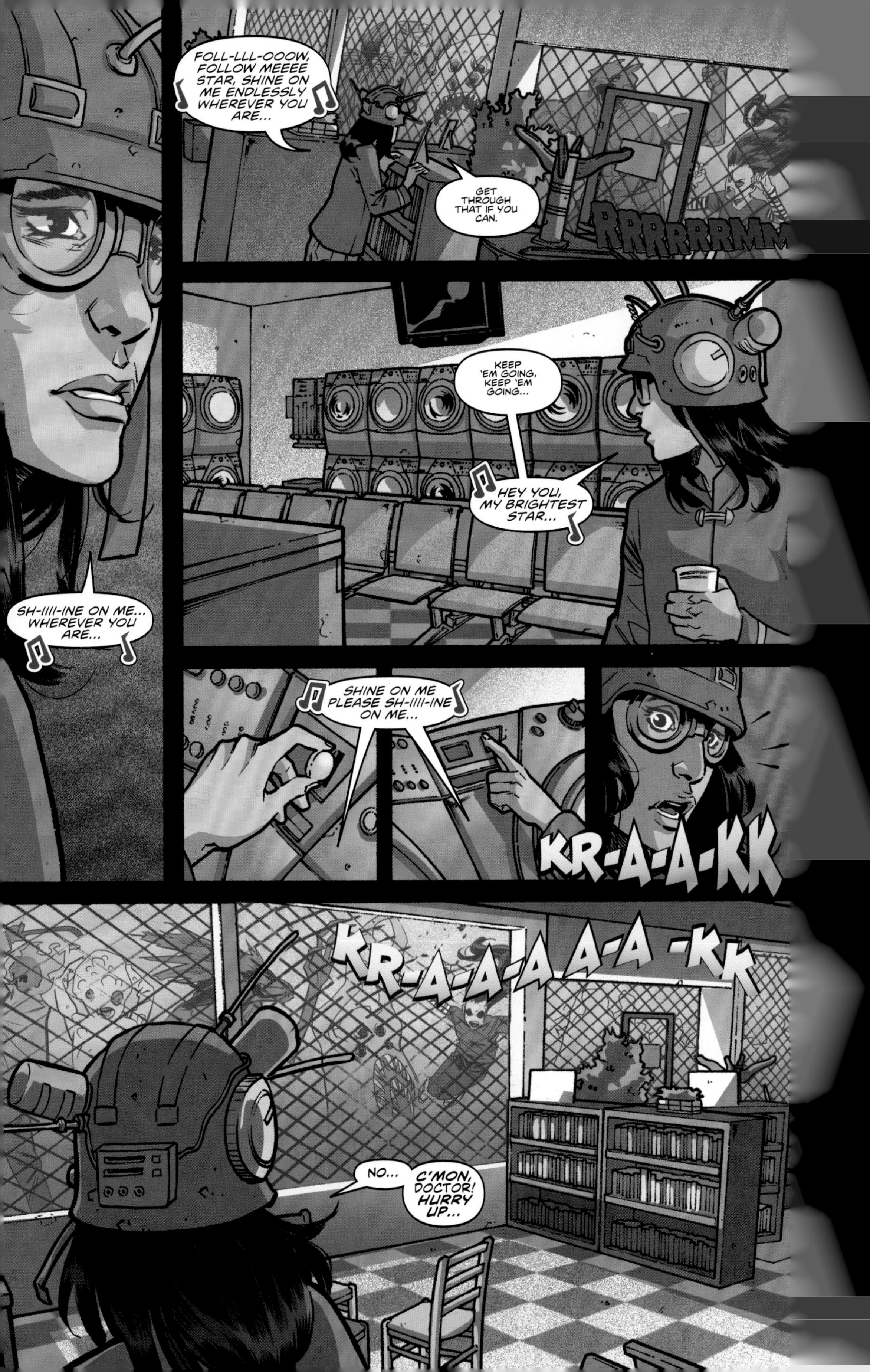

FOLL-LLL-OOOW, FOLLOW MEEEE STAR, SHINE ON ME ENDLESSLY WHEREVER YOU ARE...
GET THROUGH THAT IF YOU CAN.
RRRRRRRMM
KEEP 'EM GOING, KEEP 'EM GOING...
HEY YOU, MY BRIGHTEST STAR...
SH-IIII-INE ON ME... WHEREVER YOU ARE...
SHINE ON ME PLEASE SH-IIII-INE ON ME...
KR-A-A-KK
KR-A-A-A A-A -KK
NO...
C'MON, DOCTOR! HURRY UP...

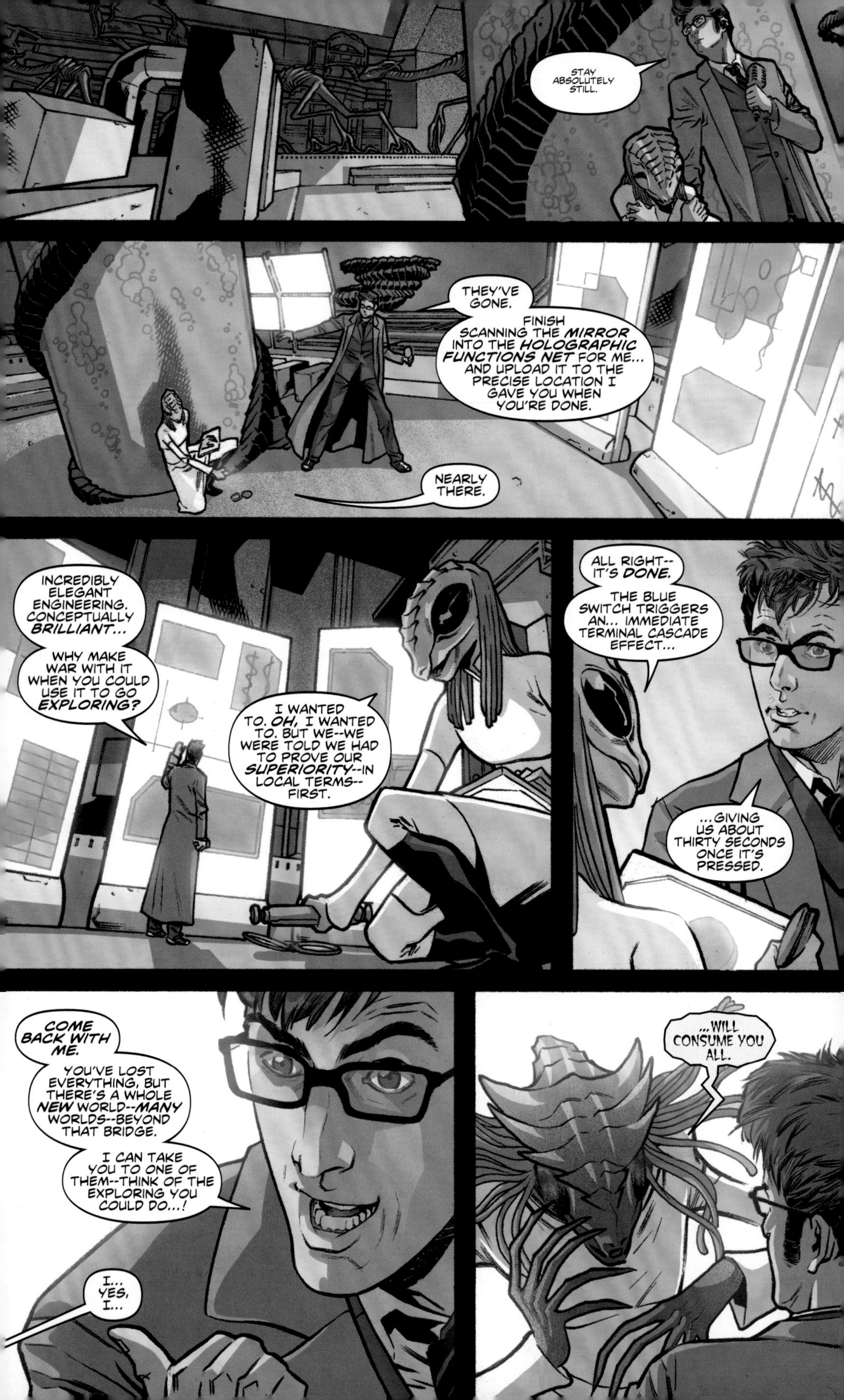

STAY ABSOLUTELY STILL.
THEY'VE GONE.
FINISH SCANNING THE MIRROR INTO THE HOLOGRAPHIC FUNCTIONS NET FOR ME... AND UPLOAD IT TO THE PRECISE LOCATION I GAVE YOU WHEN YOU'RE DONE.
NEARLY THERE.
INCREDIBLY ELEGANT ENGINEERING. CONCEPTUALLY BRILLIANT...
WHY MAKE WAR WITH IT WHEN YOU COULD USE IT TO GO EXPLORING?
I WANTED TO. OH, I WANTED TO. BUT WE--WE WERE TOLD WE HAD TO PROVE OUR SUPERIORITY--IN LOCAL TERMS--FIRST.
ALL RIGHT-- IT'S DONE.
THE BLUE SWITCH TRIGGERS AN... IMMEDIATE TERMINAL CASCADE EFFECT...
...GIVING US ABOUT THIRTY SECONDS ONCE IT'S PRESSED.
COME BACK WITH ME.
YOU'VE LOST EVERYTHING, BUT THERE'S A WHOLE NEW WORLD--MANY WORLDS--BEYOND THAT BRIDGE.
I CAN TAKE YOU TO ONE OF THEM--THINK OF THE EXPLORING YOU COULD DO...!
I... YES, I...
...WILL CONSUME YOU ALL.

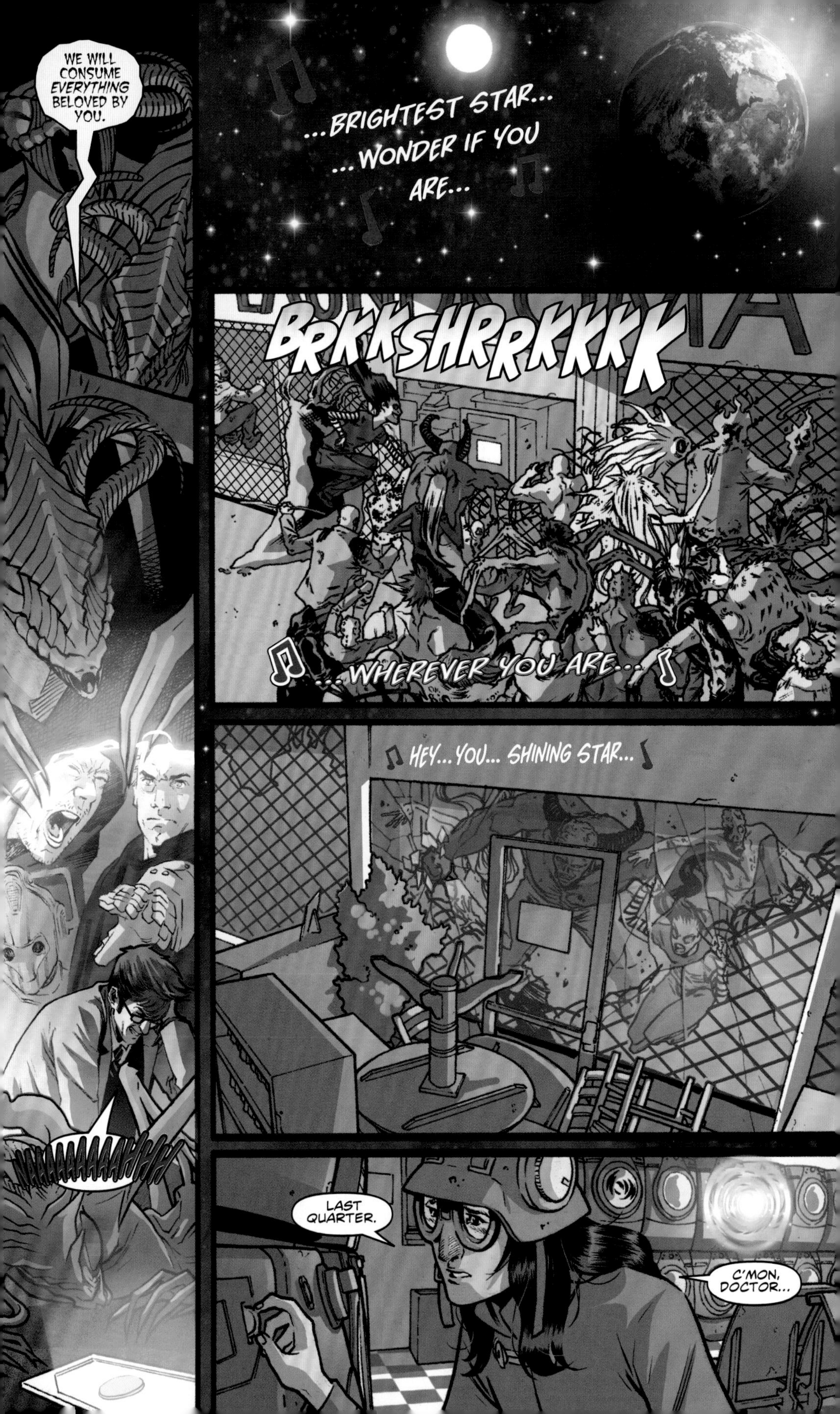
WE WILL CONSUME EVERYTHING BELOVED BY YOU.
...BRIGHTEST STAR...
...WONDER IF YOU ARE...
BRKKSHRRKKKK
...WHEREVER YOU ARE...
HEY...YOU... SHINING STAR...
NAAAAAAAAAHHHH
LAST QUARTER.
C'MON, DOCTOR...

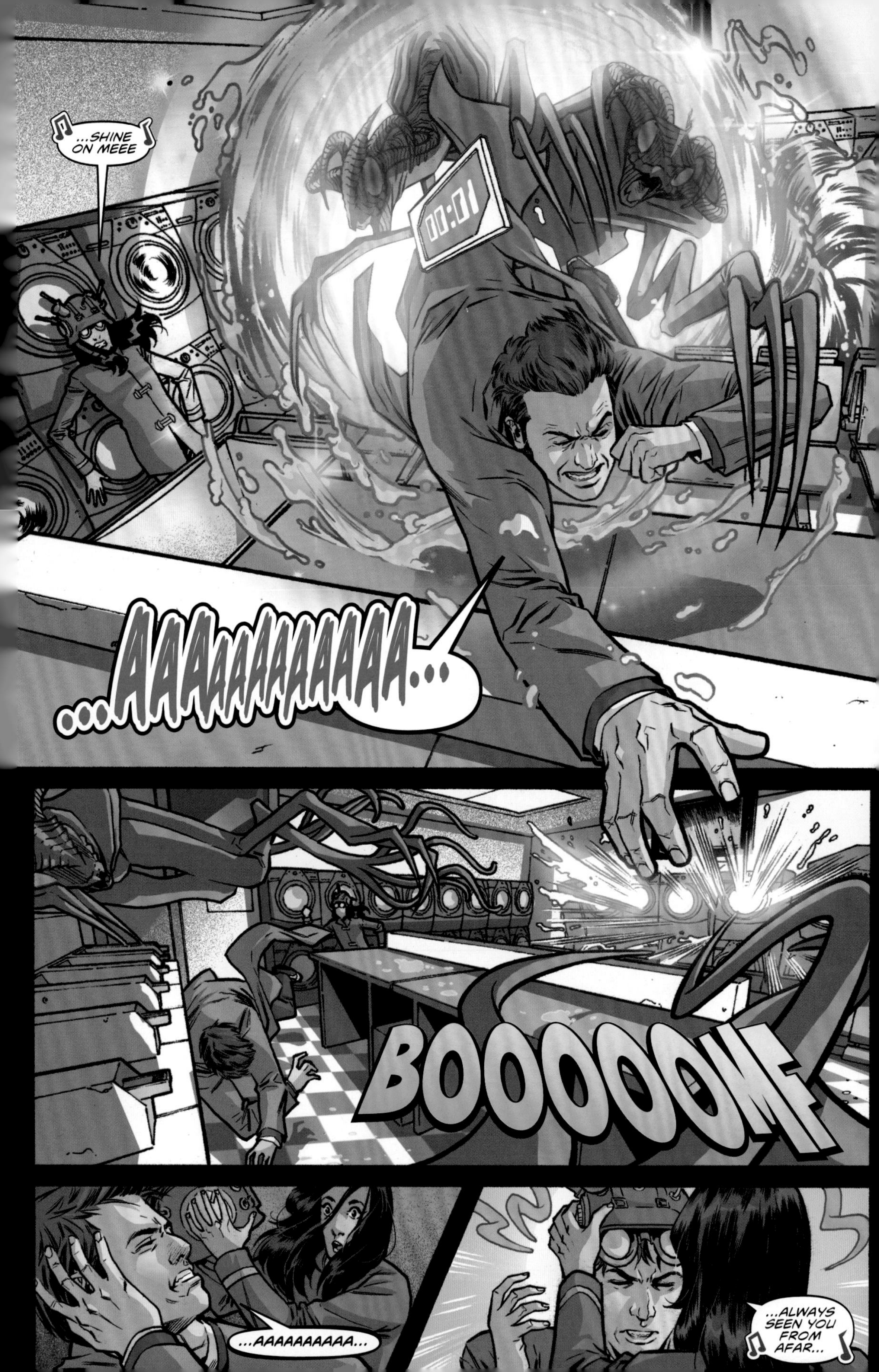
...SHINE ON MEEE
00:01
...AAAAAAAAAAAA...
BOOOOOOMF
...AAAAAAAAAA...
...ALWAYS SEEN YOU FROM AFAR...

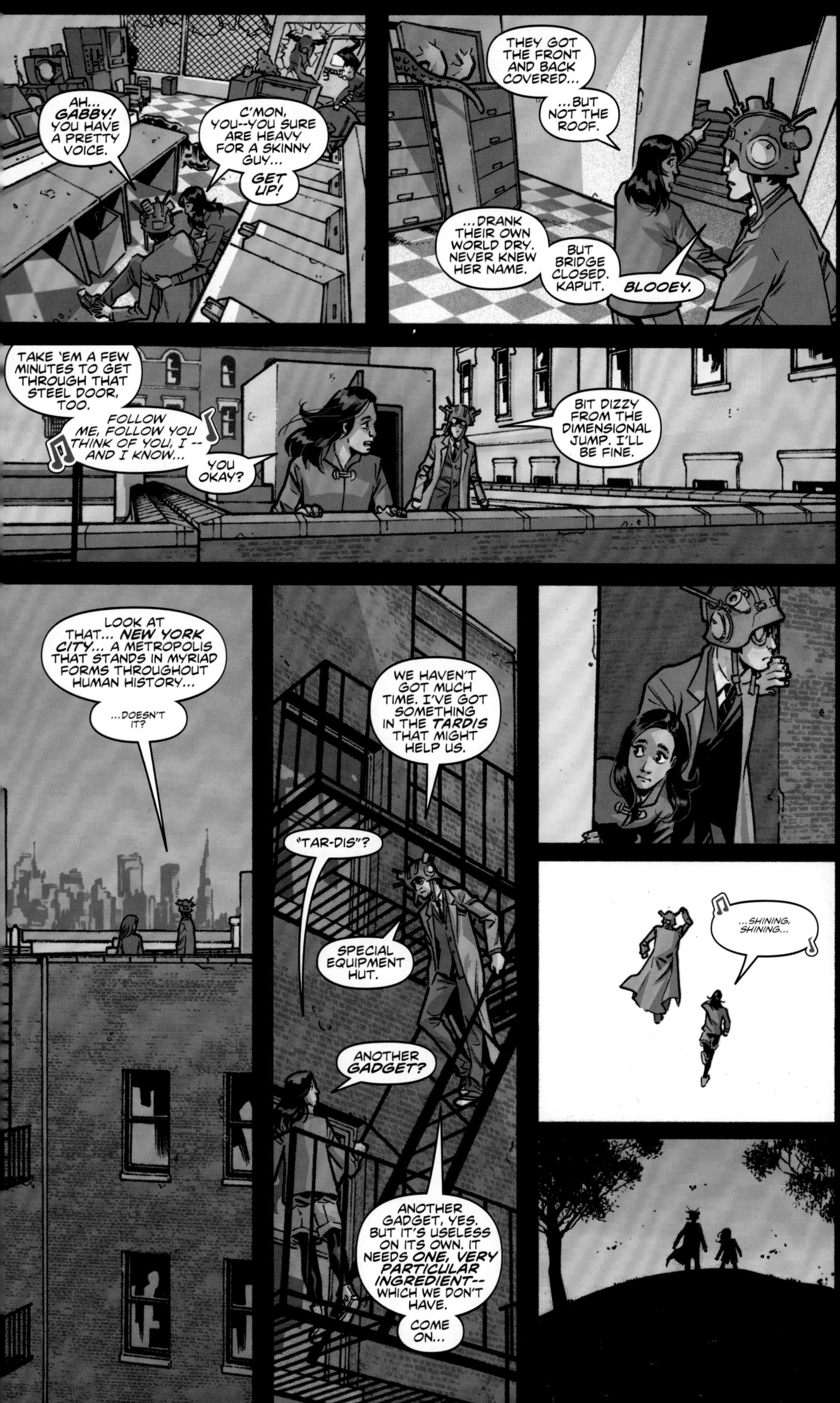
AH... GABBY! YOU HAVE A PRETTY VOICE.
C'MON, YOU--YOU SURE ARE HEAVY FOR A SKINNY GUY...
GET UP!
THEY GOT THE FRONT AND BACK COVERED...
...BUT NOT THE ROOF.
...DRANK THEIR OWN WORLD DRY. NEVER KNEW HER NAME.
BUT BRIDGE CLOSED. KAPUT.
BLOOEY.
TAKE 'EM A FEW MINUTES TO GET THROUGH THAT STEEL DOOR, TOO.
FOLLOW ME, FOLLOW YOU THINK OF YOU, I -- AND I KNOW...
YOU OKAY?
BIT DIZZY FROM THE DIMENSIONAL JUMP. I'LL BE FINE.
LOOK AT THAT... NEW YORK CITY... A METROPOLIS THAT STANDS IN MYRIAD FORMS THROUGHOUT HUMAN HISTORY...
...DOESN'T IT?
WE HAVEN'T GOT MUCH TIME. I'VE GOT SOMETHING IN THE TARDIS THAT MIGHT HELP US.
"TAR-DIS"?
SPECIAL EQUIPMENT HUT.
ANOTHER GADGET?
ANOTHER GADGET, YES. BUT IT'S USELESS ON ITS OWN. IT NEEDS ONE, VERY PARTICULAR INGREDIENT-- WHICH WE DON'T HAVE.
COME ON...
...SHINING, SHINING...

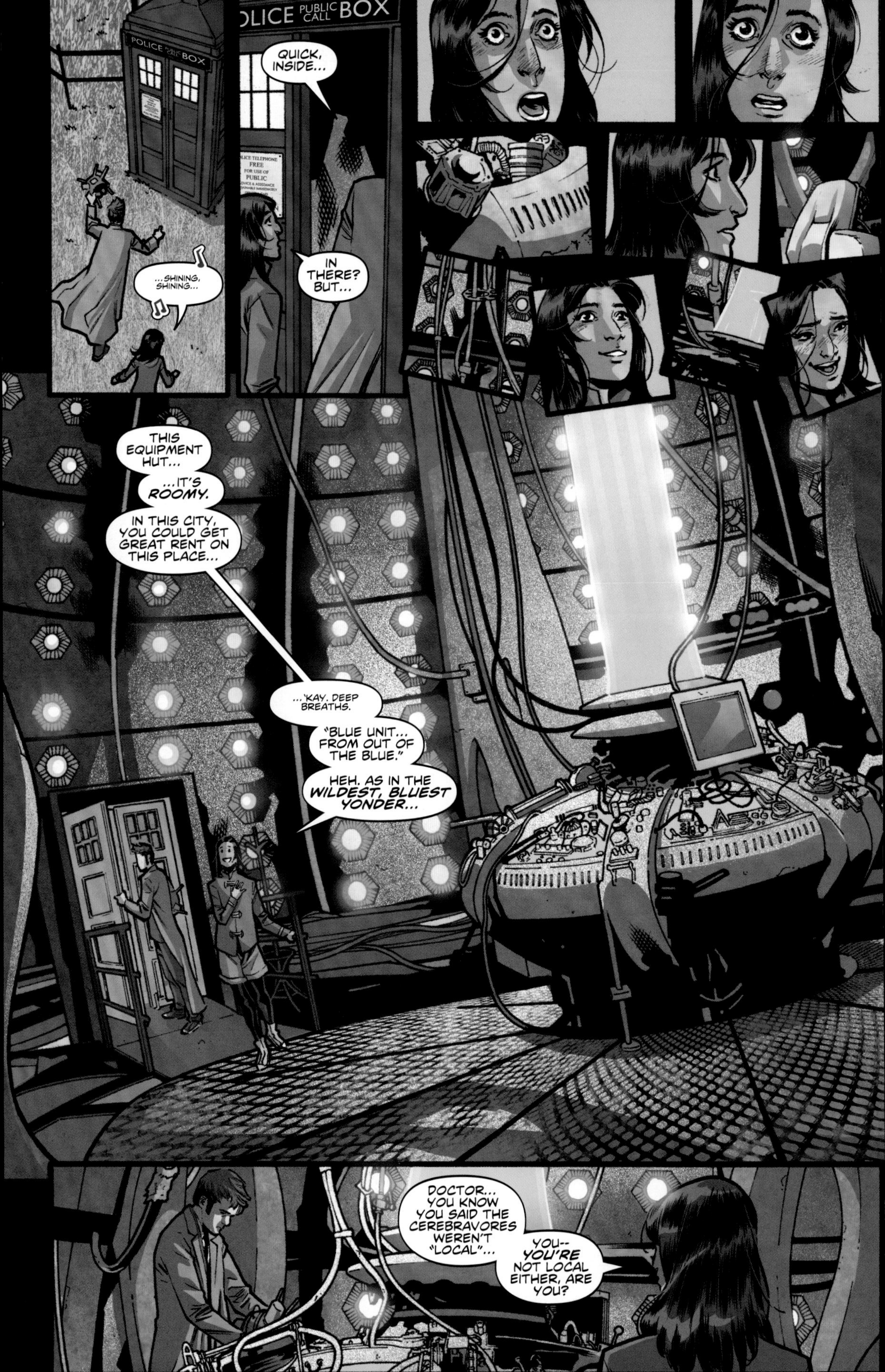
POLICE PUBLIC CALL BOX
QUICK, INSIDE...
...SHINING, SHINING...
IN THERE? BUT...
THIS EQUIPMENT HUT...
...IT'S ROOMY.
IN THIS CITY, YOU COULD GET GREAT RENT ON THIS PLACE...
...'KAY. DEEP BREATHS.
"BLUE UNIT... FROM OUT OF THE BLUE."
HEH. AS IN THE WILDEST, BLUEST YONDER...
DOCTOR... YOU KNOW YOU SAID THE CEREBRAVORES WEREN'T "LOCAL"...
YOU-- YOU'RE NOT LOCAL EITHER, ARE YOU?

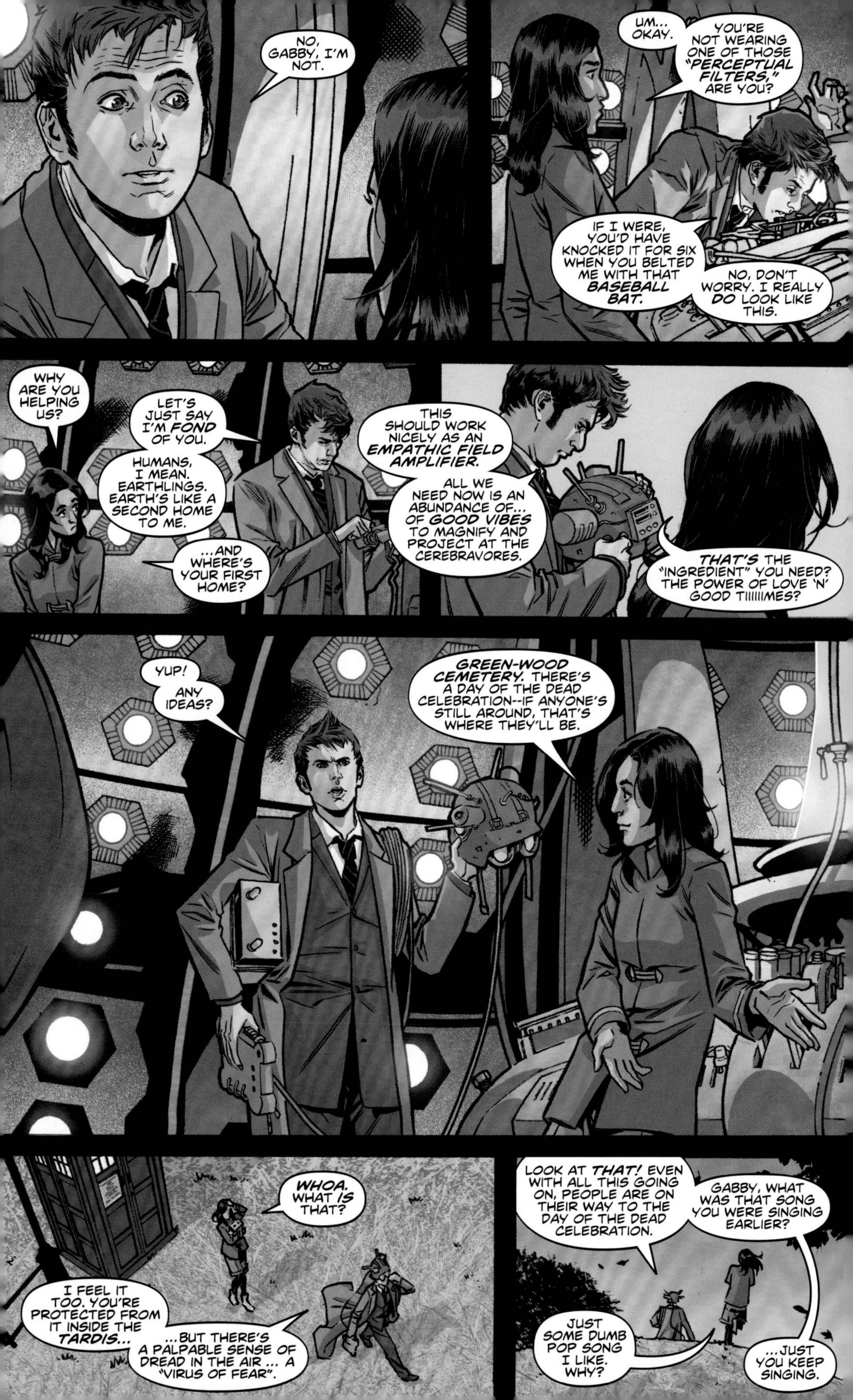
NO, GABBY, I'M NOT.
UM... OKAY.
YOU'RE NOT WEARING ONE OF THOSE "PERCEPTUAL FILTERS," ARE YOU?
IF I WERE, YOU'D HAVE KNOCKED IT FOR SIX WHEN YOU BELTED ME WITH THAT BASEBALL BAT.
NO, DON'T WORRY. I REALLY DO LOOK LIKE THIS.
WHY ARE YOU HELPING US?
LET'S JUST SAY I'M FOND OF YOU.
HUMANS, I MEAN. EARTHLINGS. EARTH'S LIKE A SECOND HOME TO ME.
...AND WHERE'S YOUR FIRST HOME?
THIS SHOULD WORK NICELY AS AN EMPATHIC FIELD AMPLIFIER.
ALL WE NEED NOW IS AN ABUNDANCE OF... OF GOOD VIBES TO MAGNIFY AND PROJECT AT THE CEREBRAVORES.
THAT'S THE "INGREDIENT" YOU NEED? THE POWER OF LOVE 'N' GOOD TIIIIIIMES?
YUP!
ANY IDEAS?
GREEN-WOOD CEMETERY. THERE'S A DAY OF THE DEAD CELEBRATION--IF ANYONE'S STILL AROUND, THAT'S WHERE THEY'LL BE.
WHOA. WHAT IS THAT?
I FEEL IT TOO. YOU'RE PROTECTED FROM IT INSIDE THE TARDIS...
...BUT THERE'S A PALPABLE SENSE OF DREAD IN THE AIR ... A "VIRUS OF FEAR".
LOOK AT THAT! EVEN WITH ALL THIS GOING ON, PEOPLE ARE ON THEIR WAY TO THE DAY OF THE DEAD CELEBRATION.
GABBY, WHAT WAS THAT SONG YOU WERE SINGING EARLIER?
JUST SOME DUMB POP SONG I LIKE. WHY?
...JUST YOU KEEP SINGING.

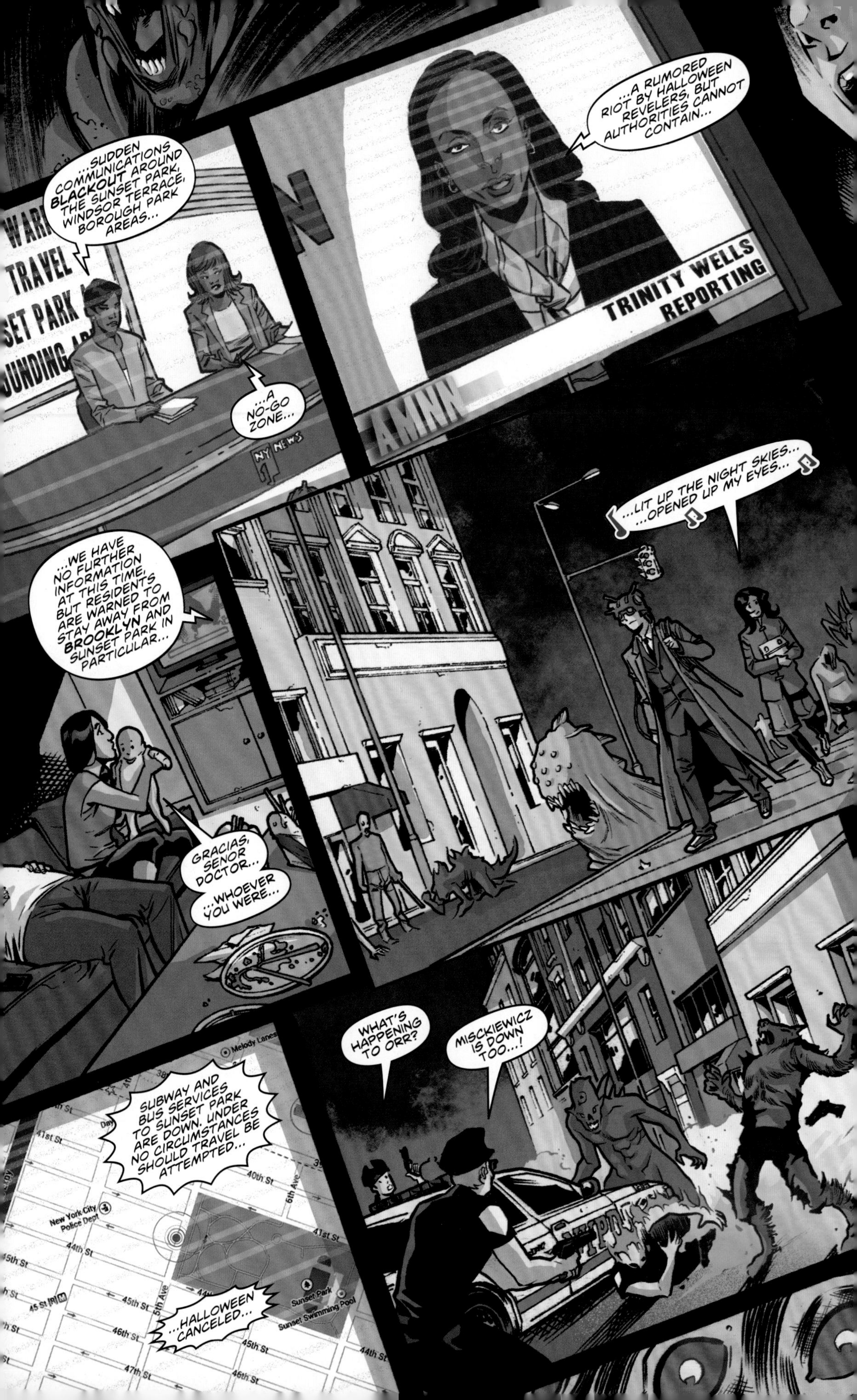

...SUDDEN COMMUNICATIONS BLACKOUT AROUND THE SUNSET PARK, WINDSOR TERRACE, BOROUGH PARK AREAS...
...A NO-GO ZONE...
NY NEWS 1
...A RUMORED RIOT BY HALLOWEEN REVELERS, BUT AUTHORITIES CANNOT CONTAIN...
TRINITY WELLS REPORTING
...WE HAVE NO FURTHER INFORMATION AT THIS TIME, BUT RESIDENTS ARE WARNED TO STAY AWAY FROM BROOKLYN AND SUNSET PARK IN PARTICULAR...
GRACIAS, SENOR DOCTOR...
...WHOEVER YOU WERE...
...LIT UP THE NIGHT SKIES... ...OPENED UP MY EYES...
SUBWAY AND BUS SERVICES TO SUNSET PARK ARE DOWN. UNDER NO CIRCUMSTANCES SHOULD TRAVEL BE ATTEMPTED...
...HALLOWEEN CANCELED...
New York City Police Dept
Sunset Park
Sunset Swimming Pool
WHAT'S HAPPENING TO ORR?
MISCKIEWICZ IS DOWN TOO...!

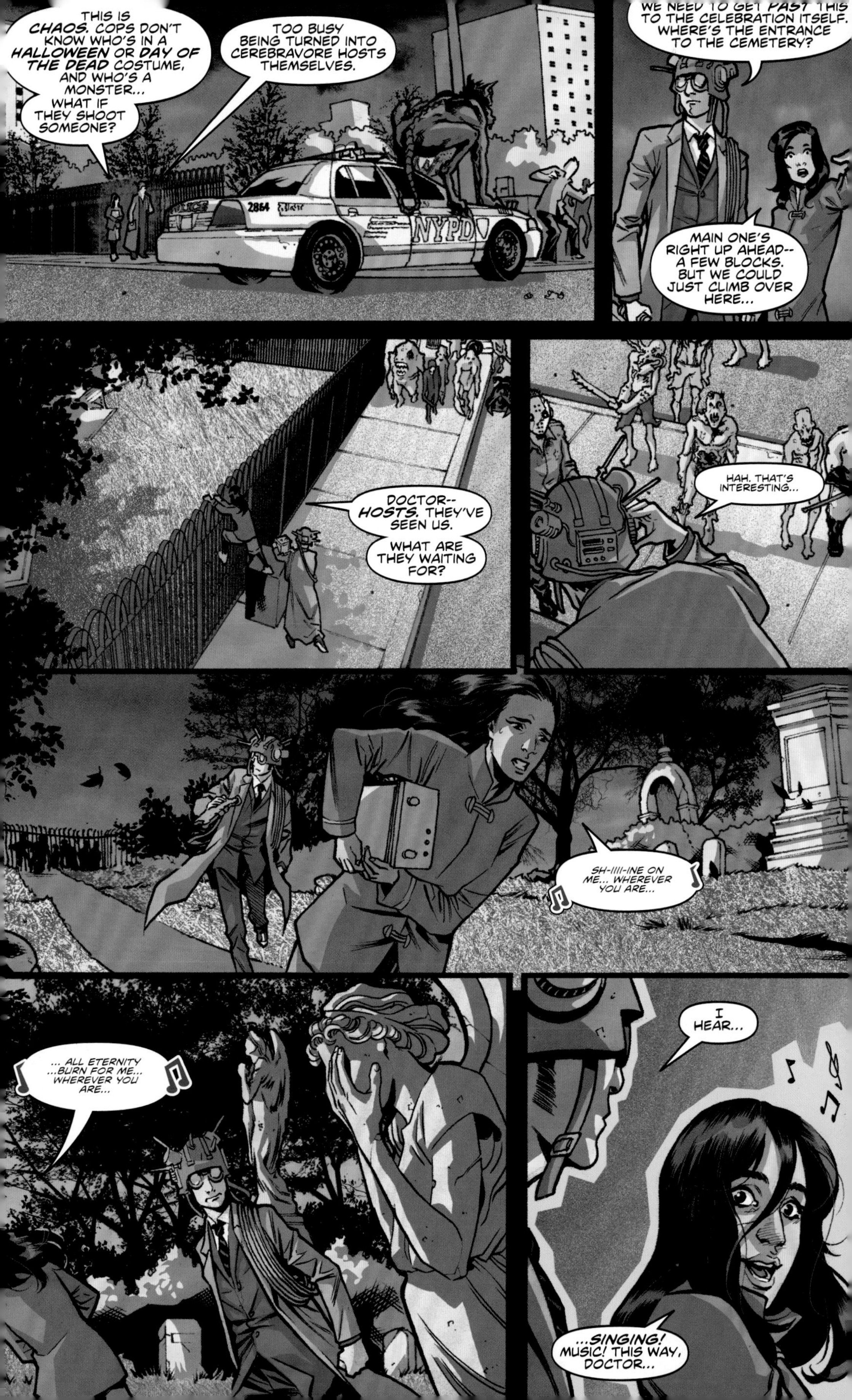

THIS IS CHAOS. COPS DON'T KNOW WHO'S IN A HALLOWEEN OR DAY OF THE DEAD COSTUME, AND WHO'S A MONSTER... WHAT IF THEY SHOOT SOMEONE?
TOO BUSY BEING TURNED INTO CEREBRAVORE HOSTS THEMSELVES.
POLICE
2864
NYPD
WE NEED TO GET PAST THIS TO THE CELEBRATION ITSELF. WHERE'S THE ENTRANCE TO THE CEMETERY?
MAIN ONE'S RIGHT UP AHEAD-- A FEW BLOCKS. BUT WE COULD JUST CLIMB OVER HERE...
DOCTOR-- HOSTS. THEY'VE SEEN US.
WHAT ARE THEY WAITING FOR?
HAH. THAT'S INTERESTING...
SH-IIII-INE ON ME... WHEREVER YOU ARE...
... ALL ETERNITY ...BURN FOR ME... WHEREVER YOU ARE...
I HEAR...
...SINGING! MUSIC! THIS WAY, DOCTOR...

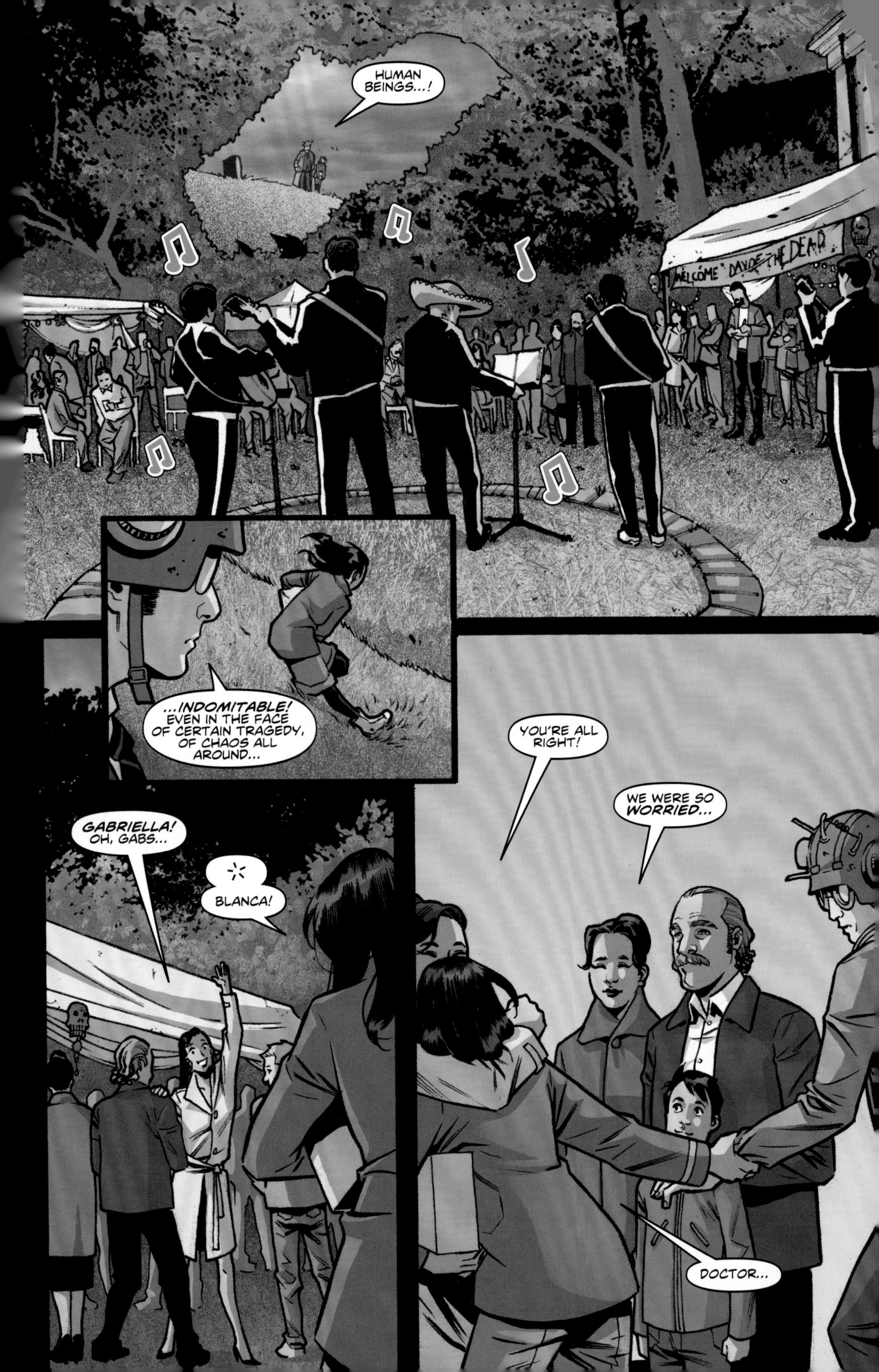
HUMAN BEINGS...!
WELCOME DAY OF THE DEAD
...INDOMITABLE! EVEN IN THE FACE OF CERTAIN TRAGEDY, OF CHAOS ALL AROUND...
YOU'RE ALL RIGHT!
WE WERE SO WORRIED...
GABRIELLA! OH, GABS...
BLANCA!
DOCTOR...

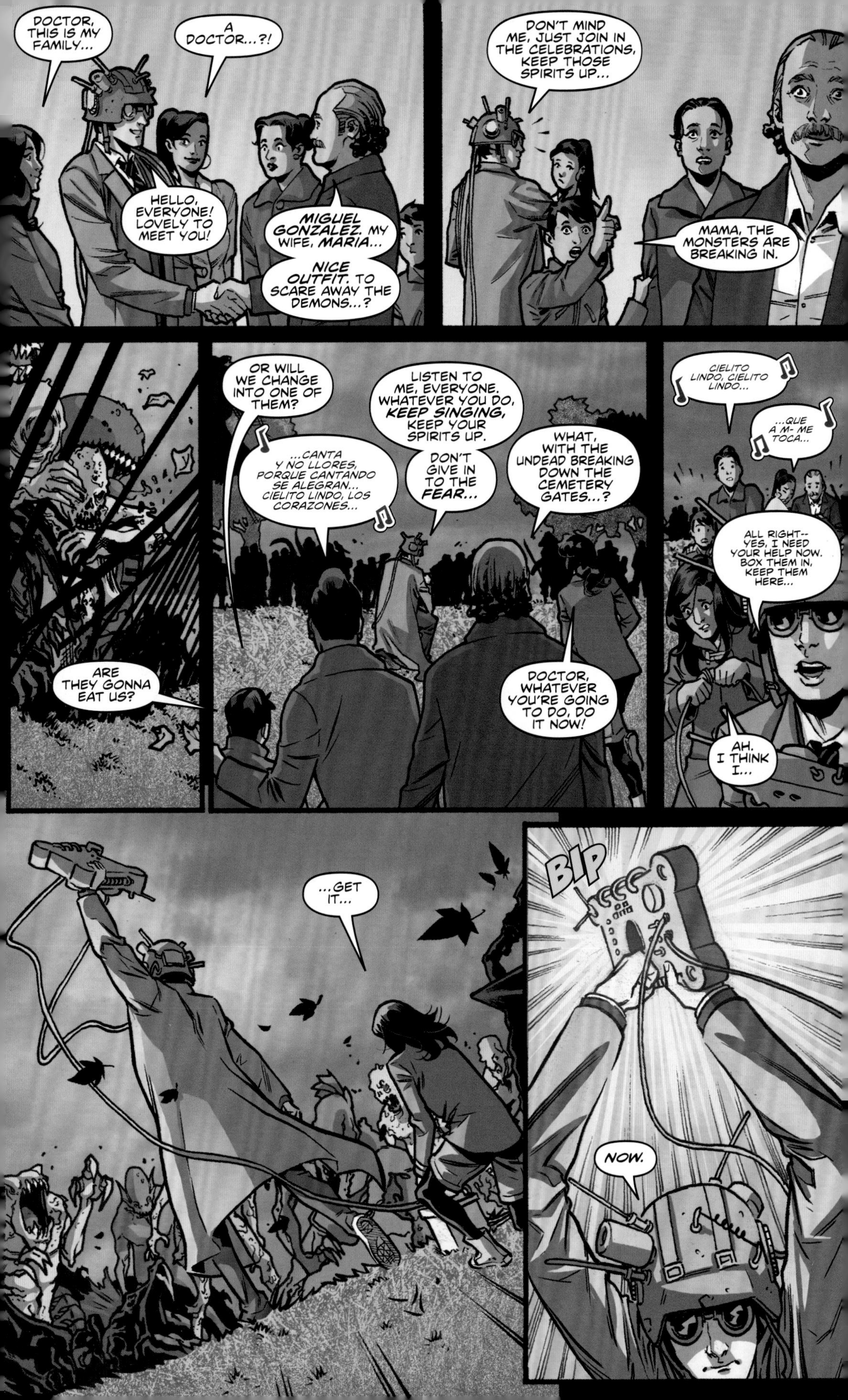
DOCTOR, THIS IS MY FAMILY...
A DOCTOR...?!
HELLO, EVERYONE! LOVELY TO MEET YOU!
MIGUEL GONZALEZ. MY WIFE, MARIA...
NICE OUTFIT. TO SCARE AWAY THE DEMONS...?
DON'T MIND ME, JUST JOIN IN THE CELEBRATIONS, KEEP THOSE SPIRITS UP...
MAMA, THE MONSTERS ARE BREAKING IN.
ARE THEY GONNA EAT US?
OR WILL WE CHANGE INTO ONE OF THEM?
...CANTA Y NO LLORES, PORQUE CANTANDO SE ALEGRAN... CIELITO LINDO, LOS CORAZONES...
LISTEN TO ME, EVERYONE. WHATEVER YOU DO, KEEP SINGING, KEEP YOUR SPIRITS UP.
DON'T GIVE IN TO THE FEAR...
WHAT, WITH THE UNDEAD BREAKING DOWN THE CEMETERY GATES...?
DOCTOR, WHATEVER YOU'RE GOING TO DO, DO IT NOW!
CIELITO LINDO, CIELITO LINDO...
...QUE A M- ME TOCA...
ALL RIGHT-- YES, I NEED YOUR HELP NOW. BOX THEM IN, KEEP THEM HERE...
AH. I THINK I...
...GET IT...
BIP
NOW.

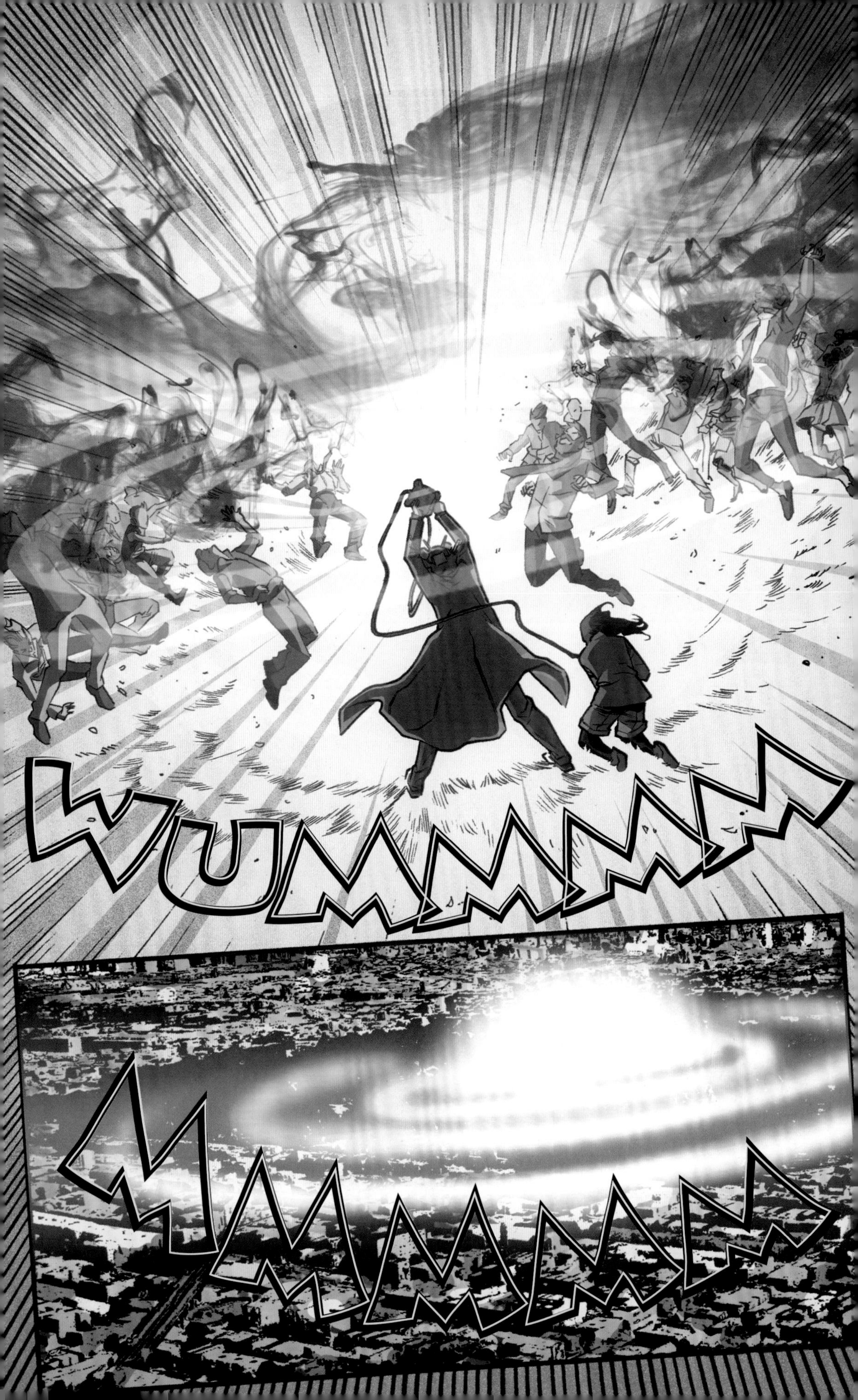
WUMMMMP
WMMMMMP

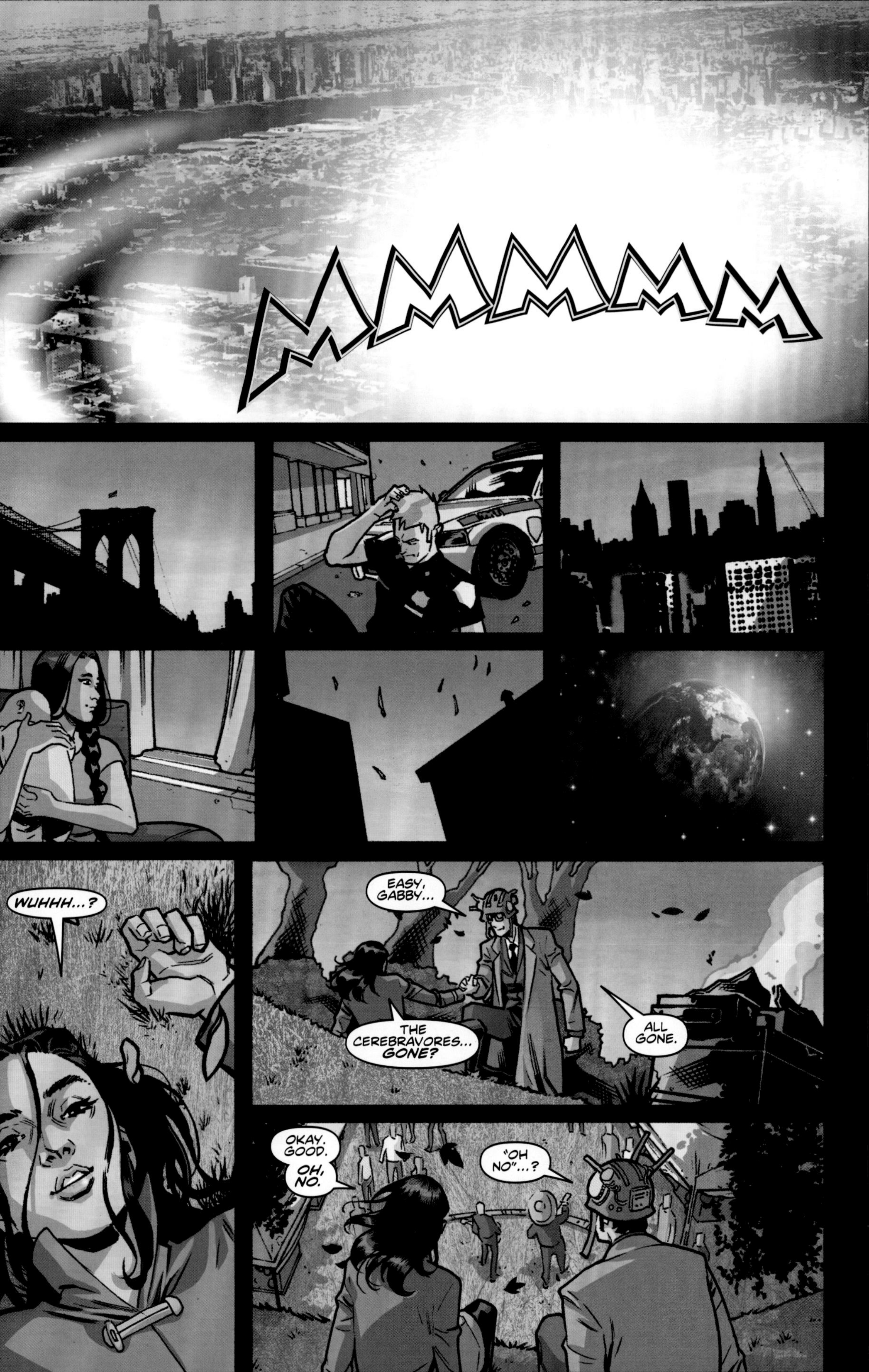
MMMMMM
WUHHH...?
EASY, GABBY...
THE CEREBRAVORES... GONE?
ALL GONE.
OKAY. GOOD. OH, NO.
"OH NO"...?

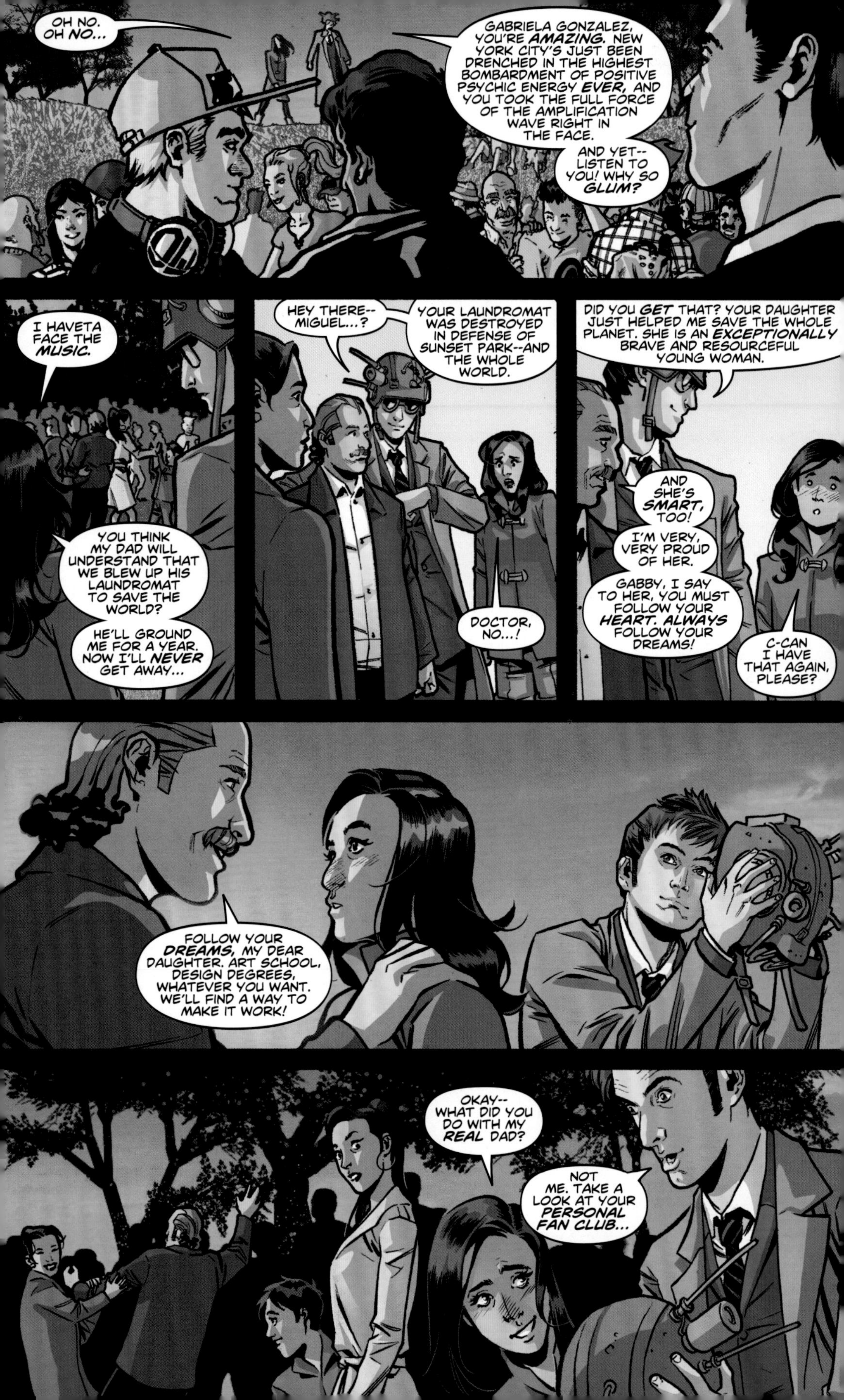
OH NO. OH NO...
GABRIELA GONZALEZ, YOU'RE AMAZING. NEW YORK CITY'S JUST BEEN DRENCHED IN THE HIGHEST BOMBARDMENT OF POSITIVE PSYCHIC ENERGY EVER, AND YOU TOOK THE FULL FORCE OF THE AMPLIFICATION WAVE RIGHT IN THE FACE.
AND YET-- LISTEN TO YOU! WHY SO GLUM?
I HAVETA FACE THE MUSIC.
YOU THINK MY DAD WILL UNDERSTAND THAT WE BLEW UP HIS LAUNDROMAT TO SAVE THE WORLD?
HE'LL GROUND ME FOR A YEAR. NOW I'LL NEVER GET AWAY...
HEY THERE-- MIGUEL...?
YOUR LAUNDROMAT WAS DESTROYED IN DEFENSE OF SUNSET PARK--AND THE WHOLE WORLD.
DOCTOR, NO...!
DID YOU GET THAT? YOUR DAUGHTER JUST HELPED ME SAVE THE WHOLE PLANET. SHE IS AN EXCEPTIONALLY BRAVE AND RESOURCEFUL YOUNG WOMAN.
AND SHE'S SMART, TOO!
I'M VERY, VERY PROUD OF HER.
GABBY, I SAY TO HER, YOU MUST FOLLOW YOUR HEART. ALWAYS FOLLOW YOUR DREAMS!
C-CAN I HAVE THAT AGAIN, PLEASE?
FOLLOW YOUR DREAMS, MY DEAR DAUGHTER. ART SCHOOL, DESIGN DEGREES, WHATEVER YOU WANT. WE'LL FIND A WAY TO MAKE IT WORK!
OKAY-- WHAT DID YOU DO WITH MY REAL DAD?
NOT ME. TAKE A LOOK AT YOUR PERSONAL FAN CLUB...

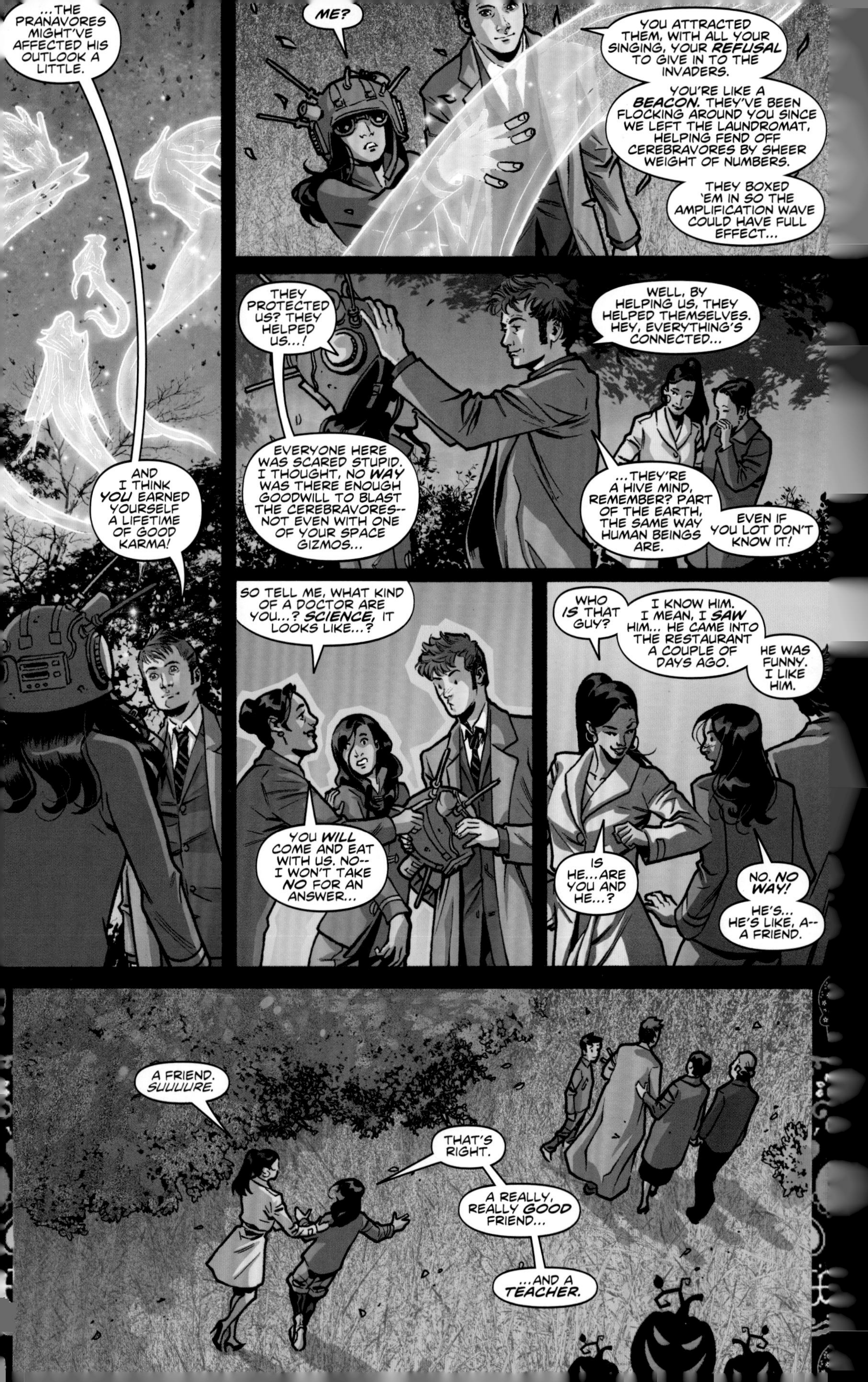

...THE PRANAVORES MIGHT'VE AFFECTED HIS OUTLOOK A LITTLE.
AND I THINK YOU EARNED YOURSELF A LIFETIME OF GOOD KARMA!
ME?
YOU ATTRACTED THEM, WITH ALL YOUR SINGING, YOUR REFUSAL TO GIVE IN TO THE INVADERS.
YOU'RE LIKE A BEACON. THEY'VE BEEN FLOCKING AROUND YOU SINCE WE LEFT THE LAUNDROMAT, HELPING FEND OFF CEREBRAVORES BY SHEER WEIGHT OF NUMBERS.
THEY BOXED 'EM IN SO THE AMPLIFICATION WAVE COULD HAVE FULL EFFECT...
THEY PROTECTED US? THEY HELPED US...!
WELL, BY HELPING US, THEY HELPED THEMSELVES. HEY, EVERYTHING'S CONNECTED...
EVERYONE HERE WAS SCARED STUPID. I THOUGHT, NO WAY WAS THERE ENOUGH GOODWILL TO BLAST THE CEREBRAVORES-- NOT EVEN WITH ONE OF YOUR SPACE GIZMOS...
...THEY'RE A HIVE MIND, REMEMBER? PART OF THE EARTH, THE SAME WAY HUMAN BEINGS ARE.
EVEN IF YOU LOT DON'T KNOW IT!
SO TELL ME, WHAT KIND OF A DOCTOR ARE YOU...? SCIENCE, IT LOOKS LIKE...?
YOU WILL COME AND EAT WITH US. NO-- I WON'T TAKE NO FOR AN ANSWER...
WHO IS THAT GUY?
I KNOW HIM. I MEAN, I SAW HIM... HE CAME INTO THE RESTAURANT A COUPLE OF DAYS AGO.
HE WAS FUNNY. I LIKE HIM.
IS HE...ARE YOU AND HE...?
NO. NO WAY! HE'S... HE'S LIKE, A-- A FRIEND.
A FRIEND. SUUUURE.
THAT'S RIGHT.
A REALLY, REALLY GOOD FRIEND...
...AND A TEACHER.

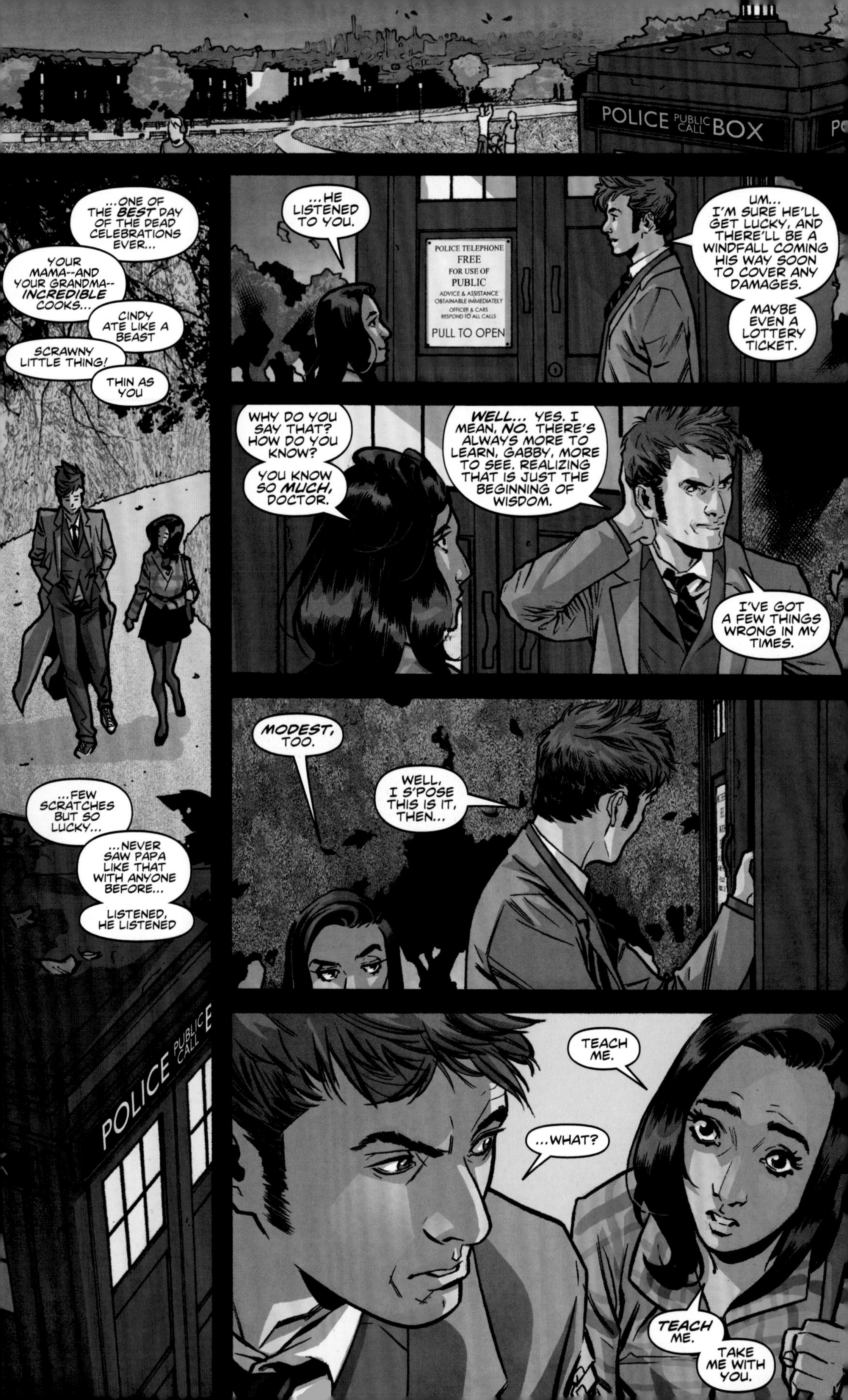
POLICE PUBLIC CALL BOX
...ONE OF THE BEST DAY OF THE DEAD CELEBRATIONS EVER...
YOUR MAMA--AND YOUR GRANDMA--INCREDIBLE COOKS...
CINDY ATE LIKE A BEAST
SCRAWNY LITTLE THING!
THIN AS YOU
...FEW SCRATCHES BUT SO LUCKY...
...NEVER SAW PAPA LIKE THAT WITH ANYONE BEFORE...
LISTENED, HE LISTENED
POLICE PUBLIC CALL
...HE LISTENED TO YOU.
POLICE TELEPHONE FREE FOR USE OF PUBLIC ADVICE & ASSISTANCE OBTAINABLE IMMEDIATELY OFFICER & CARS RESPOND TO ALL CALLS PULL TO OPEN
UM... I'M SURE HE'LL GET LUCKY, AND THERE'LL BE A WINDFALL COMING HIS WAY SOON TO COVER ANY DAMAGES.
MAYBE EVEN A LOTTERY TICKET.
WHY DO YOU SAY THAT? HOW DO YOU KNOW?
YOU KNOW SO MUCH, DOCTOR.
WELL... YES. I MEAN, NO. THERE'S ALWAYS MORE TO LEARN, GABBY, MORE TO SEE. REALIZING THAT IS JUST THE BEGINNING OF WISDOM.
I'VE GOT A FEW THINGS WRONG IN MY TIMES.
MODEST, TOO.
WELL, I S'POSE THIS IS IT, THEN...
TEACH ME.
...WHAT?
TEACH ME.
TAKE ME WITH YOU.

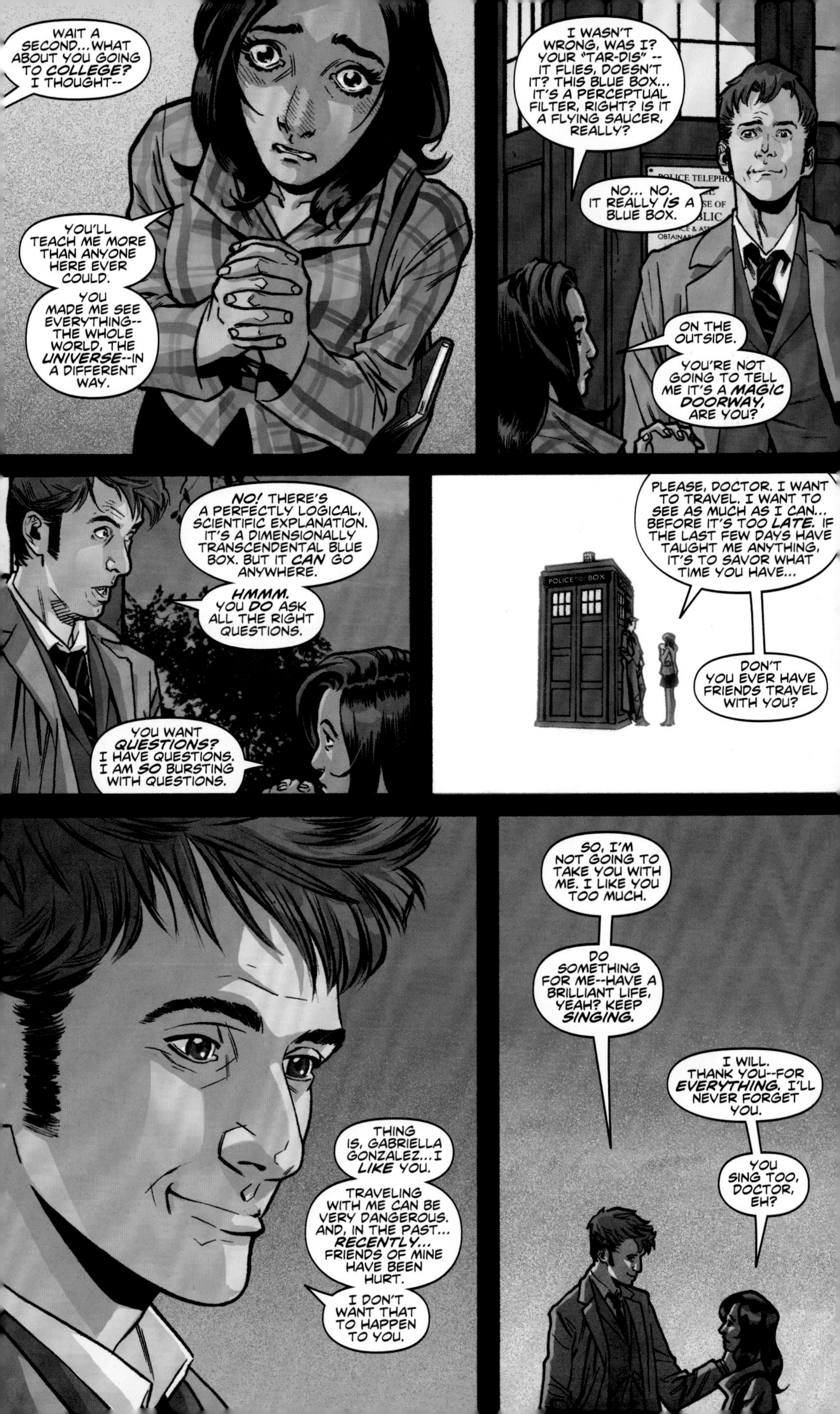
WAIT A SECOND...WHAT ABOUT YOU GOING TO COLLEGE? I THOUGHT--
YOU'LL TEACH ME MORE THAN ANYONE HERE EVER COULD.
YOU MADE ME SEE EVERYTHING--THE WHOLE WORLD, THE UNIVERSE--IN A DIFFERENT WAY.
I WASN'T WRONG, WAS I? YOUR "TAR-DIS" --IT FLIES, DOESN'T IT? THIS BLUE BOX... IT'S A PERCEPTUAL FILTER, RIGHT? IS IT A FLYING SAUCER, REALLY?
NO... NO. IT REALLY IS A BLUE BOX.
ON THE OUTSIDE.
YOU'RE NOT GOING TO TELL ME IT'S A MAGIC DOORWAY, ARE YOU?
NO! THERE'S A PERFECTLY LOGICAL, SCIENTIFIC EXPLANATION. IT'S A DIMENSIONALLY TRANSCENDENTAL BLUE BOX. BUT IT CAN GO ANYWHERE.
HMMM. YOU DO ASK ALL THE RIGHT QUESTIONS.
YOU WANT QUESTIONS? I HAVE QUESTIONS. I AM SO BURSTING WITH QUESTIONS.
PLEASE, DOCTOR. I WANT TO TRAVEL. I WANT TO SEE AS MUCH AS I CAN... BEFORE IT'S TOO LATE. IF THE LAST FEW DAYS HAVE TAUGHT ME ANYTHING, IT'S TO SAVOR WHAT TIME YOU HAVE...
DON'T YOU EVER HAVE FRIENDS TRAVEL WITH YOU?
THING IS, GABRIELLA GONZALEZ...I LIKE YOU.
TRAVELING WITH ME CAN BE VERY DANGEROUS. AND, IN THE PAST... RECENTLY... FRIENDS OF MINE HAVE BEEN HURT.
I DON'T WANT THAT TO HAPPEN TO YOU.
SO, I'M NOT GOING TO TAKE YOU WITH ME. I LIKE YOU TOO MUCH.
DO SOMETHING FOR ME--HAVE A BRILLIANT LIFE, YEAH? KEEP SINGING.
I WILL. THANK YOU--FOR EVERYTHING. I'LL NEVER FORGET YOU.
YOU SING TOO, DOCTOR, EH?

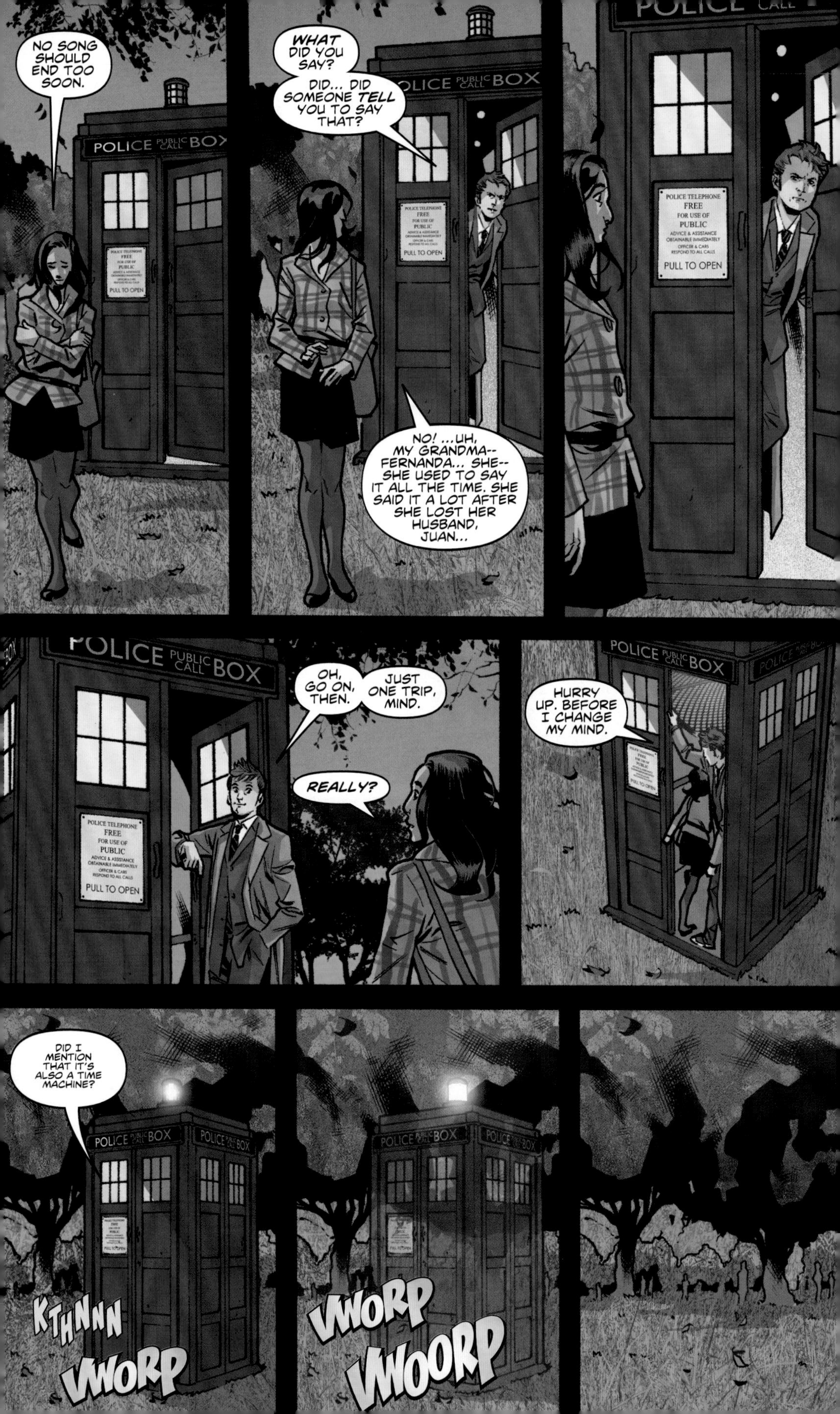
NO SONG SHOULD END TOO SOON.
WHAT DID YOU SAY?
DID... DID SOMEONE TELL YOU TO SAY THAT?
POLICE PUBLIC CALL BOX
POLICE TELEPHONE FREE FOR USE OF PUBLIC ADVICE & ASSISTANCE OBTAINABLE IMMEDIATELY OFFICER & CARS RESPOND TO ALL CALLS PULL TO OPEN
NO! ...UH, MY GRANDMA--FERNANDA... SHE--SHE USED TO SAY IT ALL THE TIME. SHE SAID IT A LOT AFTER SHE LOST HER HUSBAND, JUAN...
OH, GO ON, THEN.
JUST ONE TRIP, MIND.
REALLY?
HURRY UP. BEFORE I CHANGE MY MIND.
DID I MENTION THAT IT'S ALSO A TIME MACHINE?
KTHNNN
VWORP
VWORP
VWOORP

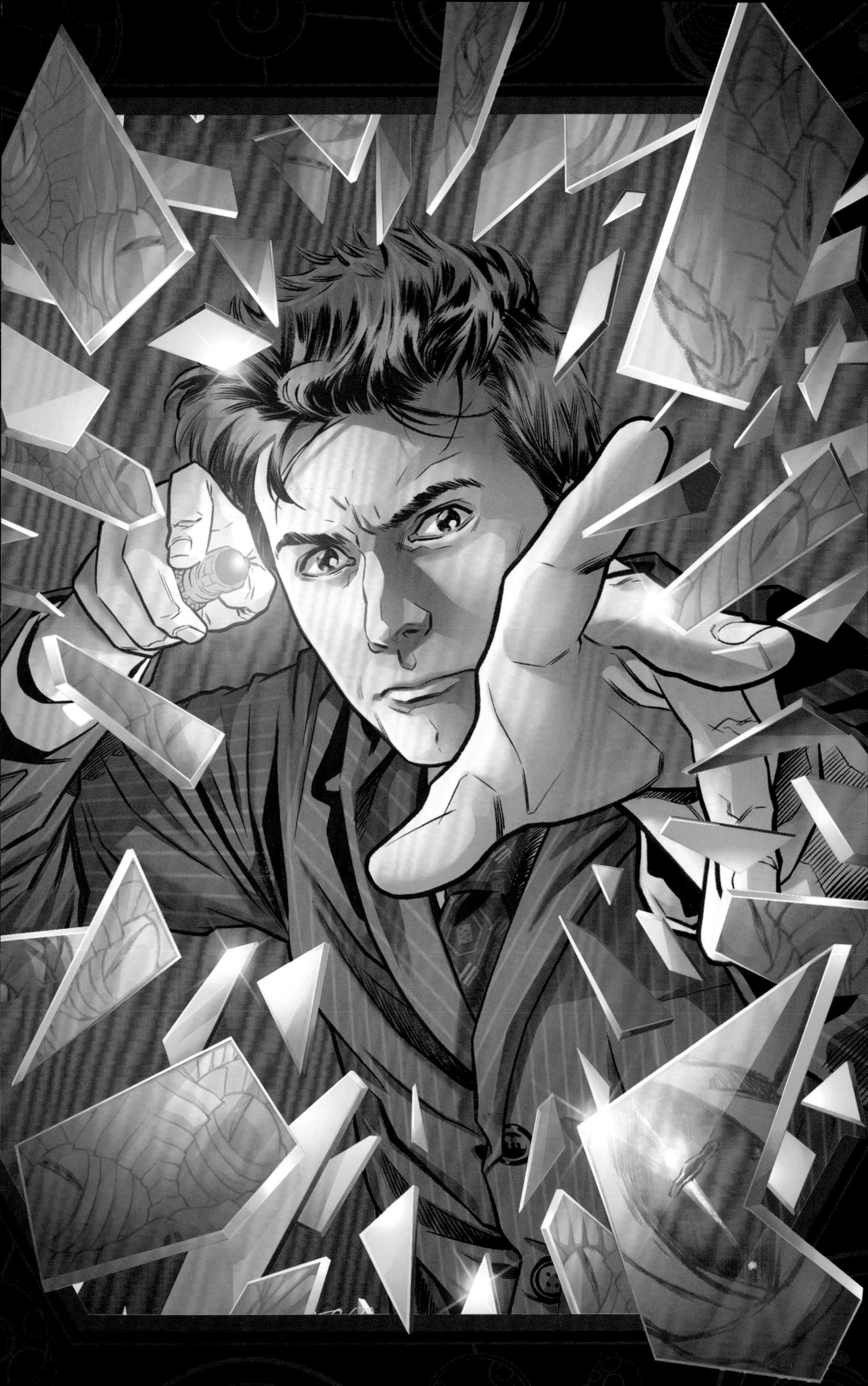

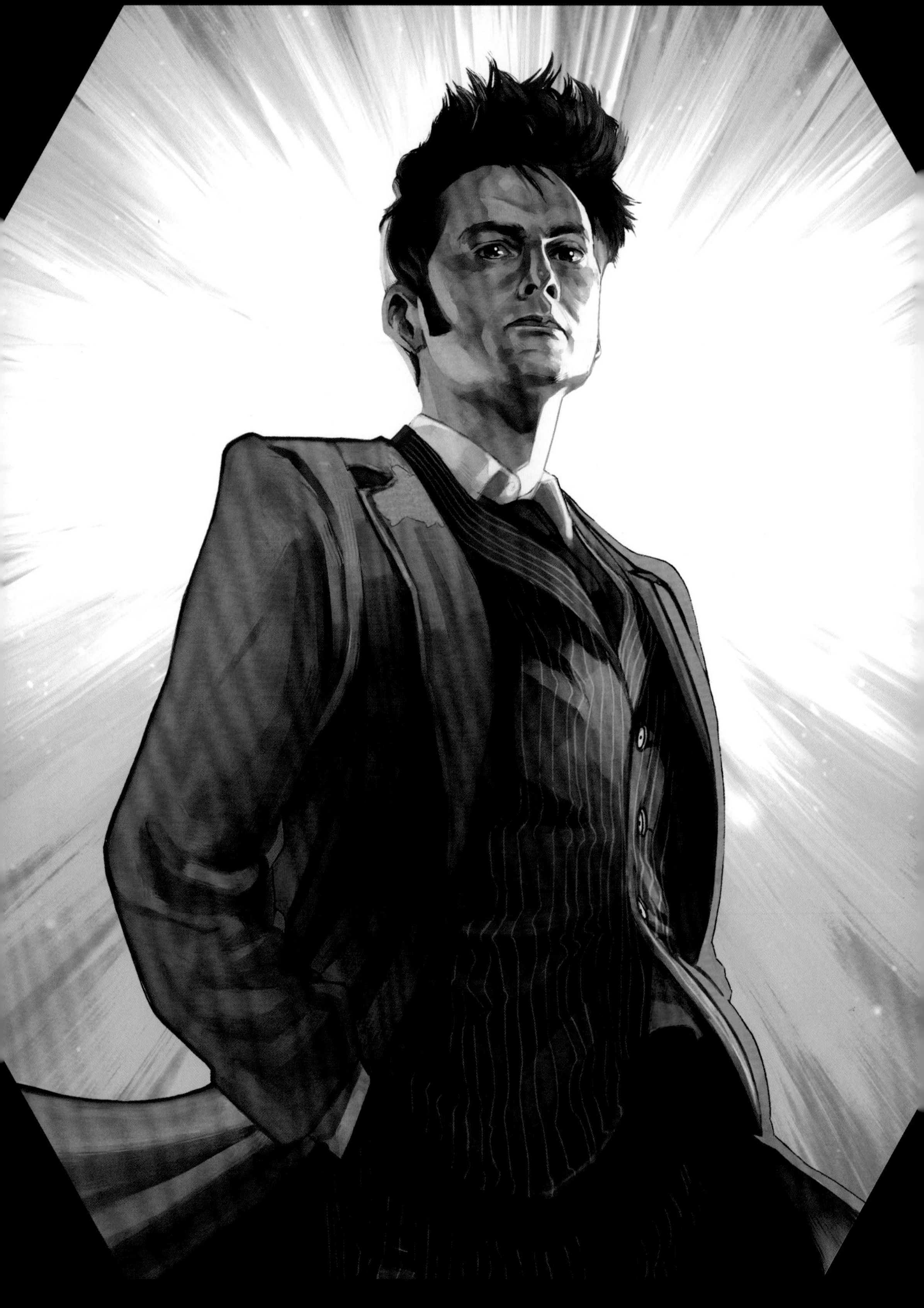

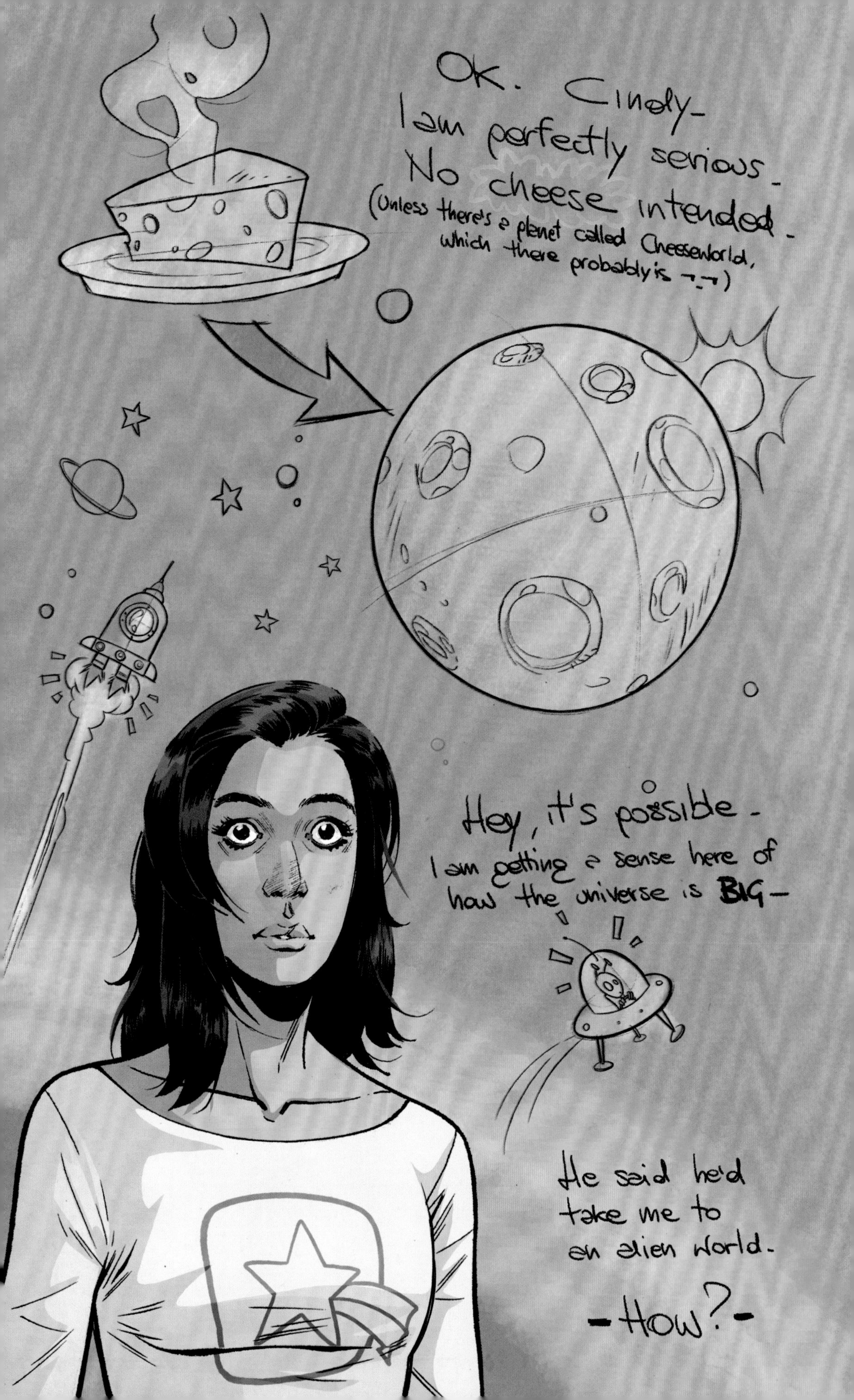
OK. Cindy-
I am perfectly serious-
No cheese intended-
(Unless there's a planet called Cheeseworld, which there probably is ¬_¬)
Hey, it's possible-
I am getting a sense here of how the universe is BIG-
He said he'd take me to an alien world-
-How?-

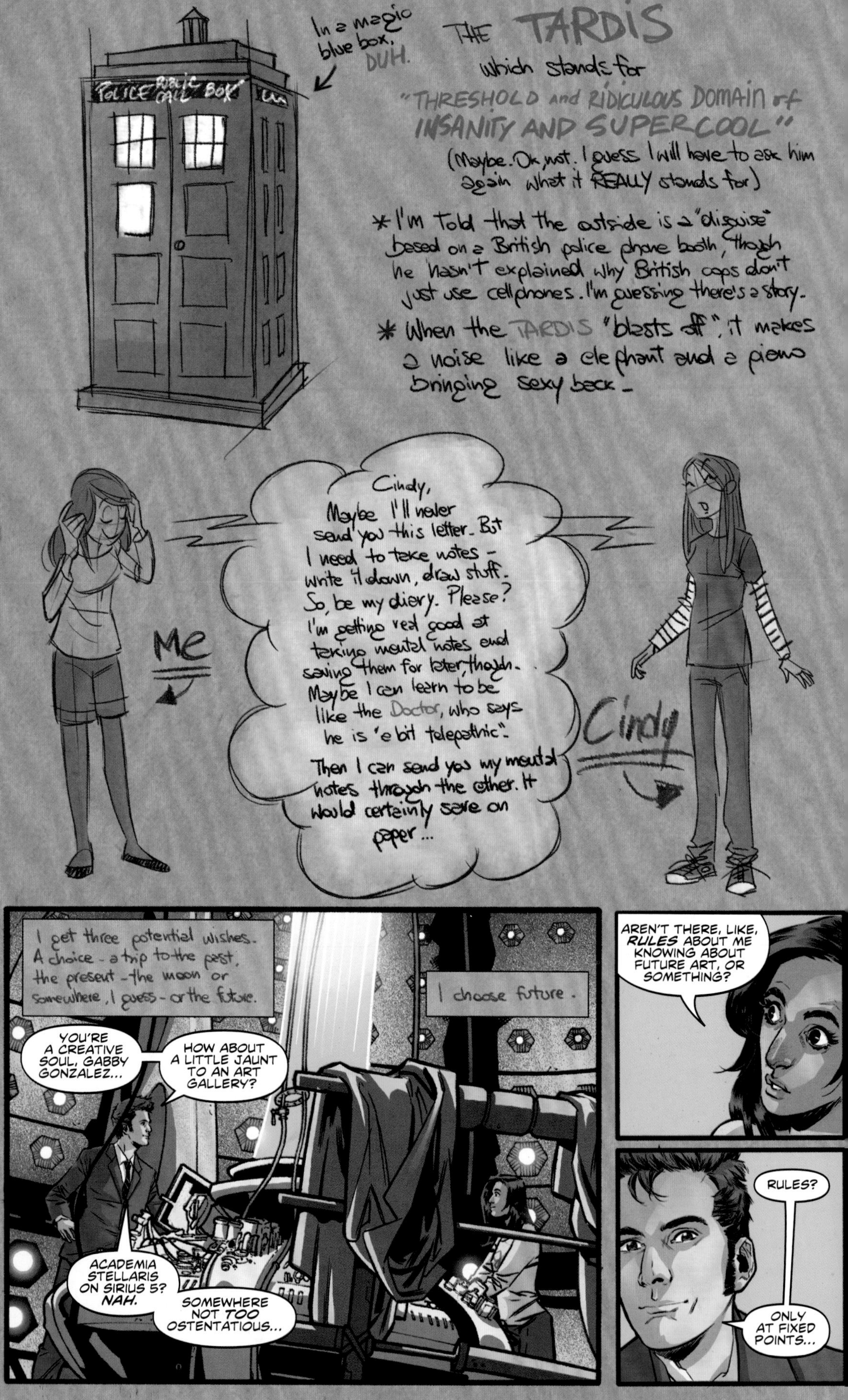
POLICE PUBLIC CALL BOX
In a magic blue box, DUH.
THE TARDIS
which stands for
"THRESHOLD and RIDICULOUS DOMAIN of INSANITY AND SUPERCOOL"
(Maybe. Ok, not. I guess I will have to ask him again what it REALLY stands for)
* I'm Told that the outside is a "disguise" based on a British police phone booth, though he hasn't explained why British cops don't just use cellphones. I'm guessing there's a story.
* When the TARDIS "blasts off", it makes a noise like a elephant and a piano bringing sexy back.
Cindy, Maybe I'll never send you this letter. But I need to take notes - write it down, draw stuff. So, be my diary. Please? I'm getting real good at taking mental notes and saving them for later, though. Maybe I can learn to be like the Doctor, who says he is 'a bit telepathic'.
Then I can send you my mental notes through the ether. It would certainly save on paper...
Me
Cindy
I get three potential wishes. A choice - a trip to the past, the present - the moon or somewhere, I guess - or the future.
I choose future.
YOU'RE A CREATIVE SOUL, GABBY GONZALEZ...
HOW ABOUT A LITTLE JAUNT TO AN ART GALLERY?
ACADEMIA STELLARIS ON SIRIUS 5? NAH.
SOMEWHERE NOT TOO OSTENTATIOUS...
AREN'T THERE, LIKE, RULES ABOUT ME KNOWING ABOUT FUTURE ART, OR SOMETHING?
RULES?
ONLY AT FIXED POINTS...

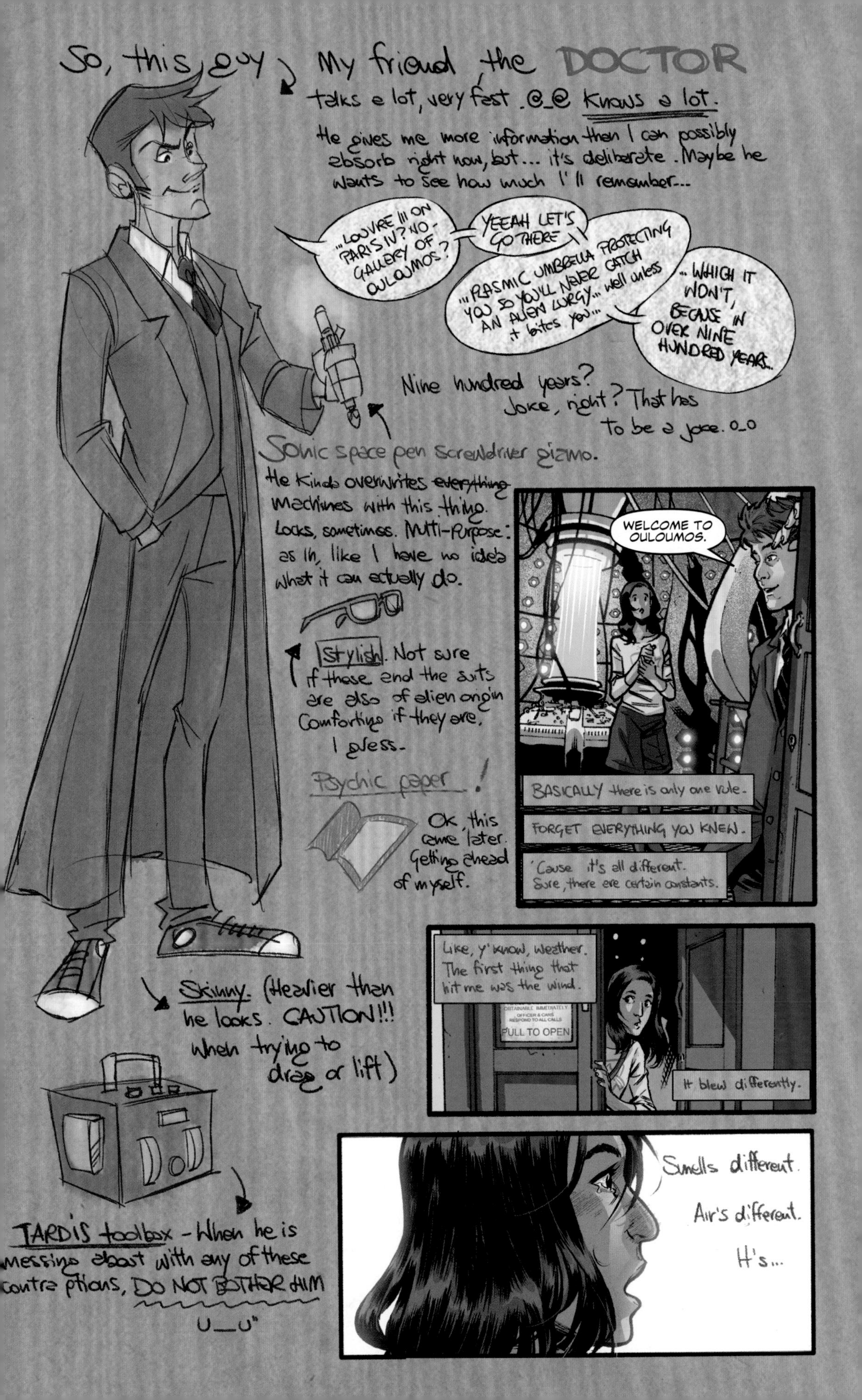

So, this guy, My friend the DOCTOR
talks a lot, very fast @_@ Knows a lot.
He gives me more information than I can possibly absorb right now, but... it's deliberate. Maybe he wants to see how much I'll remember...
...LOUVRE III ON PARIS IV? NO - GALLERY OF OULOUMOS?
YEEAH LET'S GO THERE
...PLASMIC UMBRELLA PROTECTING YOU SO YOU'LL NEVER CATCH AN ALIEN LURGY... well unless it bites you...
...WHICH IT WON'T, BECAUSE IN OVER NINE HUNDRED YEARS...
Nine hundred years? Joke, right? That has to be a joke. o_o
Sonic space pen screwdriver gizmo.
He kinda overwrites everything machines with this thing. Locks, sometimes. Multi-purpose: as in, like I have no idea what it can actually do.
Stylish. Not sure if these and the suits are also of alien origin. Comforting if they are, I guess.
Psychic paper!
Ok, this came later. Getting ahead of myself.
WELCOME TO OULOUMOS.
BASICALLY there is only one rule.
FORGET EVERYTHING YOU KNEW.
'Cause it's all different. Sure, there are certain constants.
Skinny. (Heavier than he looks. CAUTION!!! when trying to drag or lift)
Like, y'know, weather. The first thing that hit me was the wind.
PULL TO OPEN
It blew differently.
TARDIS toolbox - When he is messing about with any of these contraptions, DO NOT BOTHER HIM
U_U"
Smells different.
Air's different.
It's...

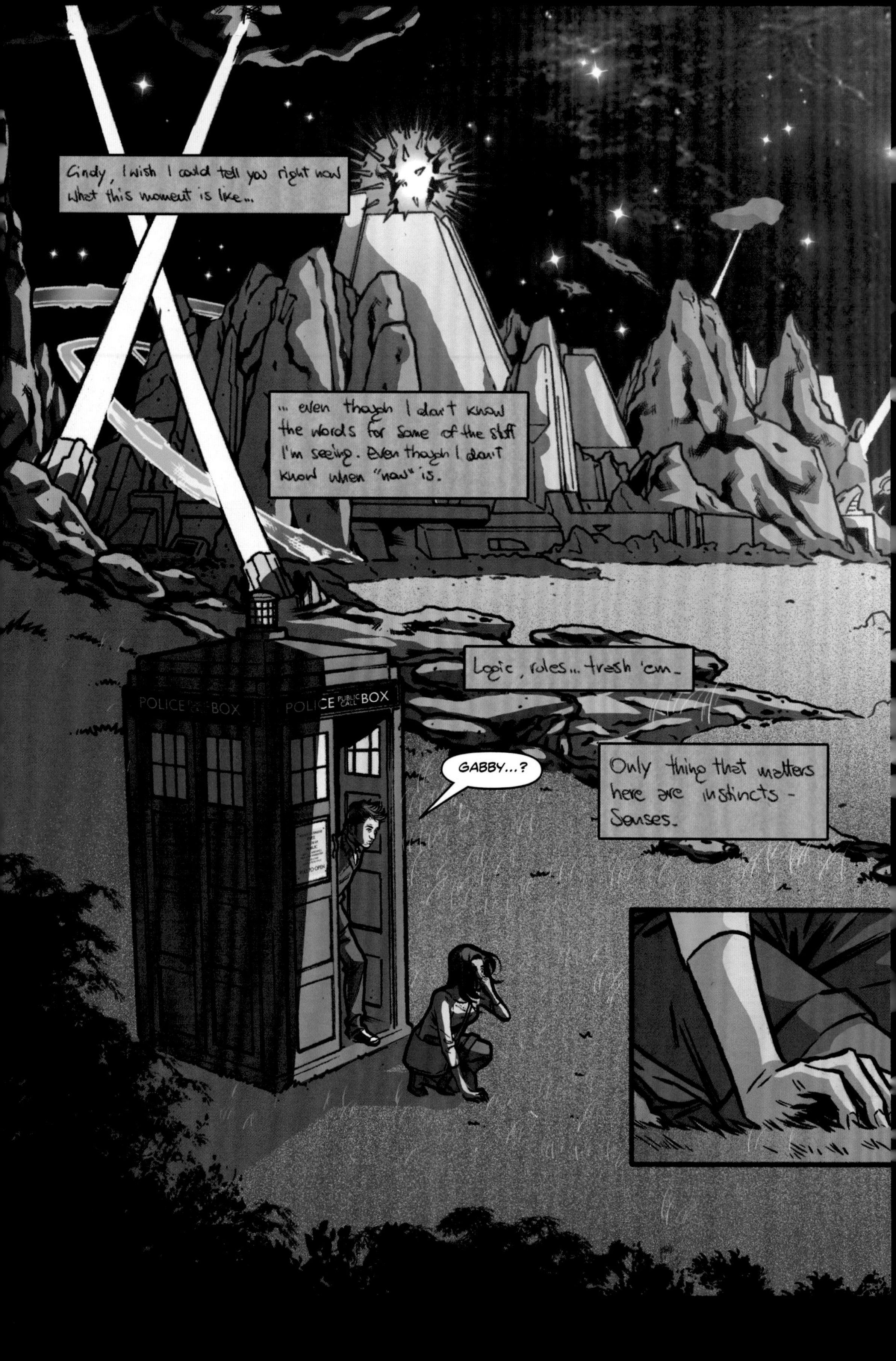
Cindy, I wish I could tell you right now what this moment is like...
... even though I don't know the words for some of the stuff I'm seeing. Even though I don't know when "now" is.
Logic, rules... trash 'em.
POLICE PUBLIC CALL BOX
GABBY...?
Only thing that matters here are instincts - Senses.

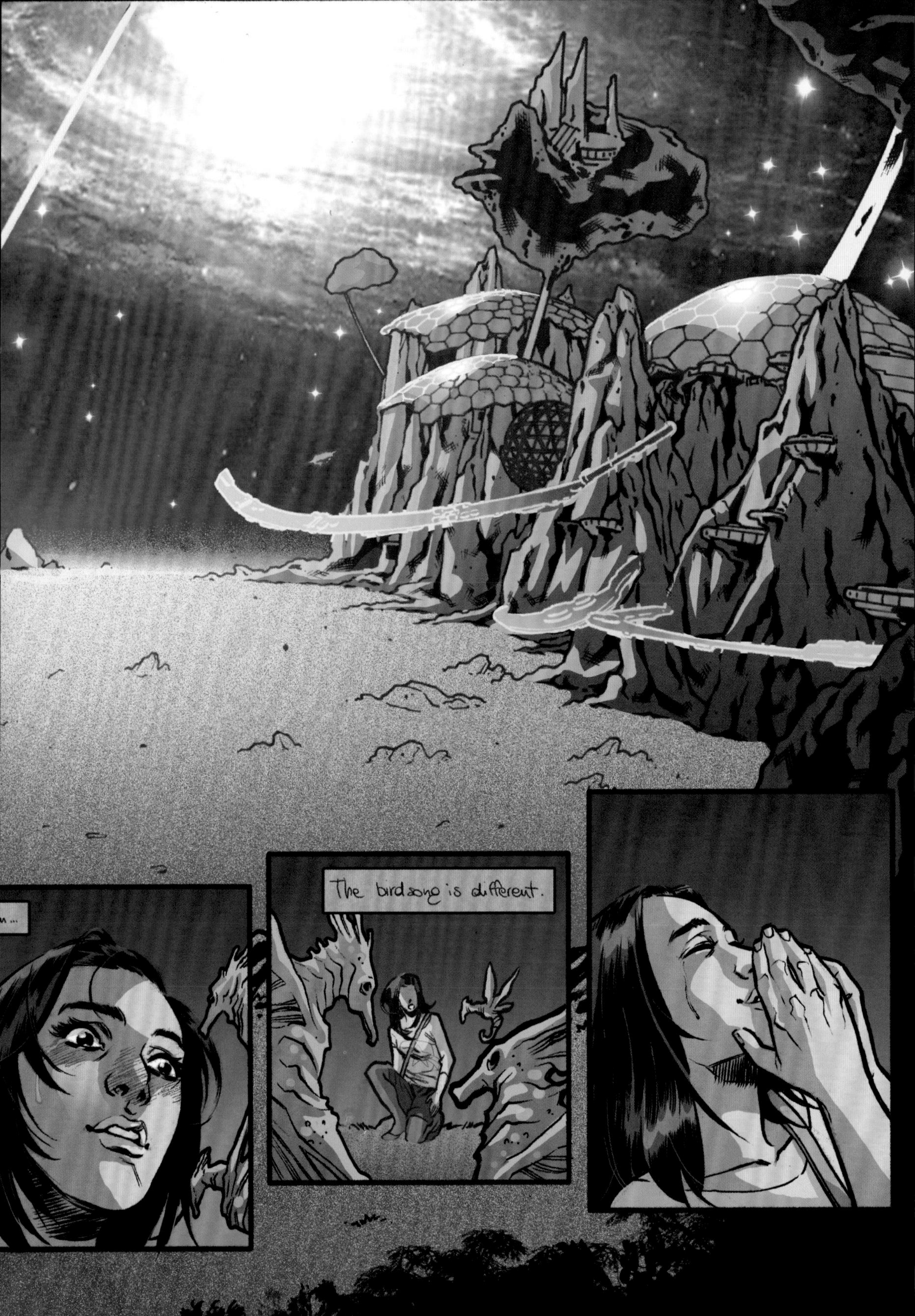
m ...
The birdsong is different.

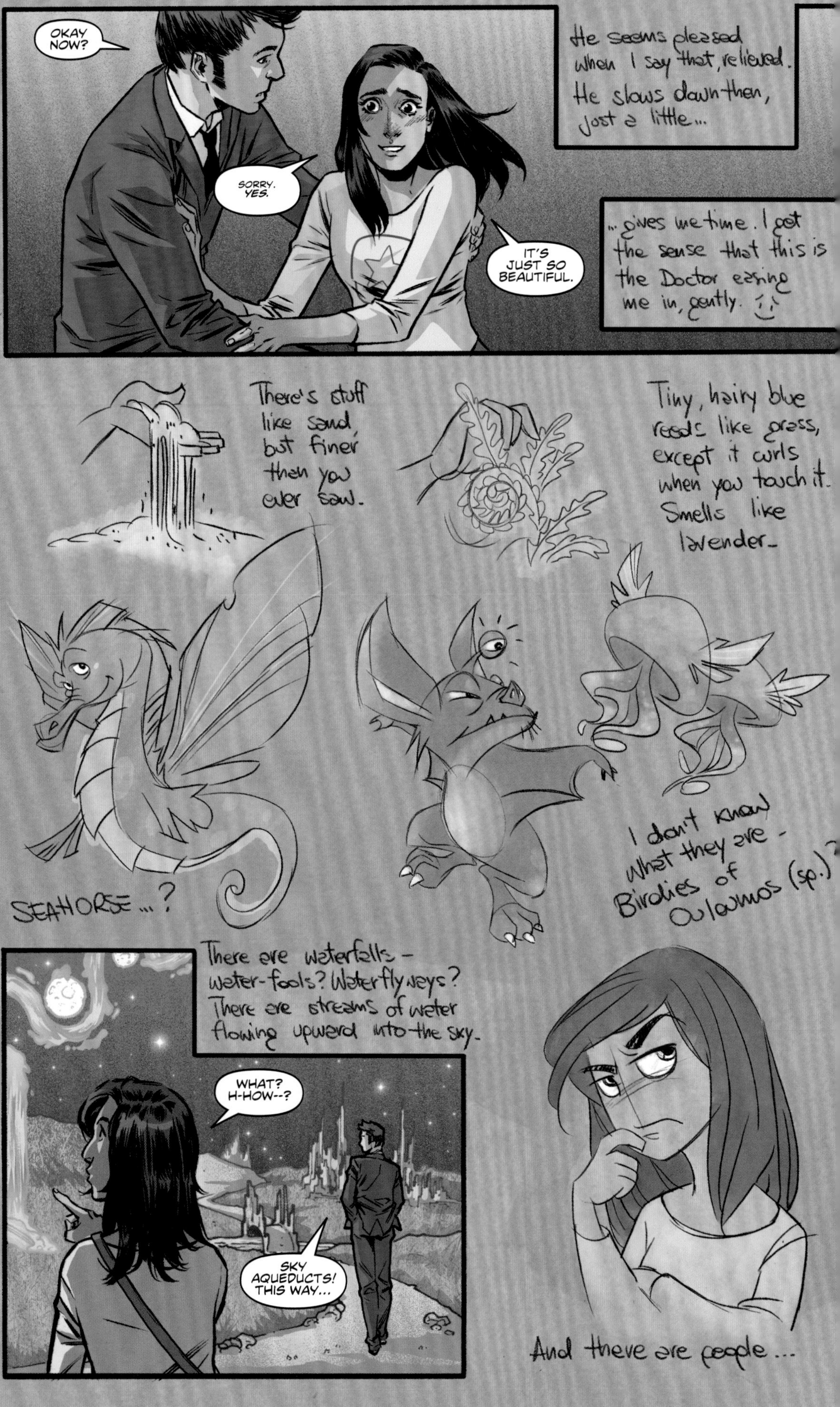
OKAY NOW?
He seems pleased when I say that, relieved. He slows down then, just a little...
SORRY. YES.
IT'S JUST SO BEAUTIFUL.
...gives me time. I got the sense that this is the Doctor easing me in, gently.
There's stuff like sand, but finer then you ever saw.
Tiny, hairy blue reeds like grass, except it curls when you touch it. Smells like lavender.
SEAHORSE...?
I don't know what they are - Birdies of Oulowmos (sp.)?
There are waterfalls - water-fools? Waterflyways? There are streams of water flowing upward into the sky.
WHAT? H-HOW--?
SKY AQUEDUCTS! THIS WAY...
And there are people...

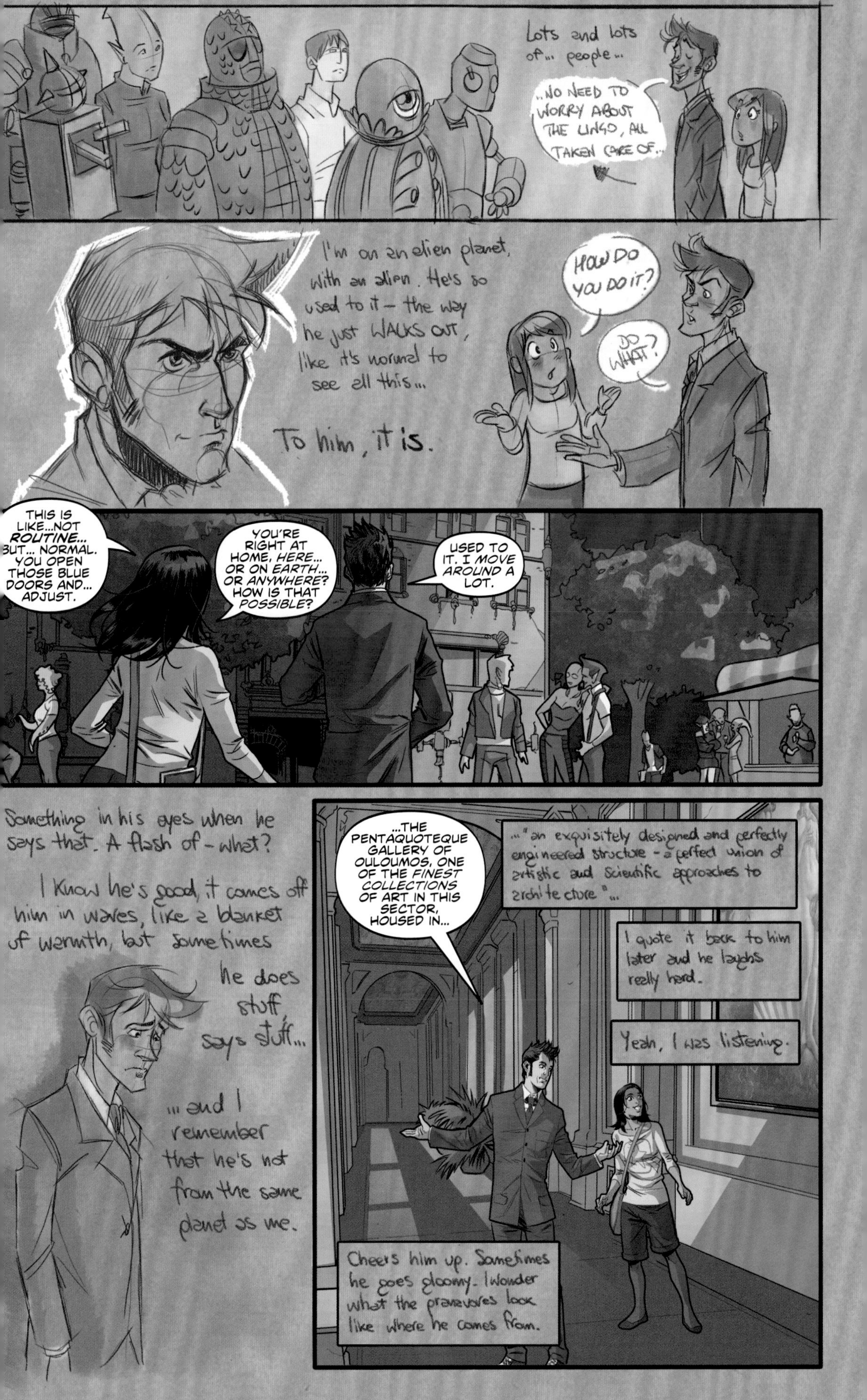

Lots and lots of... people...
...NO NEED TO WORRY ABOUT THE LINGO, ALL TAKEN CARE OF...
I'm on an alien planet, with an alien. He's so used to it – the way he just WALKS OUT, like it's normal to see all this...
To him, it is.
HOW DO YOU DO IT?
DO WHAT?
THIS IS LIKE...NOT ROUTINE... BUT... NORMAL. YOU OPEN THOSE BLUE DOORS AND... ADJUST.
YOU'RE RIGHT AT HOME, HERE... OR ON EARTH... OR ANYWHERE? HOW IS THAT POSSIBLE?
USED TO IT. I MOVE AROUND A LOT.
Something in his eyes when he says that. A flash of – what?
I know he's good, it comes off him in waves, like a blanket of warmth, but sometimes
he does stuff, says stuff...
...and I remember that he's not from the same planet as me.
...THE PENTAQUOTEQUE GALLERY OF OULOUMOS, ONE OF THE FINEST COLLECTIONS OF ART IN THIS SECTOR, HOUSED IN...
..."an exquisitely designed and perfectly engineered structure – a perfect union of artistic and scientific approaches to architecture"...
I quote it back to him later and he laughs really hard.
Yeah, I was listening.
Cheers him up. Sometimes he goes gloomy. I wonder what the gravevores look like where he comes from.

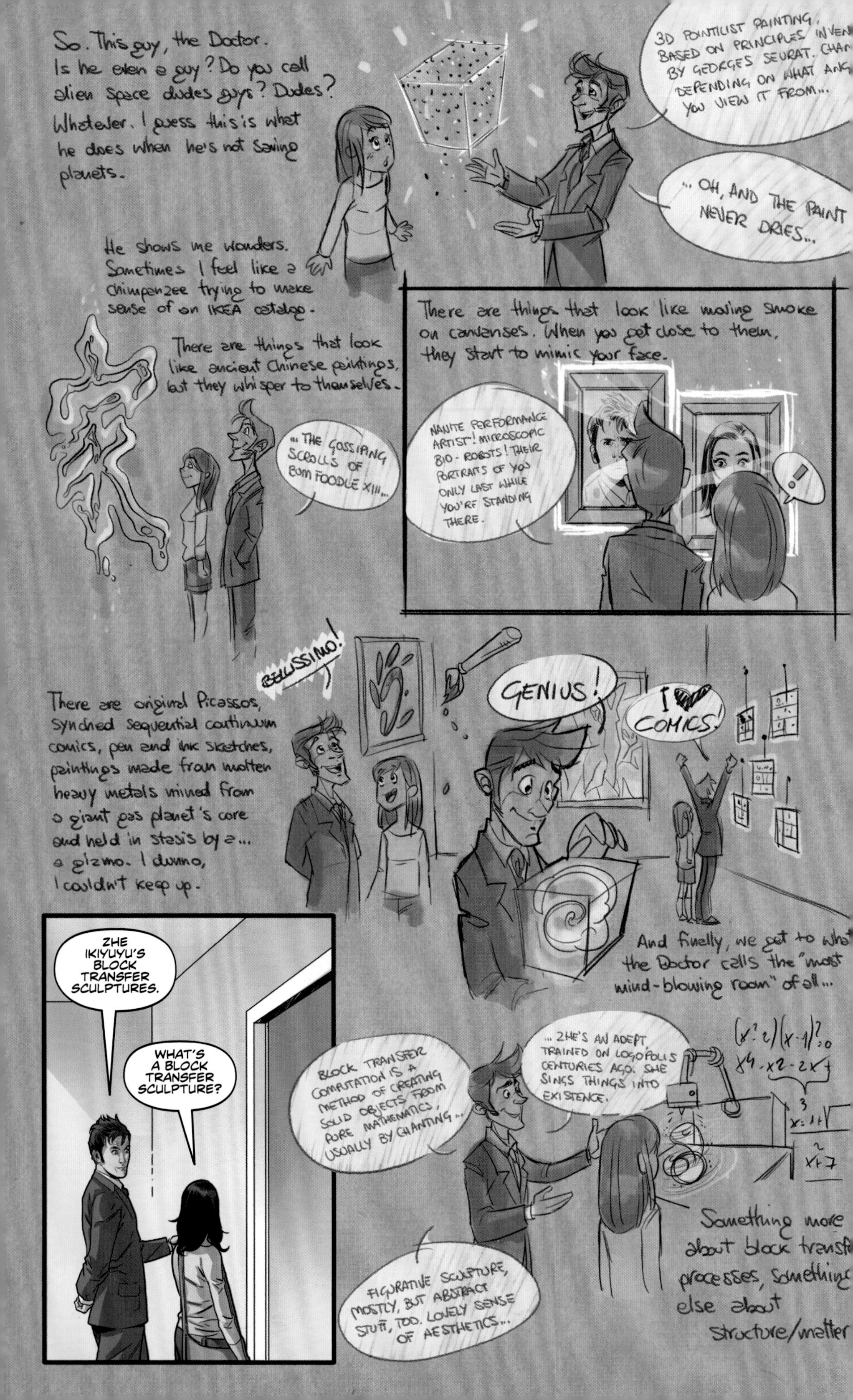

So. This guy, the Doctor. Is he even a guy? Do you call alien space dudes guys? Dudes? Whatever. I guess this is what he does when he's not saving planets.
3D POINTILIST PAINTING, BASED ON PRINCIPLES INVEN BY GEORGES SEURAT. CHAN DEPENDING ON WHAT ANG YOU VIEW IT FROM...
... OH, AND THE PAINT NEVER DRIES...
He shows me wonders. Sometimes I feel like a chimpanzee trying to make sense of an IKEA catalog.
There are things that look like ancient Chinese paintings, but they whisper to themselves.
... THE GOSSIPING SCROLLS OF BUM FOODLE XIII...
There are things that look like moving smoke on canvases. When you get close to them, they start to mimic your face.
NANITE PERFORMANCE ARTIST! MICROSCOPIC BIO-ROBOTS! THEIR PORTRAITS OF YOU ONLY LAST WHILE YOU'RE STANDING THERE.
!
There are original Picassos, synched sequential continuum comics, pen and ink sketches, paintings made from molten heavy metals mined from a giant gas planet's core and held in stasis by a... a gizmo. I dunno, I couldn't keep up.
BELLISSIMO!
GENIUS!
I ♥ COMICS!
And finally, we get to what the Doctor calls the "most mind-blowing room" of all...
ZHE IKIYUYU'S BLOCK TRANSFER SCULPTURES.
WHAT'S A BLOCK TRANSFER SCULPTURE?
BLOCK TRANSFER COMPUTATION IS A METHOD OF CREATING SOLID OBJECTS FROM PURE MATHEMATICS, USUALLY BY CHANTING...
... ZHE'S AN ADEPT, TRAINED ON LOGOPOLIS CENTURIES AGO. SHE SINGS THINGS INTO EXISTENCE.
FIGURATIVE SCULPTURE, MOSTLY, BUT ABSTRACT STUFF, TOO. LOVELY SENSE OF AESTHETICS...
Something more about block transf processes, something else about structure/matter

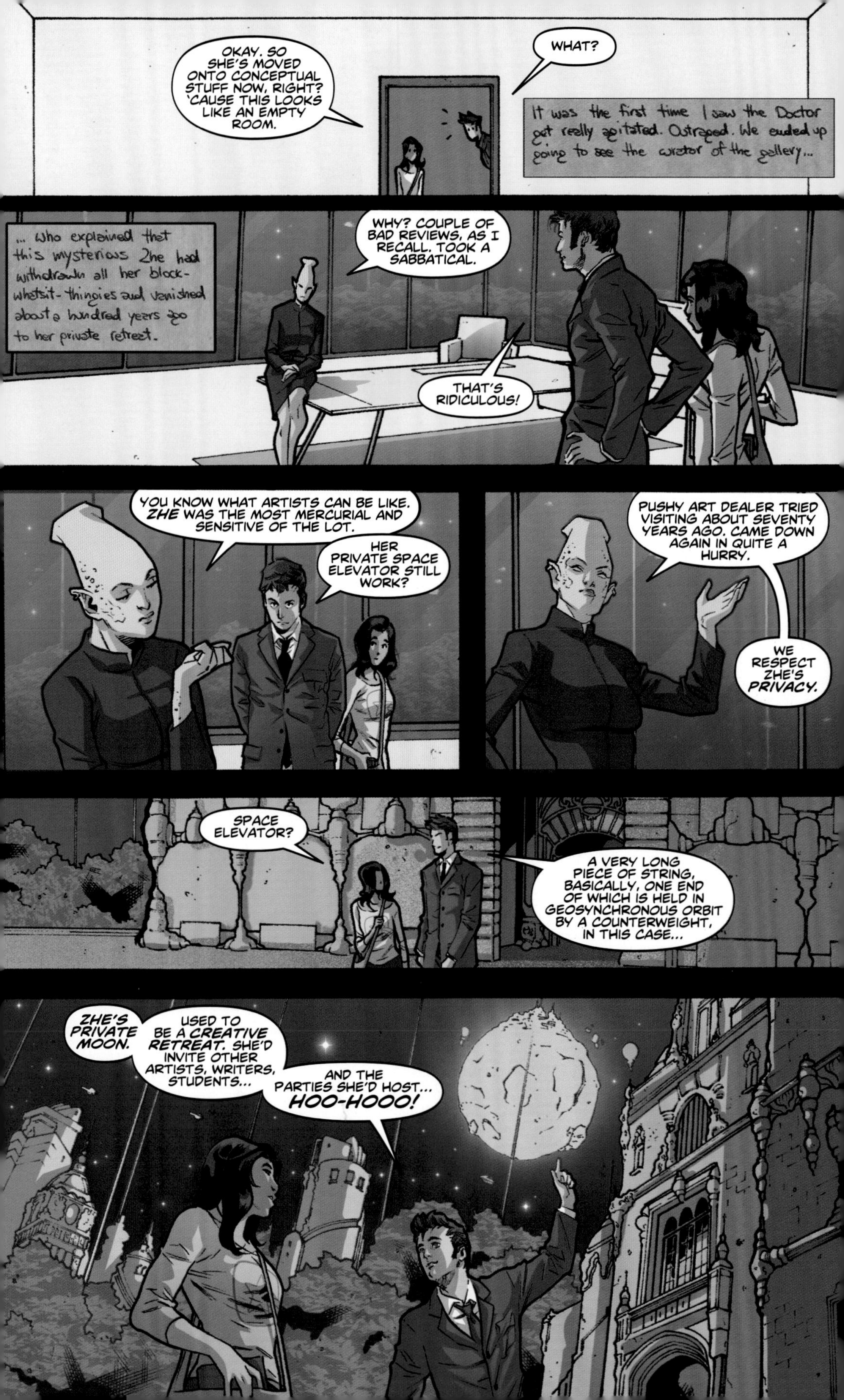
OKAY. SO SHE'S MOVED ONTO CONCEPTUAL STUFF NOW, RIGHT? 'CAUSE THIS LOOKS LIKE AN EMPTY ROOM.
WHAT?
It was the first time I saw the Doctor get really agitated. Outraged. We ended up going to see the curator of the gallery...
... who explained that this mysterious Zhe had withdrawn all her block-whatsit-thingies and vanished about a hundred years ago to her private retreat.
WHY? COUPLE OF BAD REVIEWS, AS I RECALL. TOOK A SABBATICAL.
THAT'S RIDICULOUS!
YOU KNOW WHAT ARTISTS CAN BE LIKE. *ZHE* WAS THE MOST MERCURIAL AND SENSITIVE OF THE LOT.
HER PRIVATE SPACE ELEVATOR STILL WORK?
PUSHY ART DEALER TRIED VISITING ABOUT SEVENTY YEARS AGO. CAME DOWN AGAIN IN QUITE A HURRY.
WE RESPECT ZHE'S *PRIVACY.*
SPACE ELEVATOR?
A VERY LONG PIECE OF STRING, BASICALLY, ONE END OF WHICH IS HELD IN GEOSYNCHRONOUS ORBIT BY A COUNTERWEIGHT, IN THIS CASE...
ZHE'S PRIVATE MOON.
USED TO BE A *CREATIVE RETREAT.* SHE'D INVITE OTHER ARTISTS, WRITERS, STUDENTS...
AND THE PARTIES SHE'D HOST... *HOO-HOOO!*

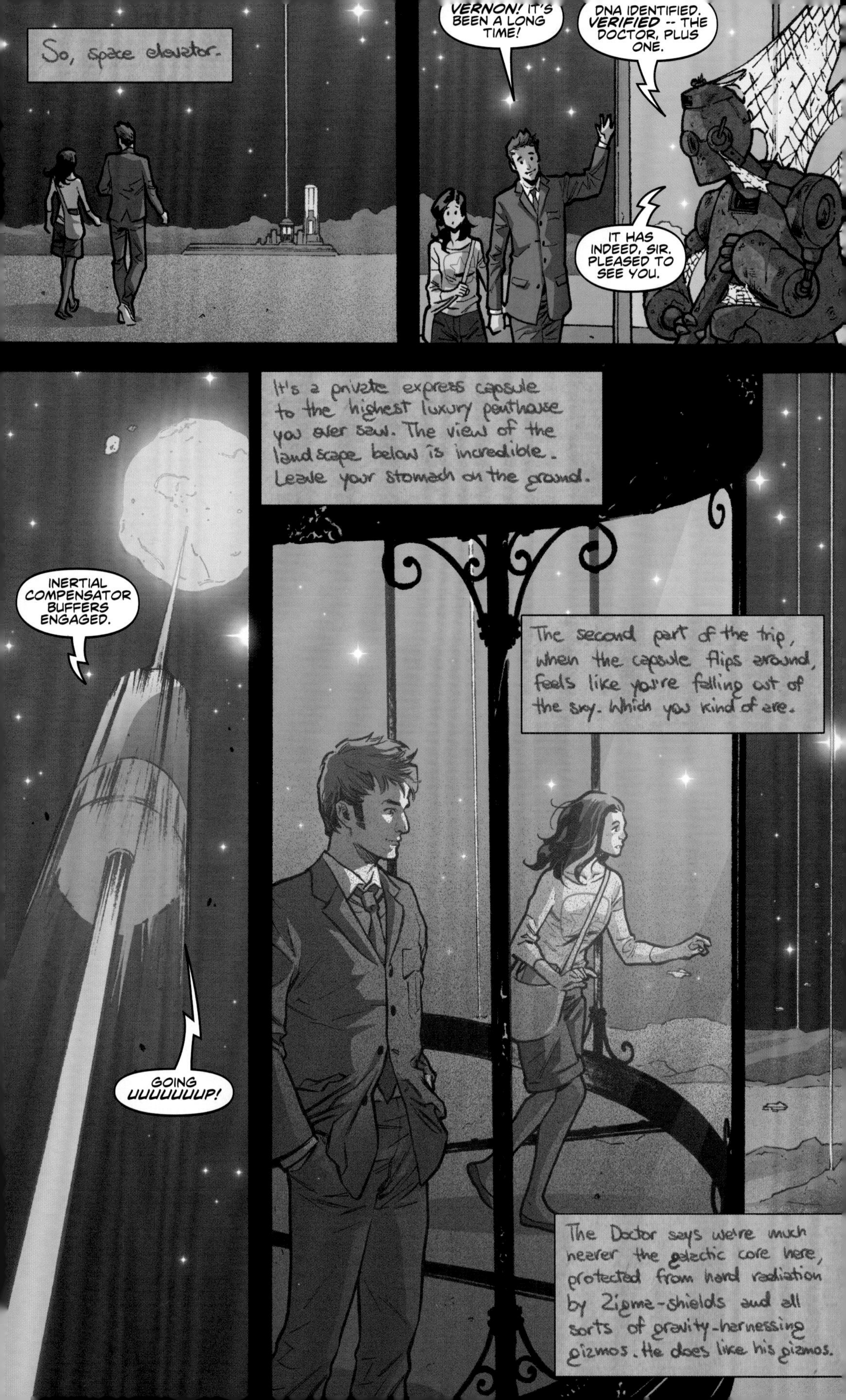

So, space elevator.
VERNON! IT'S BEEN A LONG TIME!
DNA IDENTIFIED. VERIFIED -- THE DOCTOR, PLUS ONE.
IT HAS INDEED, SIR. PLEASED TO SEE YOU.
It's a private express capsule to the highest luxury penthouse you ever saw. The view of the landscape below is incredible. Leave your stomach on the ground.
INERTIAL COMPENSATOR BUFFERS ENGAGED.
GOING UUUUUUUP!
The second part of the trip, when the capsule flips around, feels like you're falling out of the sky. Which you kind of are.
The Doctor says we're much nearer the galactic core here, protected from hard radiation by Zigma-shields and all sorts of gravity-harnessing gizmos. He does like his gizmos.

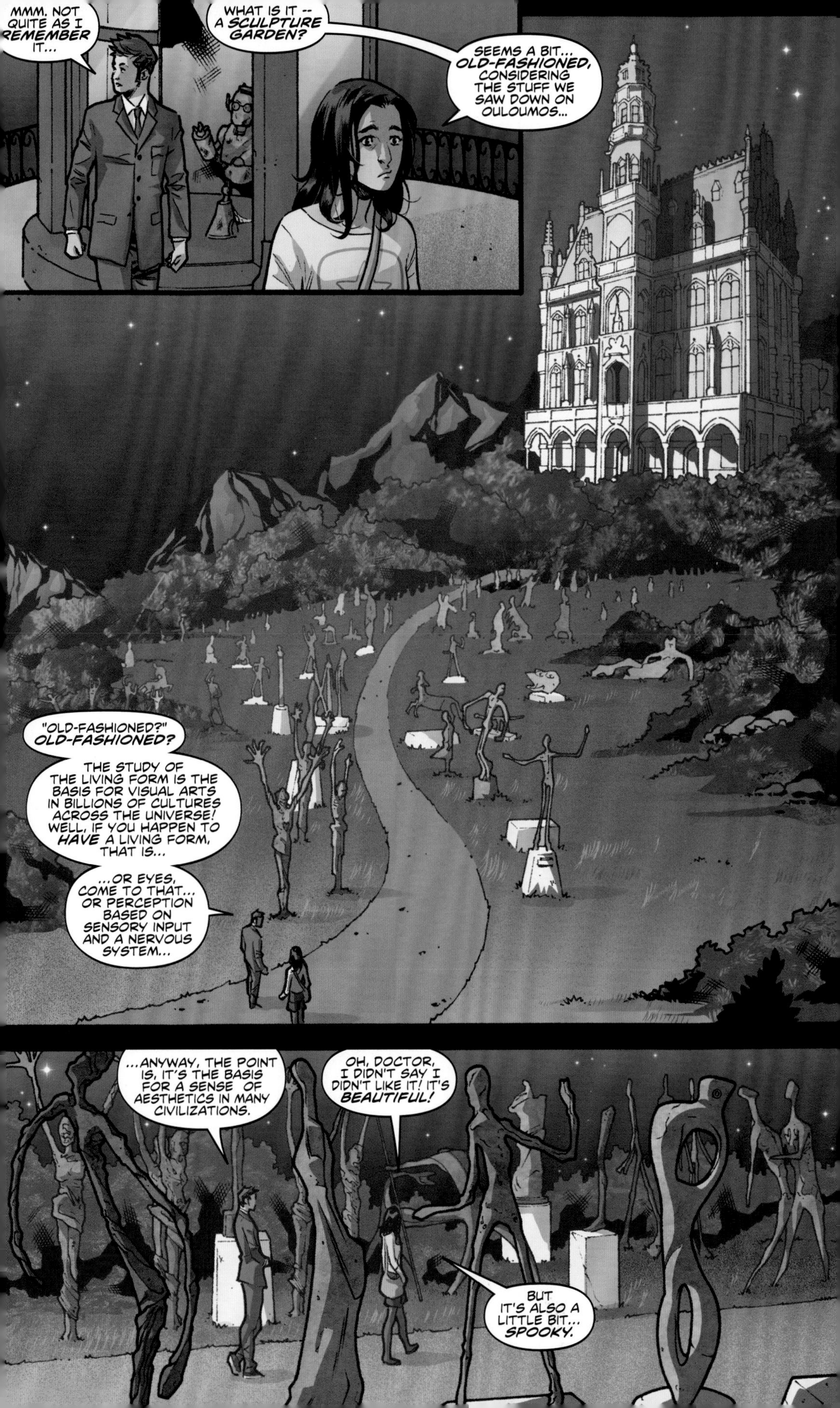

MMM. NOT QUITE AS I REMEMBER IT...
WHAT IS IT -- A SCULPTURE GARDEN?
SEEMS A BIT... OLD-FASHIONED, CONSIDERING THE STUFF WE SAW DOWN ON OULOUMOS...
"OLD-FASHIONED?" OLD-FASHIONED?
THE STUDY OF THE LIVING FORM IS THE BASIS FOR VISUAL ARTS IN BILLIONS OF CULTURES ACROSS THE UNIVERSE! WELL, IF YOU HAPPEN TO HAVE A LIVING FORM, THAT IS...
...OR EYES, COME TO THAT... OR PERCEPTION BASED ON SENSORY INPUT AND A NERVOUS SYSTEM...
...ANYWAY, THE POINT IS, IT'S THE BASIS FOR A SENSE OF AESTHETICS IN MANY CIVILIZATIONS.
OH, DOCTOR, I DIDN'T SAY I DIDN'T LIKE IT! IT'S BEAUTIFUL!
BUT IT'S ALSO A LITTLE BIT... SPOOKY.

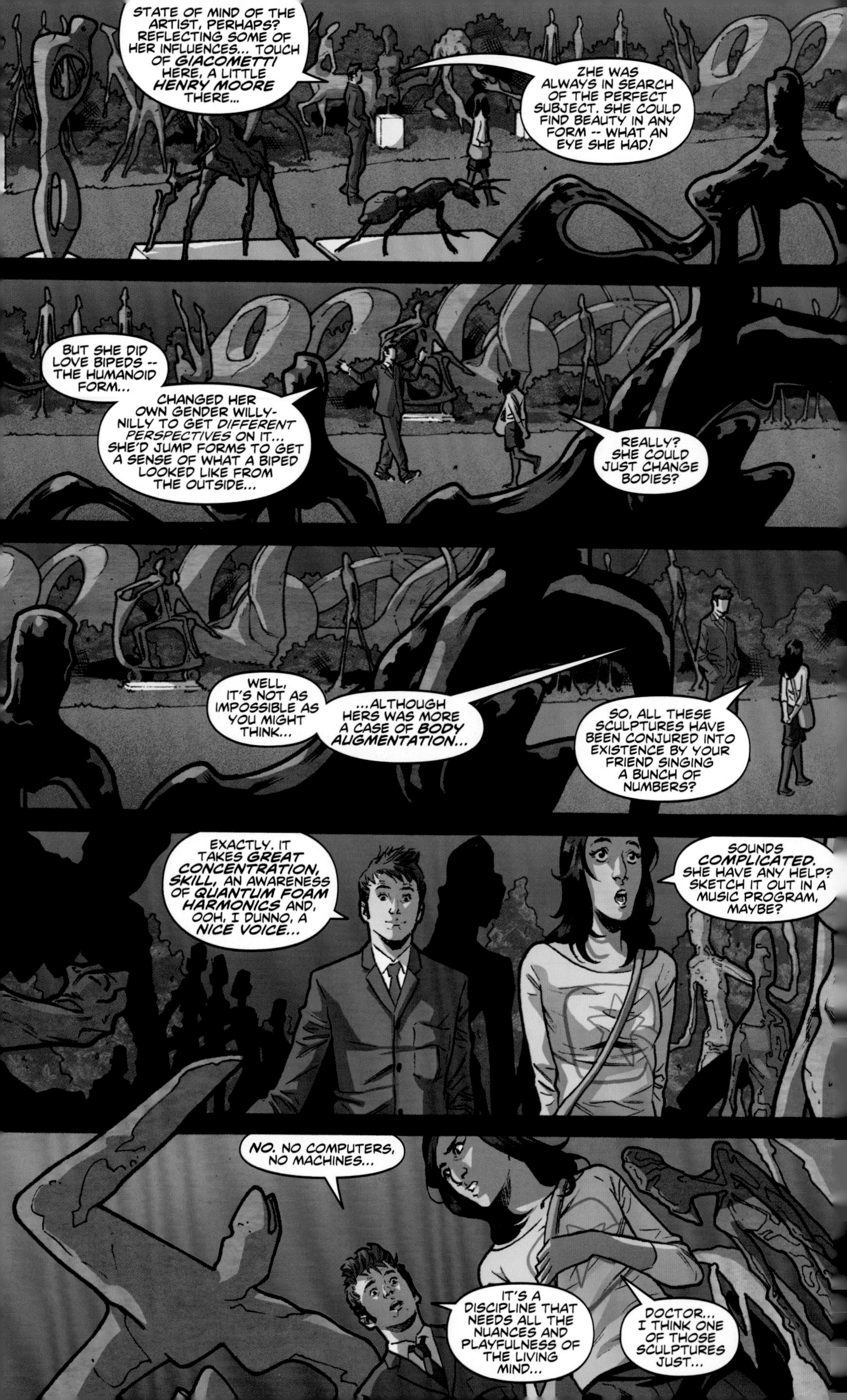
STATE OF MIND OF THE ARTIST, PERHAPS? REFLECTING SOME OF HER INFLUENCES... TOUCH OF GIACOMETTI HERE, A LITTLE HENRY MOORE THERE...
ZHE WAS ALWAYS IN SEARCH OF THE PERFECT SUBJECT. SHE COULD FIND BEAUTY IN ANY FORM -- WHAT AN EYE SHE HAD!
BUT SHE DID LOVE BIPEDS -- THE HUMANOID FORM...
CHANGED HER OWN GENDER WILLY-NILLY TO GET DIFFERENT PERSPECTIVES ON IT... SHE'D JUMP FORMS TO GET A SENSE OF WHAT A BIPED LOOKED LIKE FROM THE OUTSIDE...
REALLY? SHE COULD JUST CHANGE BODIES?
WELL, IT'S NOT AS IMPOSSIBLE AS YOU MIGHT THINK...
...ALTHOUGH HERS WAS MORE A CASE OF BODY AUGMENTATION...
SO, ALL THESE SCULPTURES HAVE BEEN CONJURED INTO EXISTENCE BY YOUR FRIEND SINGING A BUNCH OF NUMBERS?
EXACTLY. IT TAKES GREAT CONCENTRATION, SKILL, AN AWARENESS OF QUANTUM FOAM HARMONICS AND, OOH, I DUNNO, A NICE VOICE...
SOUNDS COMPLICATED. SHE HAVE ANY HELP? SKETCH IT OUT IN A MUSIC PROGRAM, MAYBE?
NO. NO COMPUTERS, NO MACHINES...
IT'S A DISCIPLINE THAT NEEDS ALL THE NUANCES AND PLAYFULNESS OF THE LIVING MIND...
DOCTOR... I THINK ONE OF THOSE SCULPTURES JUST...

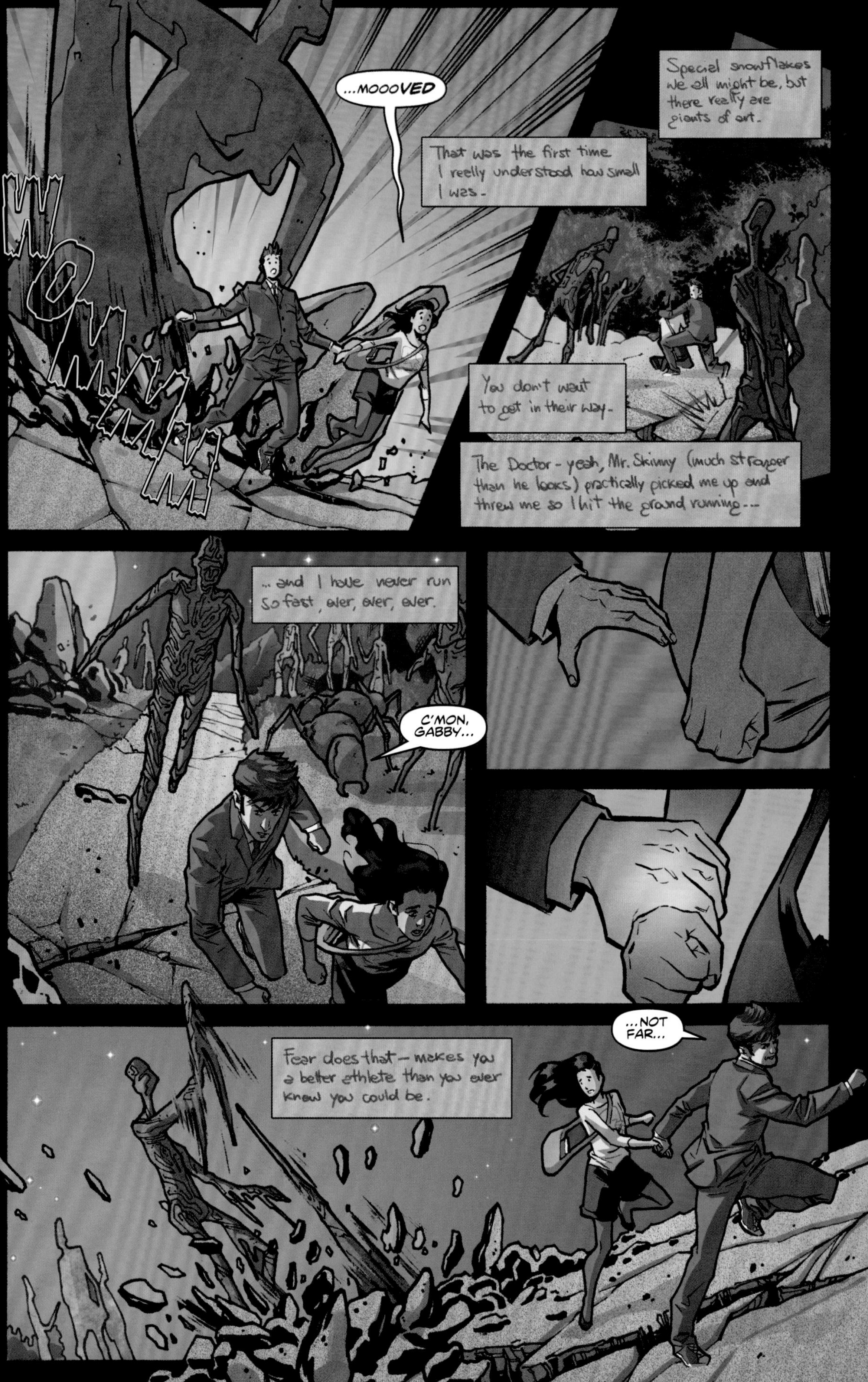
...MOOOVED
WOMMMM
That was the first time I reelly understood how small I was.
Special snowflakes we all might be, but there really are giants of art.
You don't want to get in their way.
The Doctor - yeah, Mr. Skinny (much stranger than he looks) practically picked me up and threw me so I hit the ground running...
.. and I have never run so fast, ever, ever, ever.
C'MON, GABBY...
Fear does that - makes you a better athlete than you ever knew you could be.
...NOT FAR...

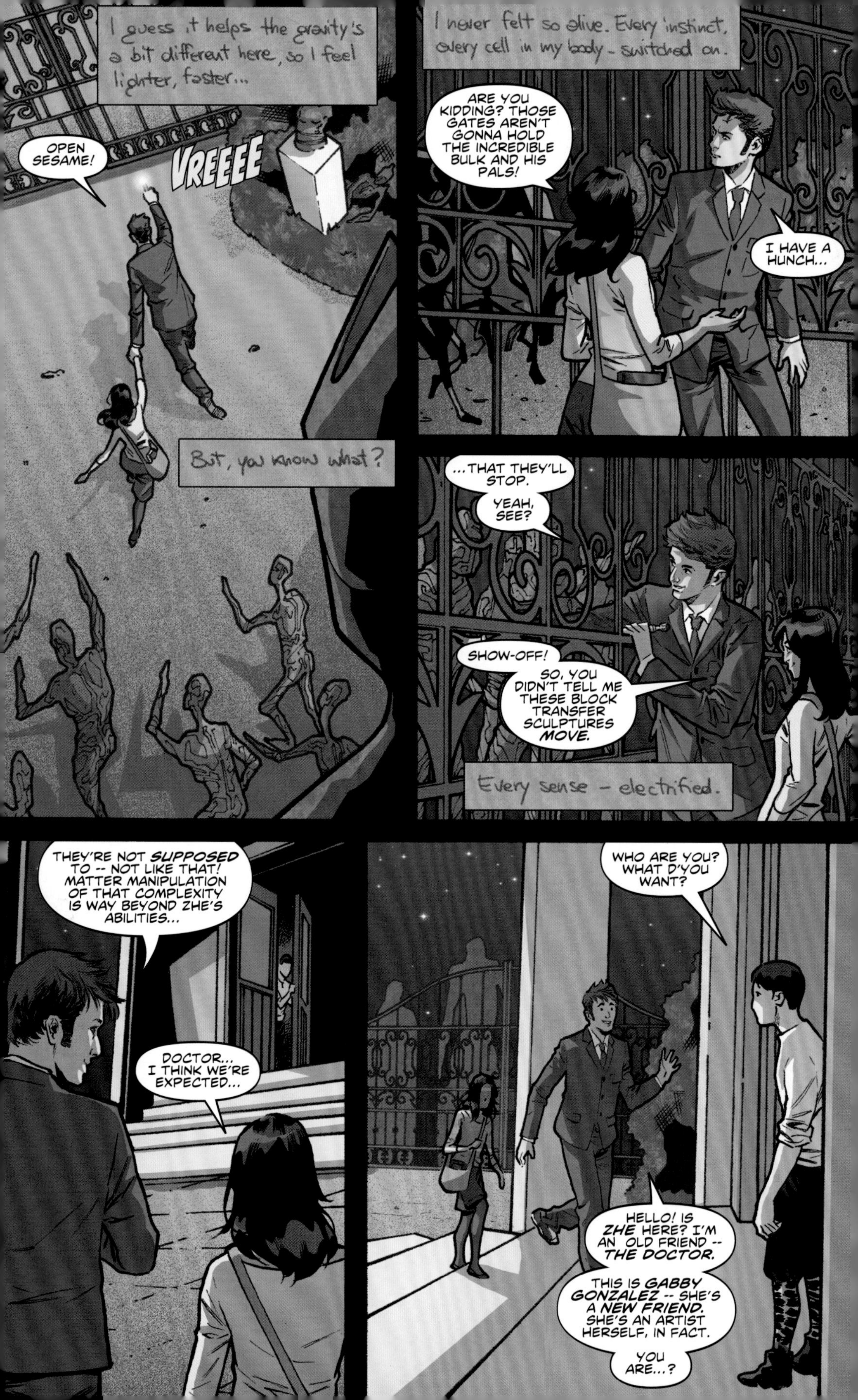
I guess it helps the gravity's a bit different here, so I feel lighter, faster...
OPEN SESAME!
VREEEE
But, you know what?
I never felt so alive. Every instinct, every cell in my body - switched on.
ARE YOU KIDDING? THOSE GATES AREN'T GONNA HOLD THE INCREDIBLE BULK AND HIS PALS!
I HAVE A HUNCH...
...THAT THEY'LL STOP.
YEAH, SEE?
SHOW-OFF!
SO, YOU DIDN'T TELL ME THESE BLOCK TRANSFER SCULPTURES MOVE.
Every sense - electrified.
THEY'RE NOT SUPPOSED TO -- NOT LIKE THAT! MATTER MANIPULATION OF THAT COMPLEXITY IS WAY BEYOND ZHE'S ABILITIES...
DOCTOR... I THINK WE'RE EXPECTED...
WHO ARE YOU? WHAT D'YOU WANT?
HELLO! IS ZHE HERE? I'M AN OLD FRIEND -- THE DOCTOR.
THIS IS GABBY GONZALEZ -- SHE'S A NEW FRIEND. SHE'S AN ARTIST HERSELF, IN FACT.
YOU ARE...?

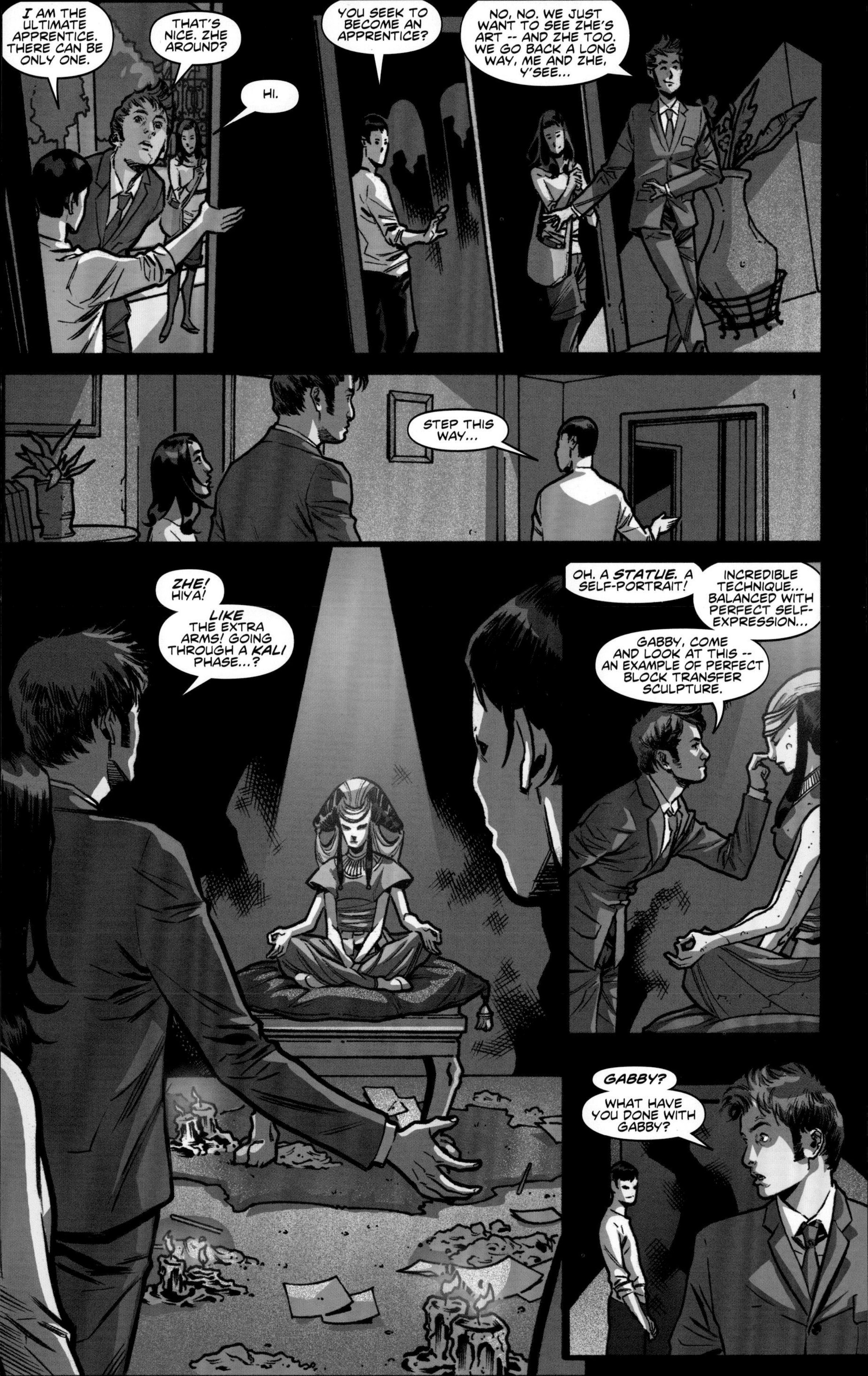

I AM THE ULTIMATE APPRENTICE. THERE CAN BE ONLY ONE.
THAT'S NICE. ZHE AROUND?
HI.
YOU SEEK TO BECOME AN APPRENTICE?
NO, NO. WE JUST WANT TO SEE ZHE'S ART -- AND ZHE TOO. WE GO BACK A LONG WAY, ME AND ZHE, Y'SEE...
STEP THIS WAY...
ZHE! HIYA!
LIKE THE EXTRA ARMS! GOING THROUGH A KALI PHASE...?
OH. A STATUE. A SELF-PORTRAIT!
INCREDIBLE TECHNIQUE... BALANCED WITH PERFECT SELF-EXPRESSION...
GABBY, COME AND LOOK AT THIS -- AN EXAMPLE OF PERFECT BLOCK TRANSFER SCULPTURE.
GABBY?
WHAT HAVE YOU DONE WITH GABBY?

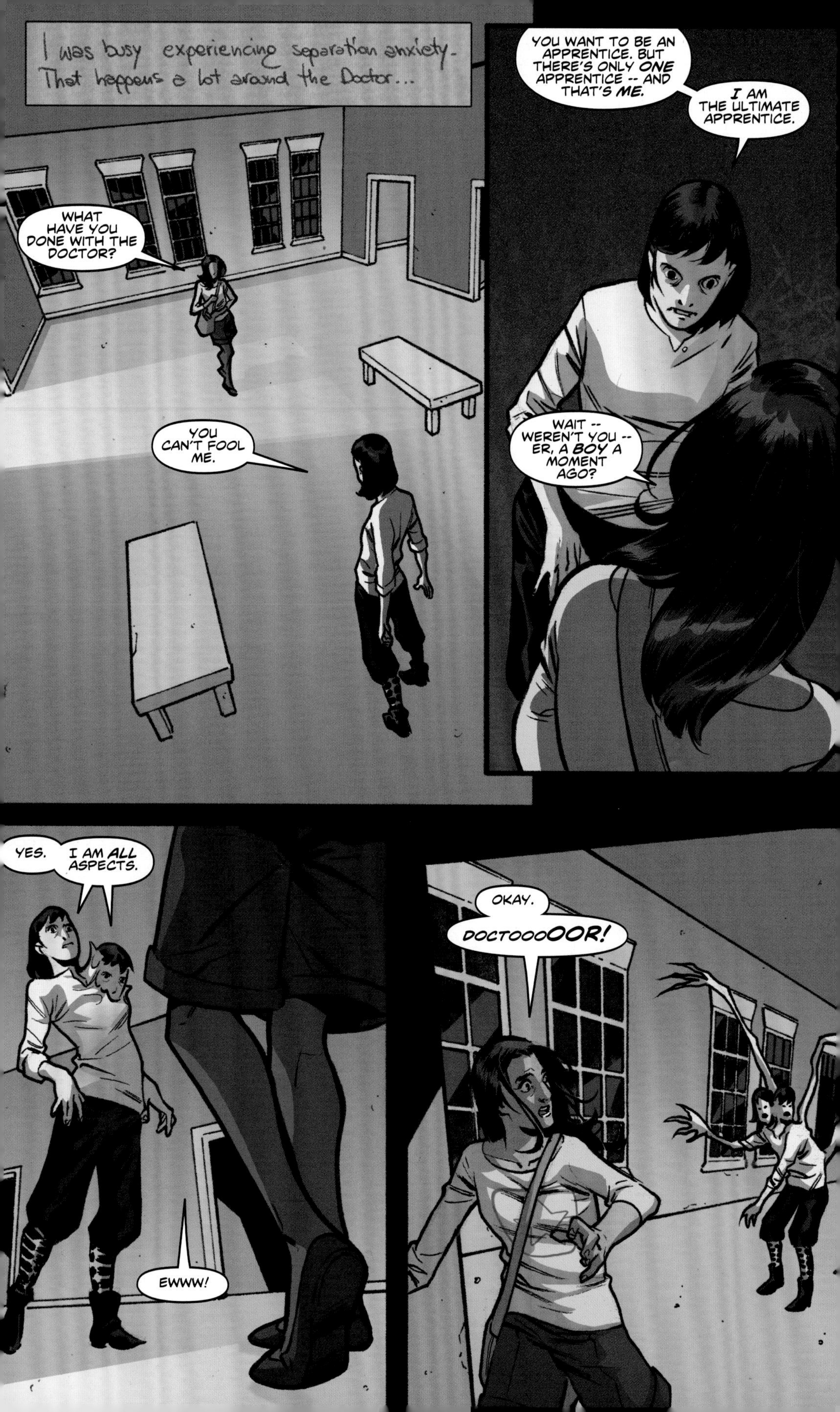
I was busy experiencing separation anxiety. That happens a lot around the Doctor...
WHAT HAVE YOU DONE WITH THE DOCTOR?
YOU CAN'T FOOL ME.
YOU WANT TO BE AN APPRENTICE. BUT THERE'S ONLY ONE APPRENTICE -- AND THAT'S ME.
I AM THE ULTIMATE APPRENTICE.
WAIT -- WEREN'T YOU -- ER, A BOY A MOMENT AGO?
YES.
I AM ALL ASPECTS.
EWWW!
OKAY.
DOCTOOOOOOR!

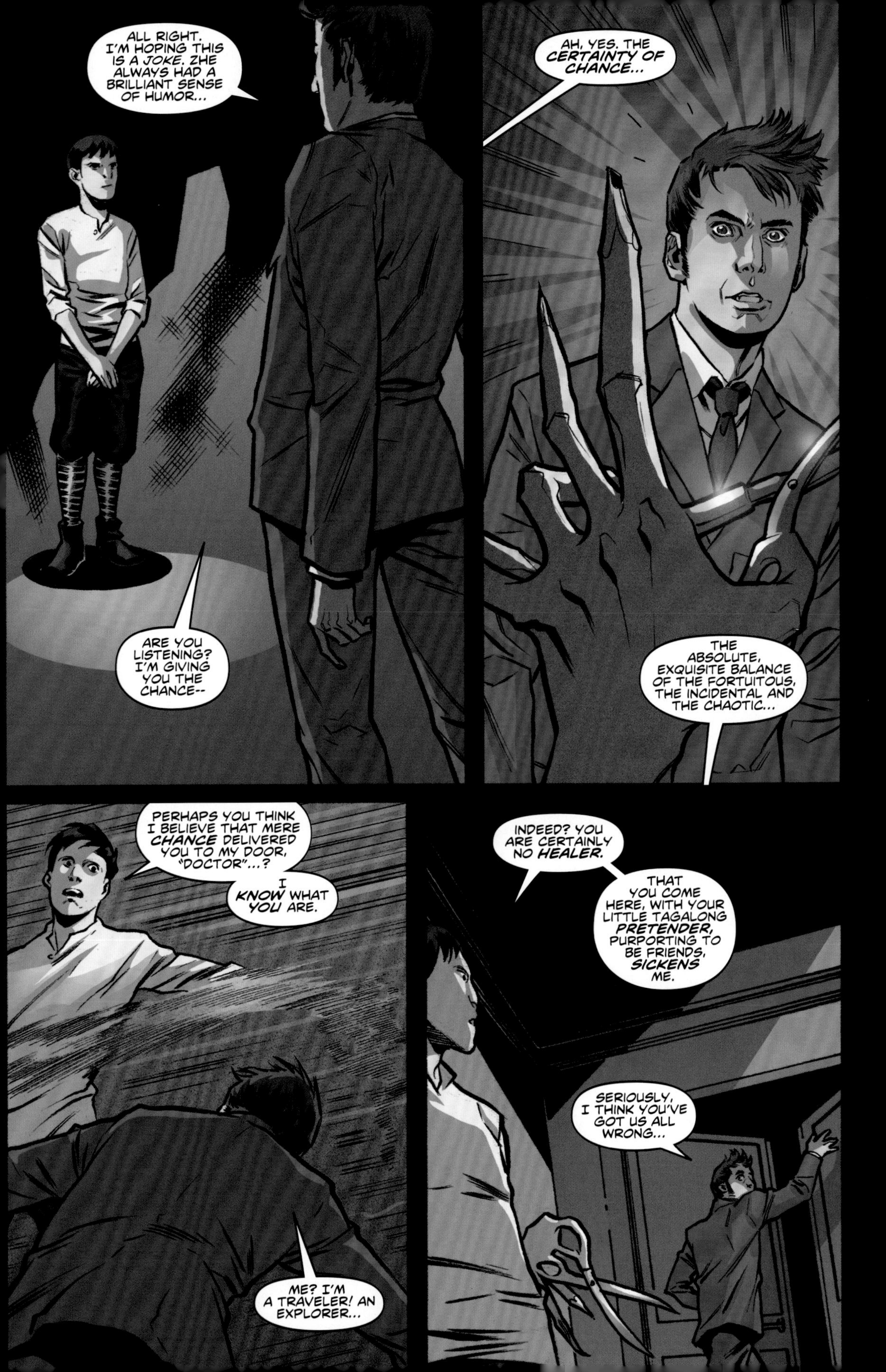
ALL RIGHT. I'M HOPING THIS IS A JOKE. ZHE ALWAYS HAD A BRILLIANT SENSE OF HUMOR...
ARE YOU LISTENING? I'M GIVING YOU THE CHANCE--
AH, YES. THE CERTAINTY OF CHANCE...
THE ABSOLUTE, EXQUISITE BALANCE OF THE FORTUITOUS, THE INCIDENTAL AND THE CHAOTIC...
PERHAPS YOU THINK I BELIEVE THAT MERE CHANCE DELIVERED YOU TO MY DOOR, "DOCTOR"...?
I KNOW WHAT YOU ARE.
ME? I'M A TRAVELER! AN EXPLORER...
INDEED? YOU ARE CERTAINLY NO HEALER.
THAT YOU COME HERE, WITH YOUR LITTLE TAGALONG PRETENDER, PURPORTING TO BE FRIENDS, SICKENS ME.
SERIOUSLY, I THINK YOU'VE GOT US ALL WRONG...

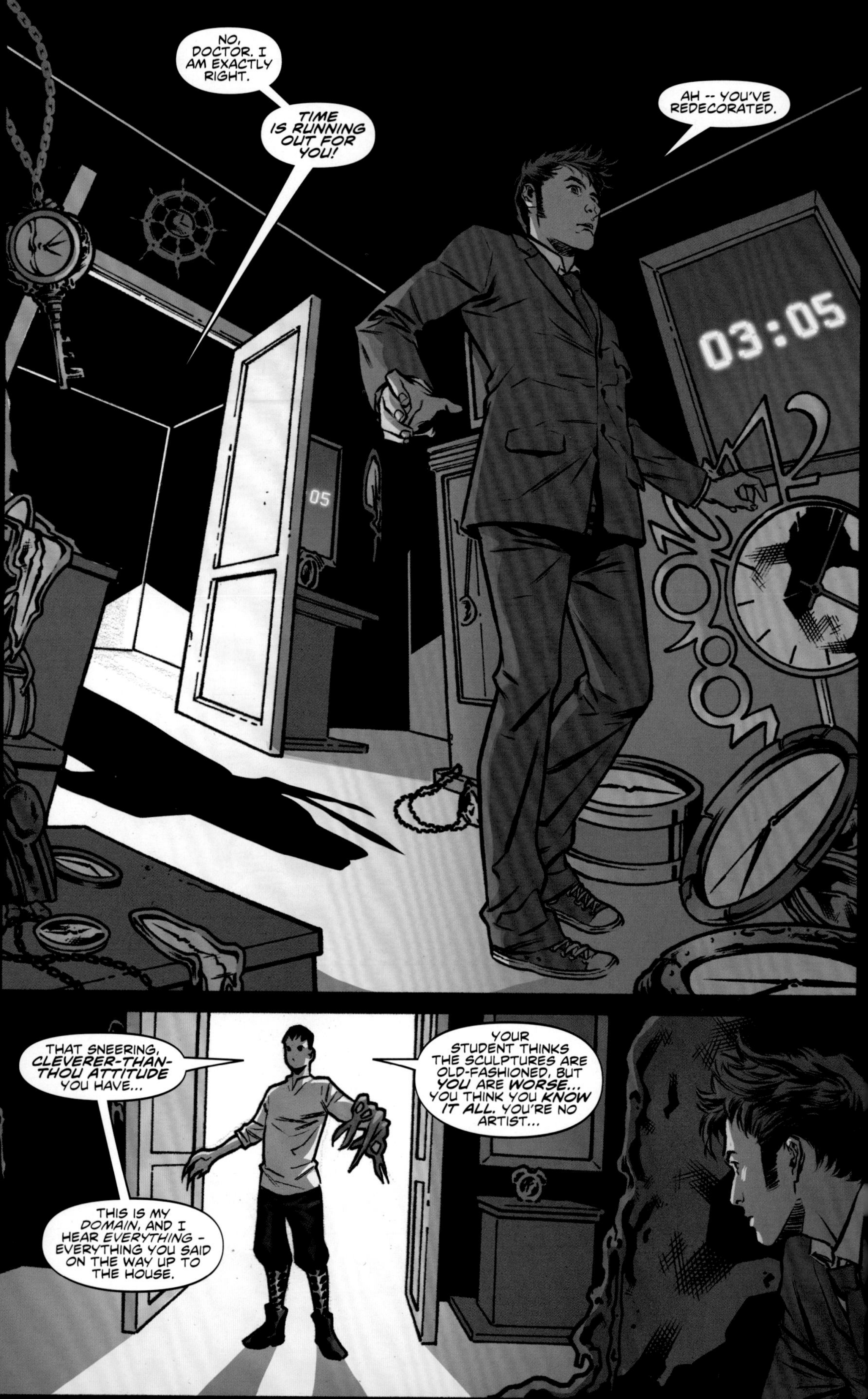

NO, DOCTOR. I AM EXACTLY RIGHT.
TIME IS RUNNING OUT FOR YOU!
AH -- YOU'VE REDECORATED.
03:05
05
THAT SNEERING, CLEVERER-THAN-THOU ATTITUDE YOU HAVE...
THIS IS MY DOMAIN, AND I HEAR EVERYTHING - EVERYTHING YOU SAID ON THE WAY UP TO THE HOUSE.
YOUR STUDENT THINKS THE SCULPTURES ARE OLD-FASHIONED, BUT YOU ARE WORSE... YOU THINK YOU KNOW IT ALL. YOU'RE NO ARTIST...

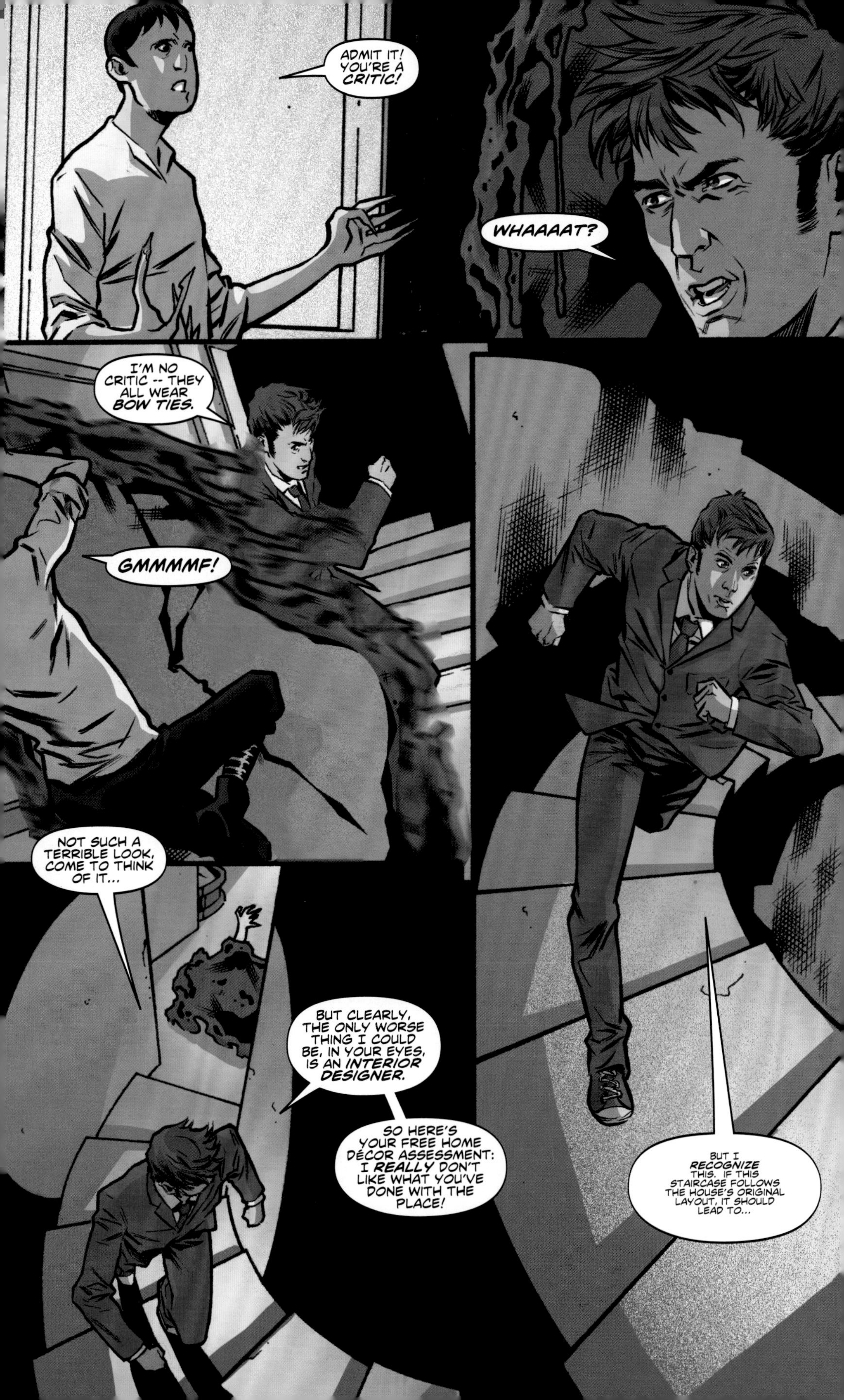
ADMIT IT! YOU'RE A CRITIC!
WHAAAAT?
I'M NO CRITIC -- THEY ALL WEAR BOW TIES.
GMMMMF!
NOT SUCH A TERRIBLE LOOK, COME TO THINK OF IT...
BUT CLEARLY, THE ONLY WORSE THING I COULD BE, IN YOUR EYES, IS AN INTERIOR DESIGNER.
SO HERE'S YOUR FREE HOME DÉCOR ASSESSMENT: I REALLY DON'T LIKE WHAT YOU'VE DONE WITH THE PLACE!
BUT I RECOGNIZE THIS. IF THIS STAIRCASE FOLLOWS THE HOUSE'S ORIGINAL LAYOUT, IT SHOULD LEAD TO...

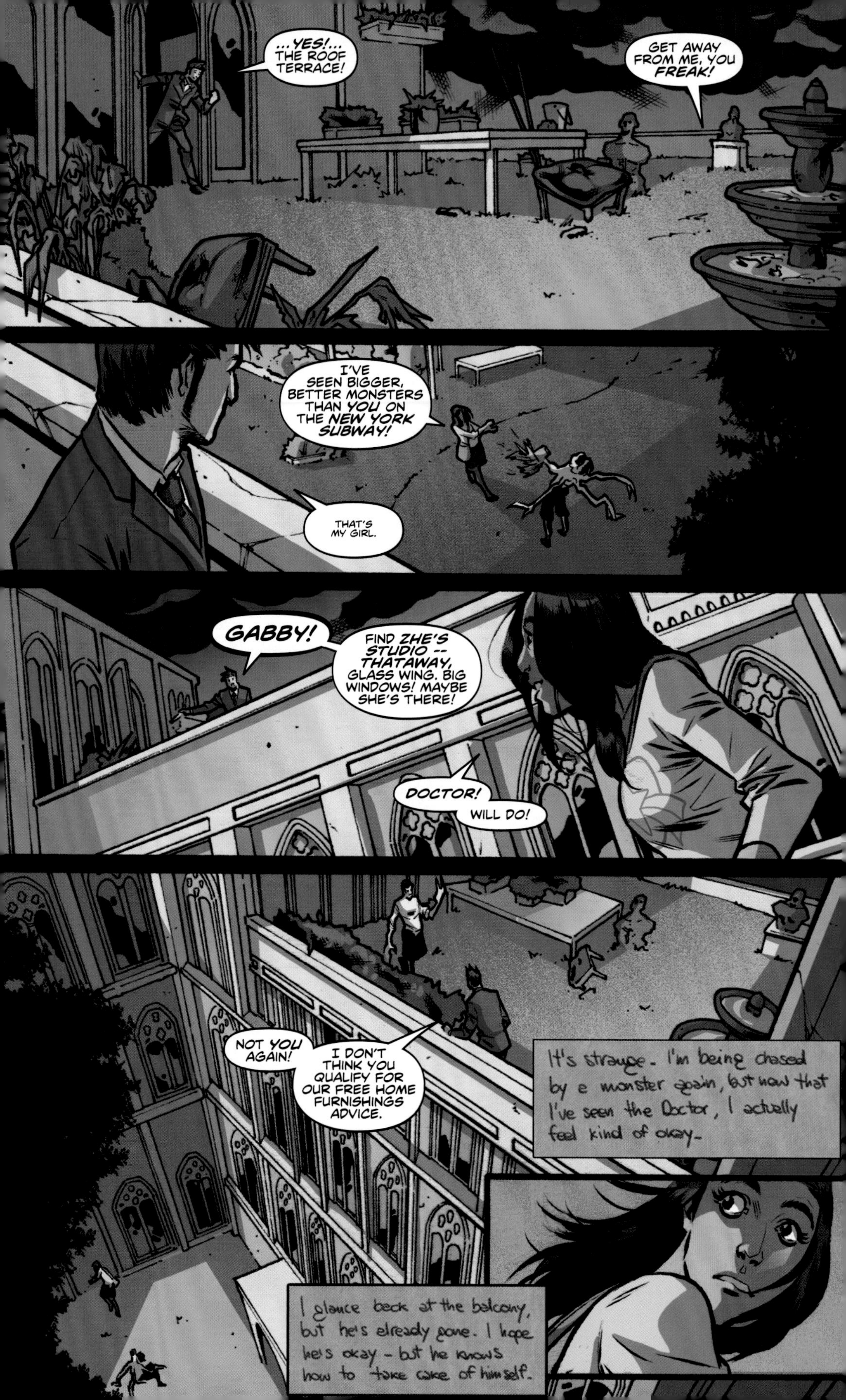
...YES!... THE ROOF TERRACE!
GET AWAY FROM ME, YOU FREAK!
I'VE SEEN BIGGER, BETTER MONSTERS THAN YOU ON THE NEW YORK SUBWAY!
THAT'S MY GIRL.
GABBY!
FIND ZHE'S STUDIO -- THATAWAY, GLASS WING. BIG WINDOWS! MAYBE SHE'S THERE!
DOCTOR!
WILL DO!
NOT YOU AGAIN!
I DON'T THINK YOU QUALIFY FOR OUR FREE HOME FURNISHINGS ADVICE.
It's strange. I'm being chased by a monster again, but now that I've seen the Doctor, I actually feel kind of okay.
I glance back at the balcony, but he's already gone. I hope he's okay – but he knows how to take care of himself.

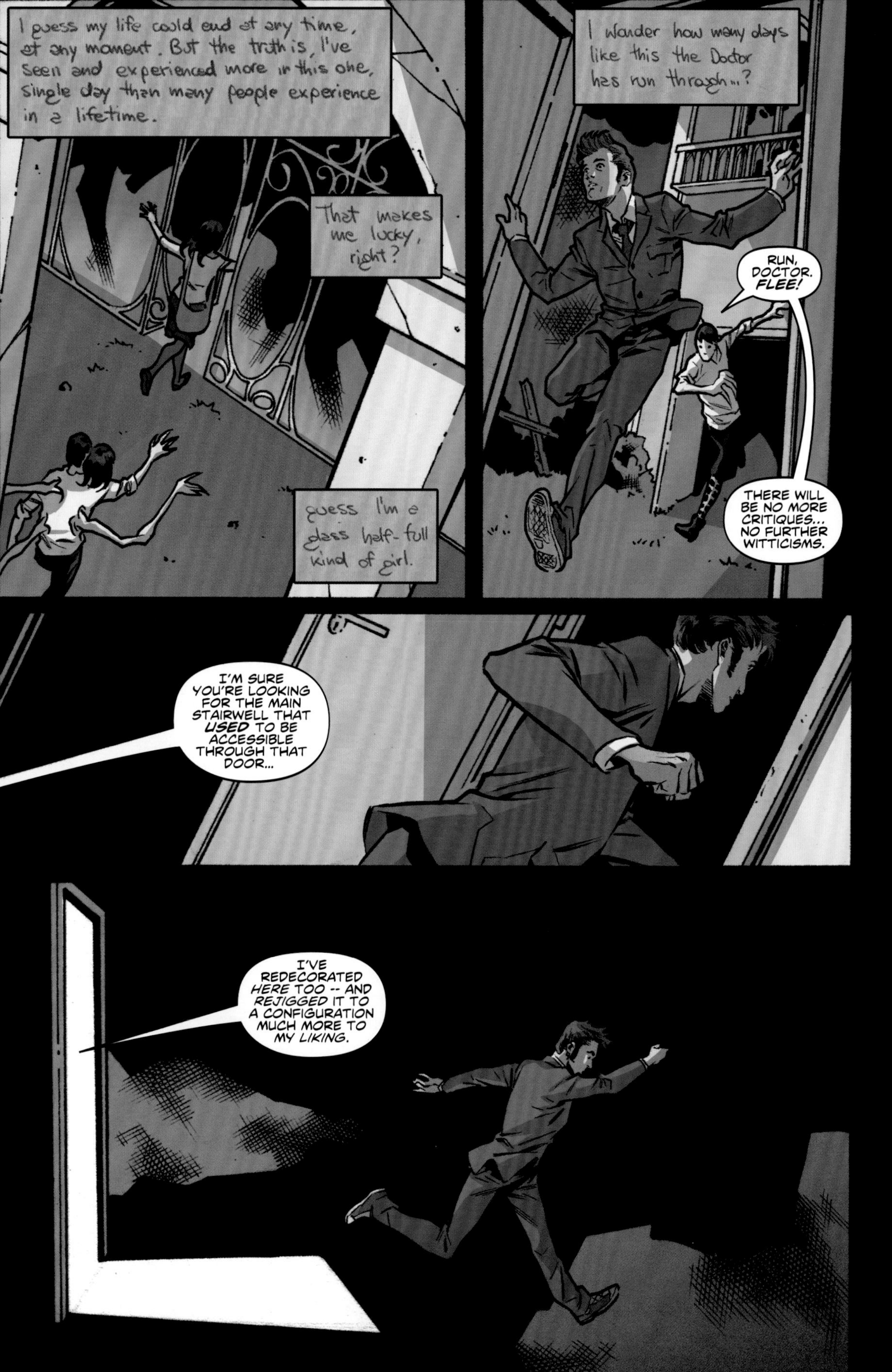

I guess my life could end at any time, at any moment. But the truth is, I've seen and experienced more in this one, single day than many people experience in a lifetime.
That makes me lucky, right?
Guess I'm a glass half-full kind of girl.
I wander how many days like this the Doctor has run through...?
RUN, DOCTOR. FLEE!
THERE WILL BE NO MORE CRITIQUES... NO FURTHER WITTICISMS.
I'M SURE YOU'RE LOOKING FOR THE MAIN STAIRWELL THAT USED TO BE ACCESSIBLE THROUGH THAT DOOR...
I'VE REDECORATED HERE TOO -- AND REJIGGED IT TO A CONFIGURATION MUCH MORE TO MY LIKING.

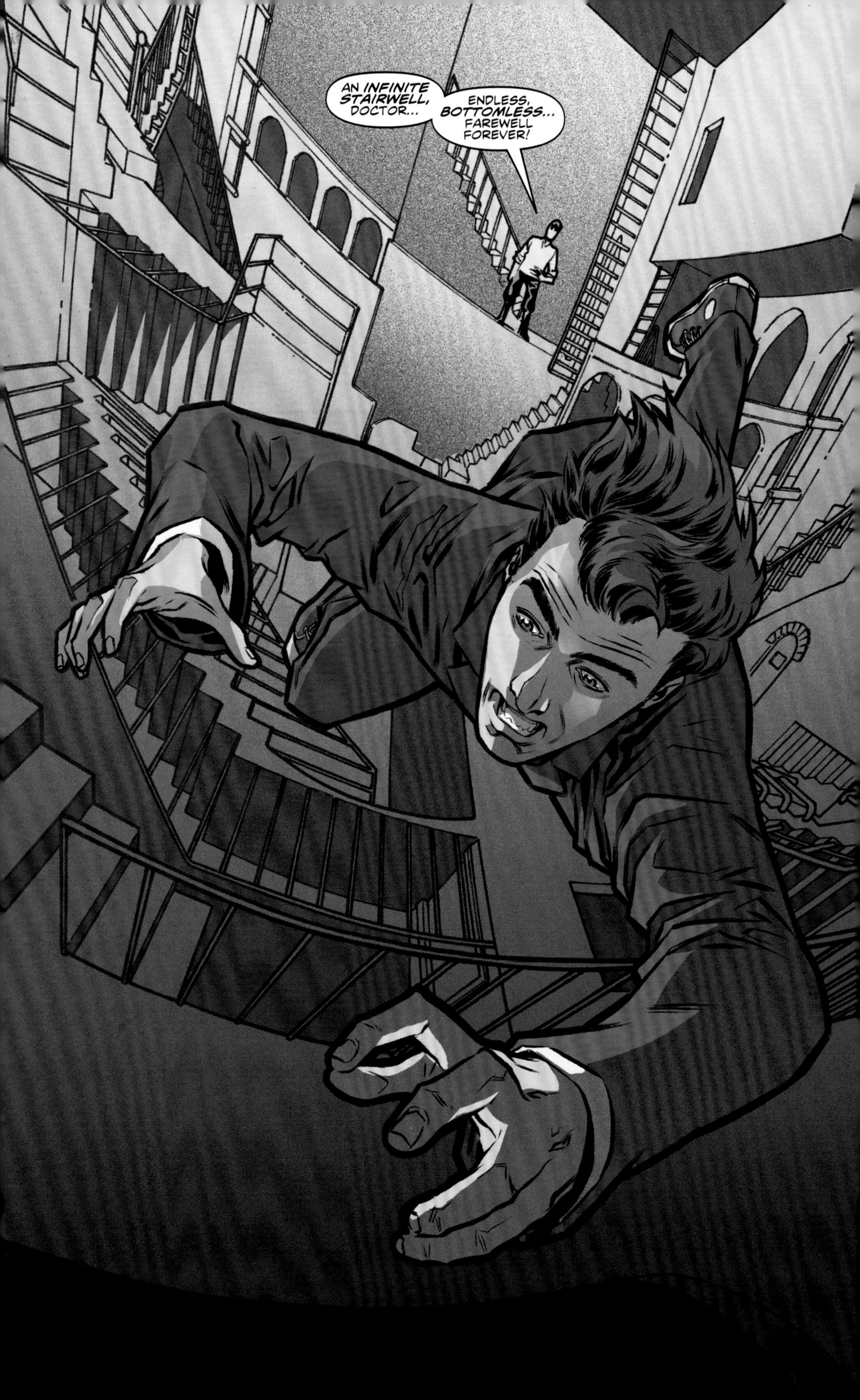
AN INFINITE STAIRWELL, DOCTOR...
ENDLESS, BOTTOMLESS... FAREWELL FOREVER!

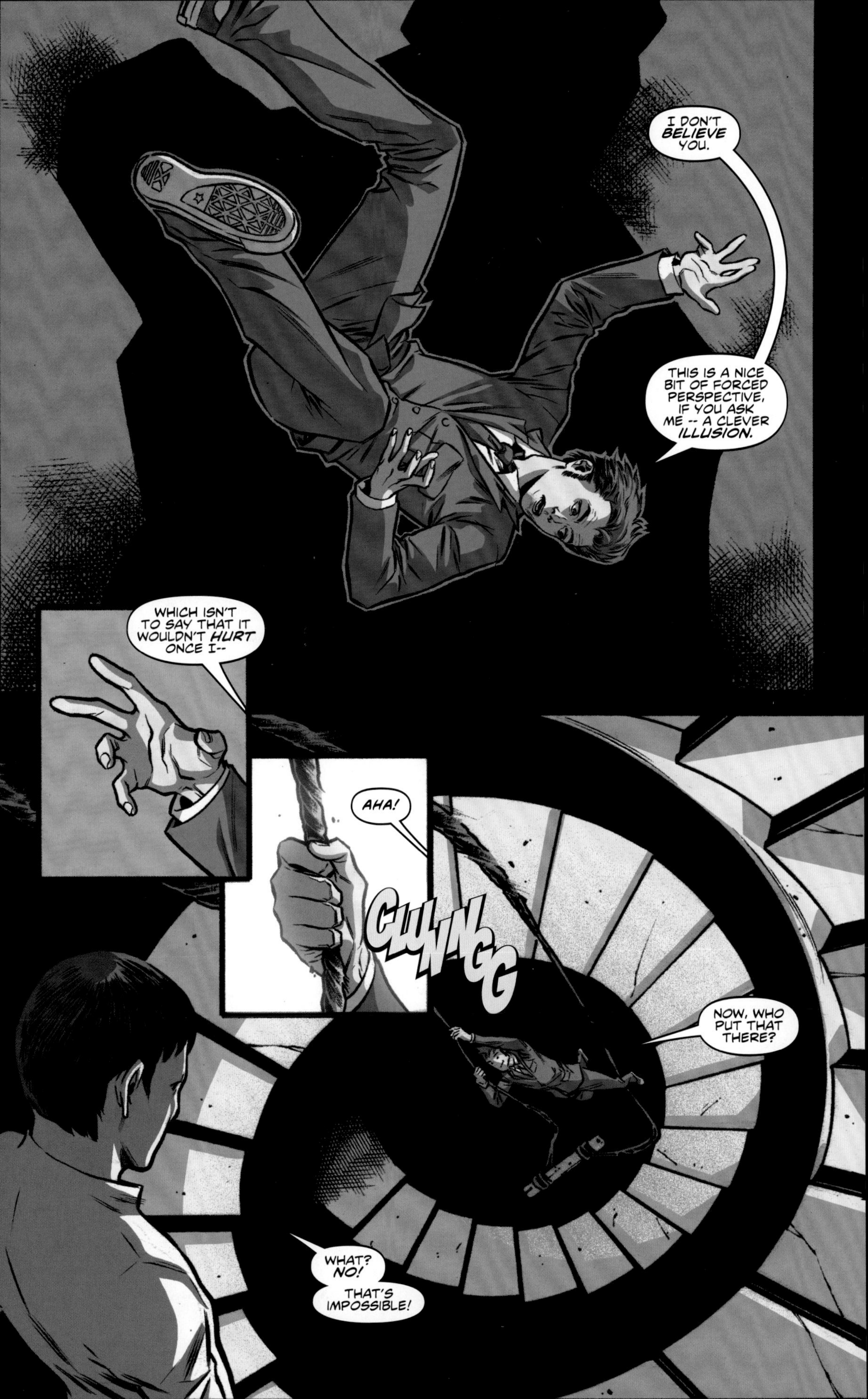
I DON'T BELIEVE YOU.
THIS IS A NICE BIT OF FORCED PERSPECTIVE, IF YOU ASK ME -- A CLEVER ILLUSION.
WHICH ISN'T TO SAY THAT IT WOULDN'T HURT ONCE I--
AHA!
CLUNNGG
NOW, WHO PUT THAT THERE?
WHAT? NO!
THAT'S IMPOSSIBLE!

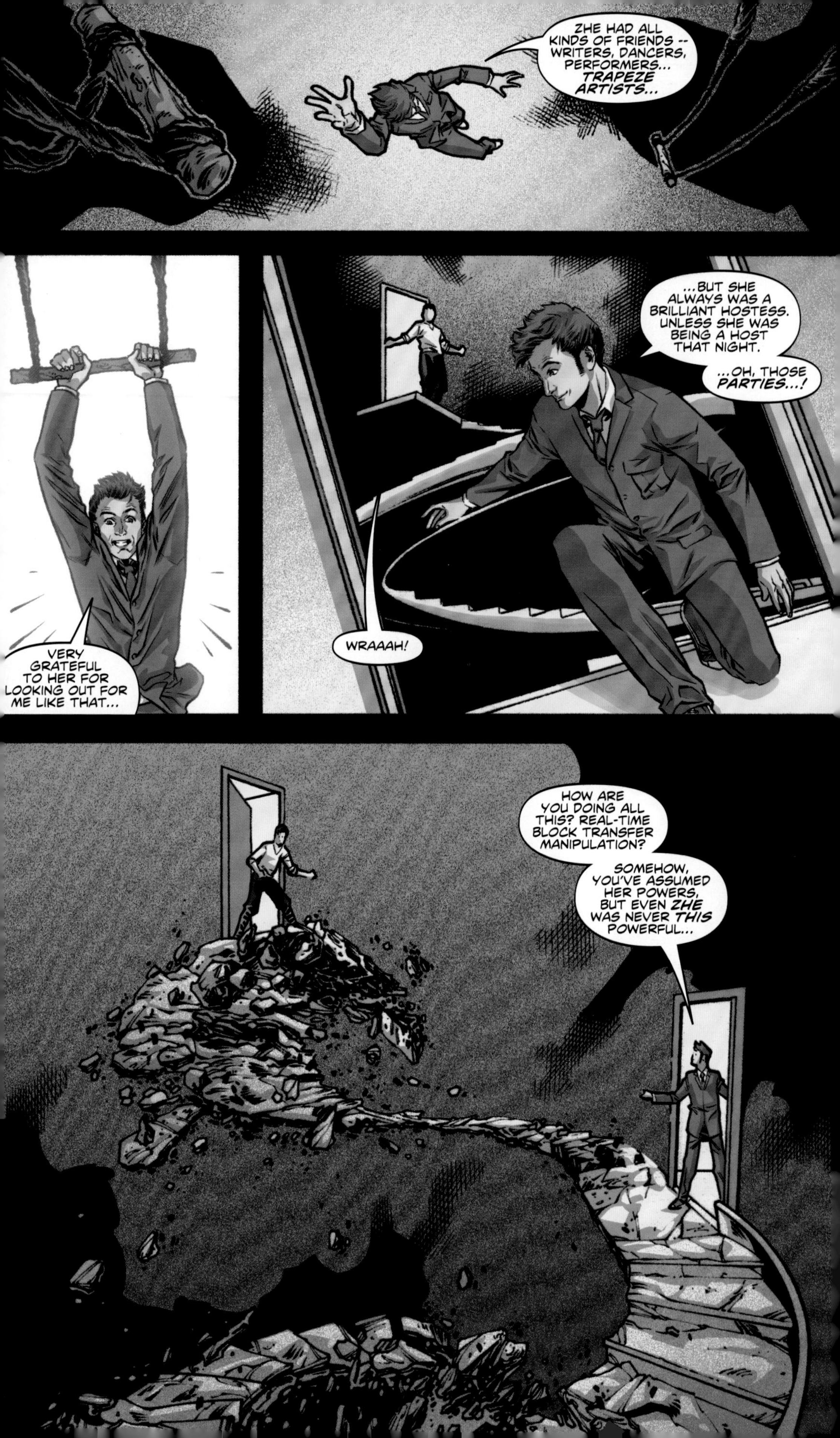
ZHE HAD ALL KINDS OF FRIENDS -- WRITERS, DANCERS, PERFORMERS... TRAPEZE ARTISTS...
VERY GRATEFUL TO HER FOR LOOKING OUT FOR ME LIKE THAT...
...BUT SHE ALWAYS WAS A BRILLIANT HOSTESS. UNLESS SHE WAS BEING A HOST THAT NIGHT.
...OH, THOSE PARTIES...!
WRAAAH!
HOW ARE YOU DOING ALL THIS? REAL-TIME BLOCK TRANSFER MANIPULATION?
SOMEHOW, YOU'VE ASSUMED HER POWERS, BUT EVEN ZHE WAS NEVER THIS POWERFUL...

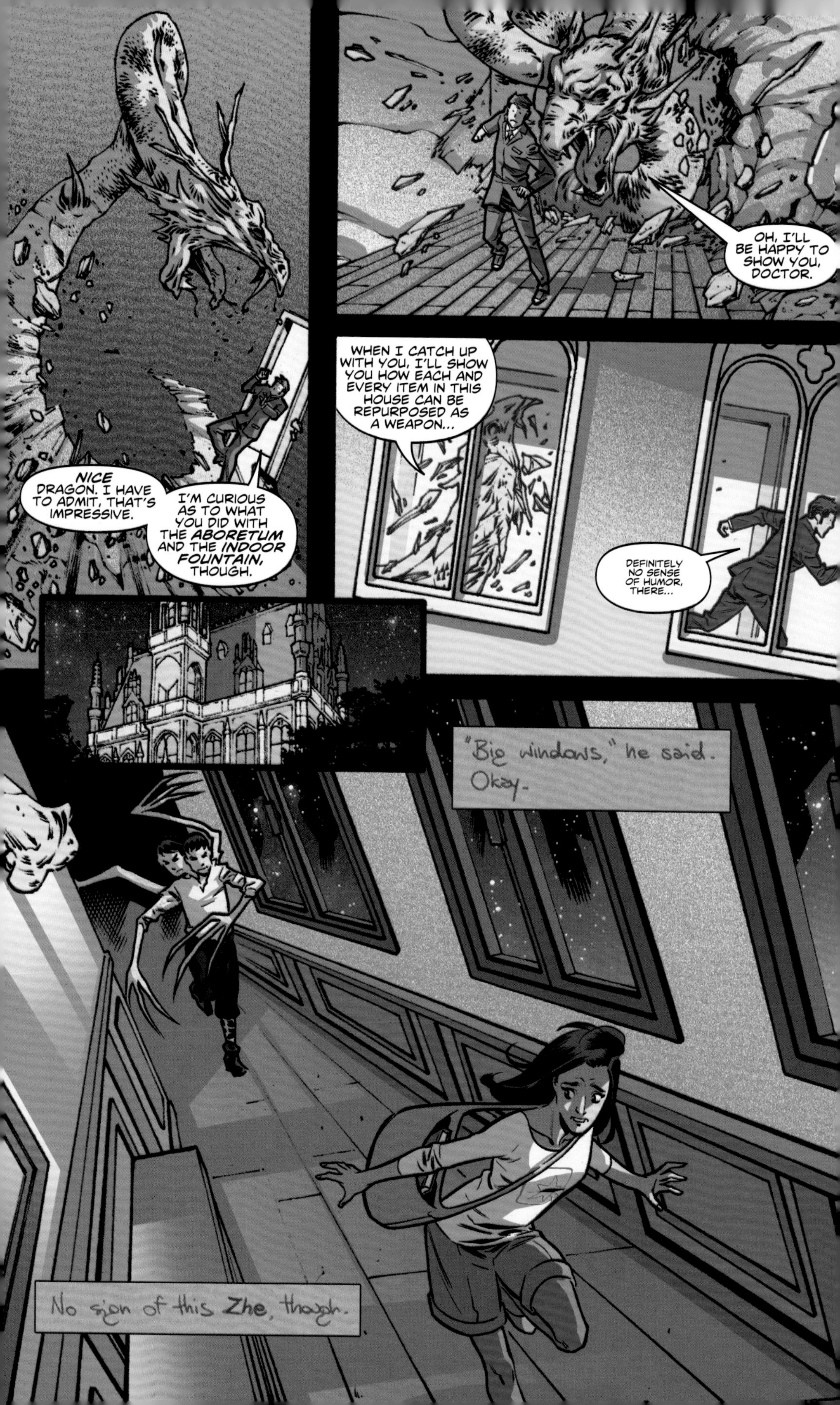
NICE DRAGON. I HAVE TO ADMIT, THAT'S IMPRESSIVE.
I'M CURIOUS AS TO WHAT YOU DID WITH THE ABORETUM AND THE INDOOR FOUNTAIN, THOUGH.
OH, I'LL BE HAPPY TO SHOW YOU, DOCTOR.
WHEN I CATCH UP WITH YOU, I'LL SHOW YOU HOW EACH AND EVERY ITEM IN THIS HOUSE CAN BE REPURPOSED AS A WEAPON...
DEFINITELY NO SENSE OF HUMOR, THERE...
"Big windows," he said. Okay.
No sign of this Zhe, though.

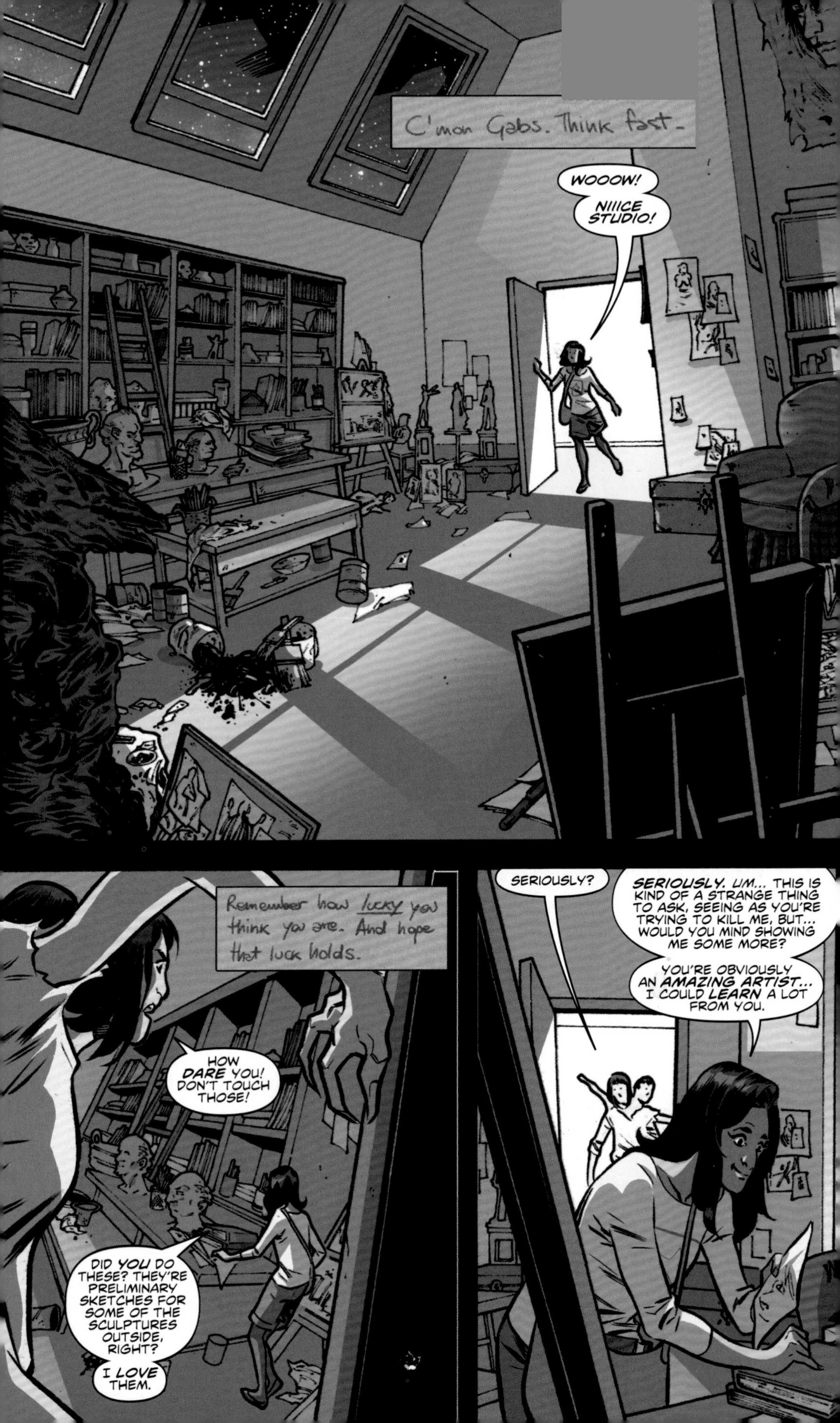
C'mon Gabs. Think fast.
WOOOW! NIIICE STUDIO!
Remember how lucky you think you are. And hope that luck holds.
HOW DARE YOU! DON'T TOUCH THOSE!
DID YOU DO THESE? THEY'RE PRELIMINARY SKETCHES FOR SOME OF THE SCULPTURES OUTSIDE, RIGHT?
I LOVE THEM.
SERIOUSLY?
SERIOUSLY. UM... THIS IS KIND OF A STRANGE THING TO ASK, SEEING AS YOU'RE TRYING TO KILL ME, BUT... WOULD YOU MIND SHOWING ME SOME MORE?
YOU'RE OBVIOUSLY AN AMAZING ARTIST... I COULD LEARN A LOT FROM YOU.

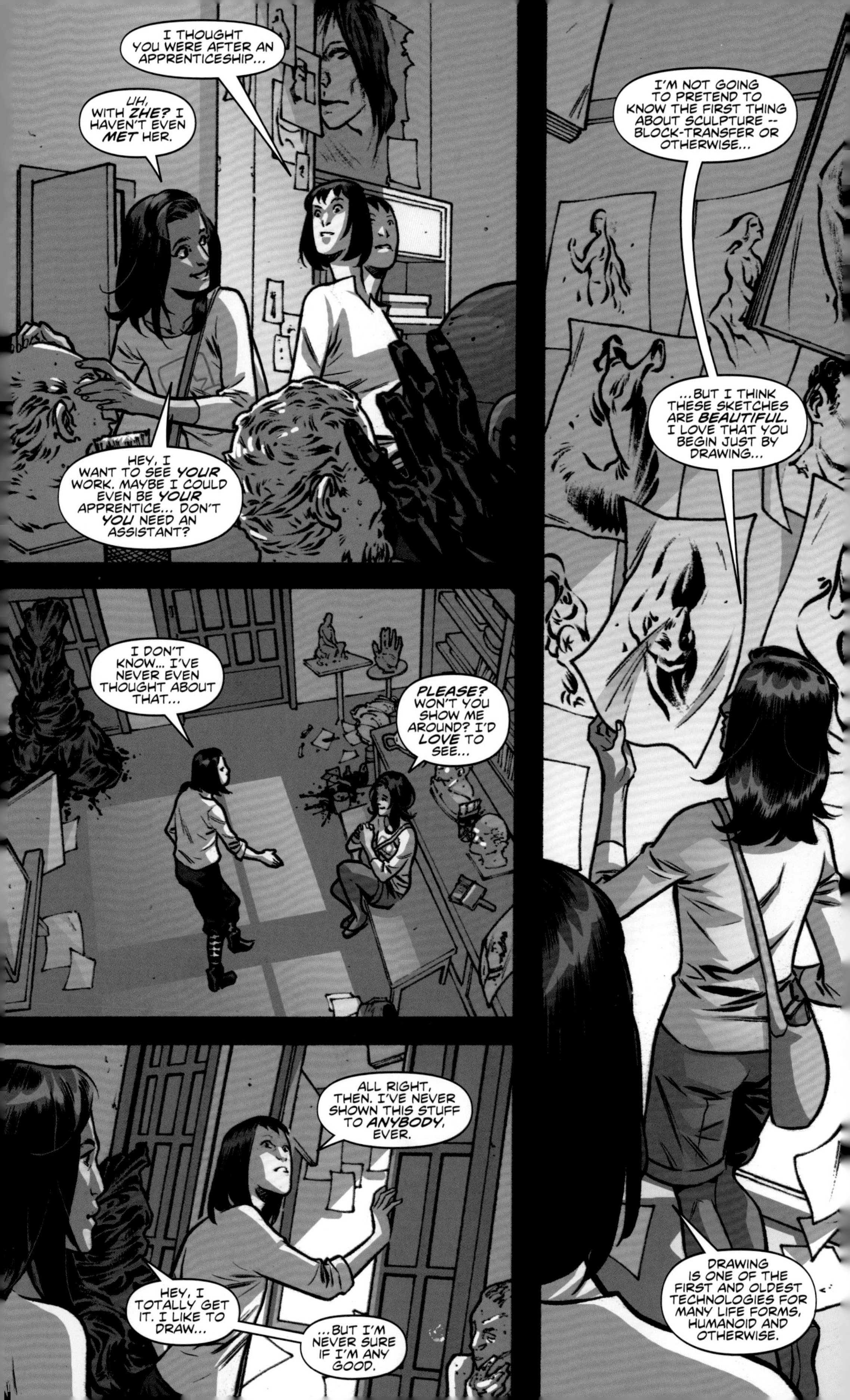
I THOUGHT YOU WERE AFTER AN APPRENTICESHIP...
UH, WITH ZHE? I HAVEN'T EVEN MET HER.
HEY, I WANT TO SEE YOUR WORK. MAYBE I COULD EVEN BE YOUR APPRENTICE... DON'T YOU NEED AN ASSISTANT?
I DON'T KNOW... I'VE NEVER EVEN THOUGHT ABOUT THAT...
PLEASE? WON'T YOU SHOW ME AROUND? I'D LOVE TO SEE...
ALL RIGHT, THEN. I'VE NEVER SHOWN THIS STUFF TO ANYBODY, EVER.
HEY, I TOTALLY GET IT. I LIKE TO DRAW...
...BUT I'M NEVER SURE IF I'M ANY GOOD.
I'M NOT GOING TO PRETEND TO KNOW THE FIRST THING ABOUT SCULPTURE -- BLOCK-TRANSFER OR OTHERWISE...
...BUT I THINK THESE SKETCHES ARE BEAUTIFUL. I LOVE THAT YOU BEGIN JUST BY DRAWING...
DRAWING IS ONE OF THE FIRST AND OLDEST TECHNOLOGIES FOR MANY LIFE FORMS, HUMANOID AND OTHERWISE.

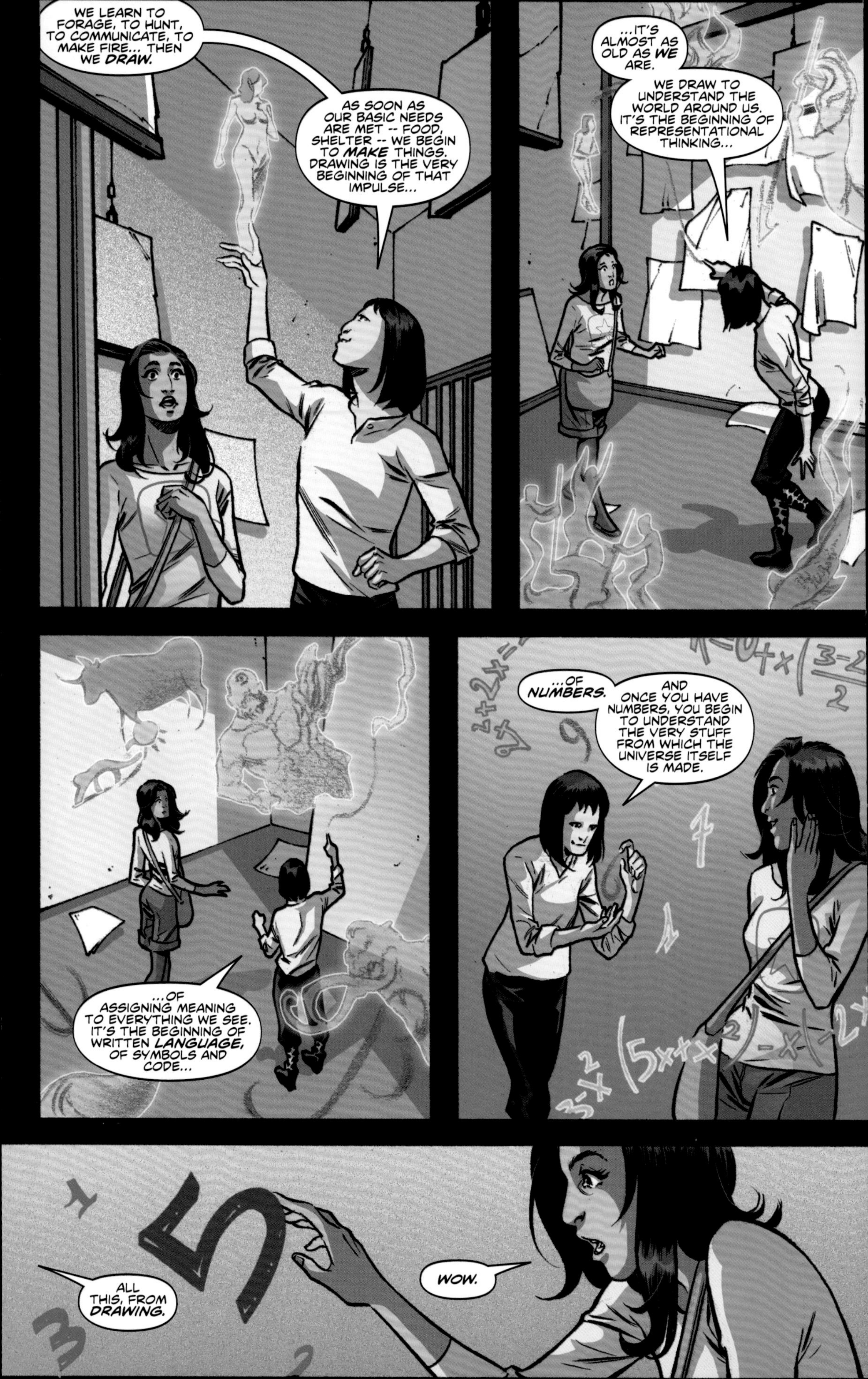
WE LEARN TO FORAGE, TO HUNT, TO COMMUNICATE, TO MAKE FIRE... THEN WE *DRAW.*
AS SOON AS OUR BASIC NEEDS ARE MET -- FOOD, SHELTER -- WE BEGIN TO *MAKE* THINGS. DRAWING IS THE VERY BEGINNING OF THAT IMPULSE...
...IT'S ALMOST AS OLD AS *WE* ARE.
WE DRAW TO UNDERSTAND THE WORLD AROUND US. IT'S THE BEGINNING OF REPRESENTATIONAL THINKING...
...OF ASSIGNING MEANING TO EVERYTHING WE SEE. IT'S THE BEGINNING OF WRITTEN *LANGUAGE,* OF SYMBOLS AND CODE...
...OF *NUMBERS.*
AND ONCE YOU HAVE NUMBERS, YOU BEGIN TO UNDERSTAND THE VERY STUFF FROM WHICH THE UNIVERSE ITSELF IS MADE.
ALL THIS, FROM *DRAWING.*
WOW.

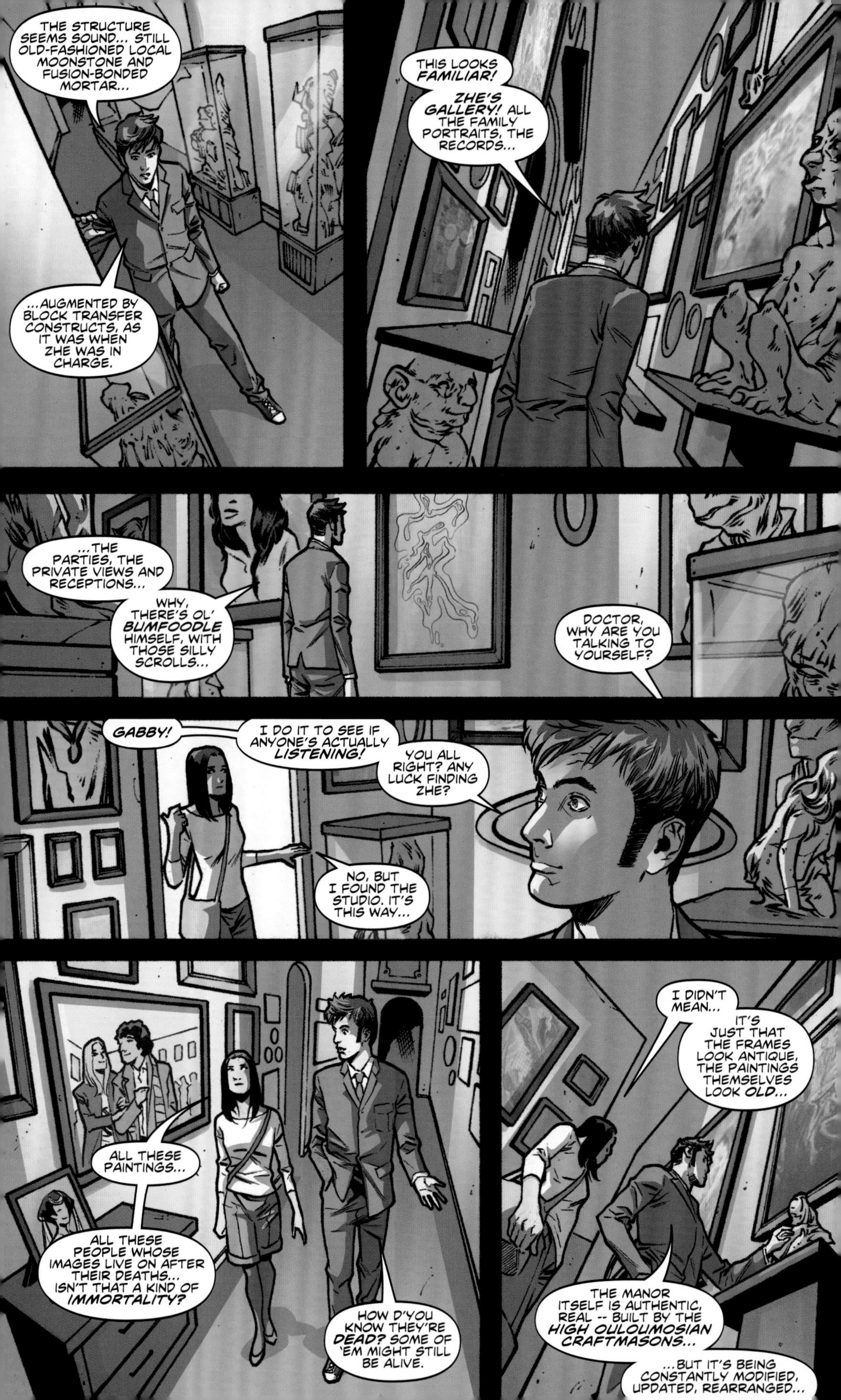
THE STRUCTURE SEEMS SOUND... STILL OLD-FASHIONED LOCAL MOONSTONE AND FUSION-BONDED MORTAR...
...AUGMENTED BY BLOCK TRANSFER CONSTRUCTS, AS IT WAS WHEN ZHE WAS IN CHARGE.
THIS LOOKS FAMILIAR!
ZHE'S GALLERY! ALL THE FAMILY PORTRAITS, THE RECORDS...
...THE PARTIES, THE PRIVATE VIEWS AND RECEPTIONS...
WHY, THERE'S OL' BUMFOODLE HIMSELF, WITH THOSE SILLY SCROLLS...
DOCTOR, WHY ARE YOU TALKING TO YOURSELF?
GABBY!
I DO IT TO SEE IF ANYONE'S ACTUALLY LISTENING!
YOU ALL RIGHT? ANY LUCK FINDING ZHE?
NO, BUT I FOUND THE STUDIO. IT'S THIS WAY...
ALL THESE PAINTINGS...
ALL THESE PEOPLE WHOSE IMAGES LIVE ON AFTER THEIR DEATHS... ISN'T THAT A KIND OF IMMORTALITY?
HOW D'YOU KNOW THEY'RE DEAD? SOME OF 'EM MIGHT STILL BE ALIVE.
I DIDN'T MEAN...
IT'S JUST THAT THE FRAMES LOOK ANTIQUE, THE PAINTINGS THEMSELVES LOOK OLD...
THE MANOR ITSELF IS AUTHENTIC, REAL -- BUILT BY THE HIGH OULOUMOSIAN CRAFTMASONS...
...BUT IT'S BEING CONSTANTLY MODIFIED, UPDATED, REARRANGED...

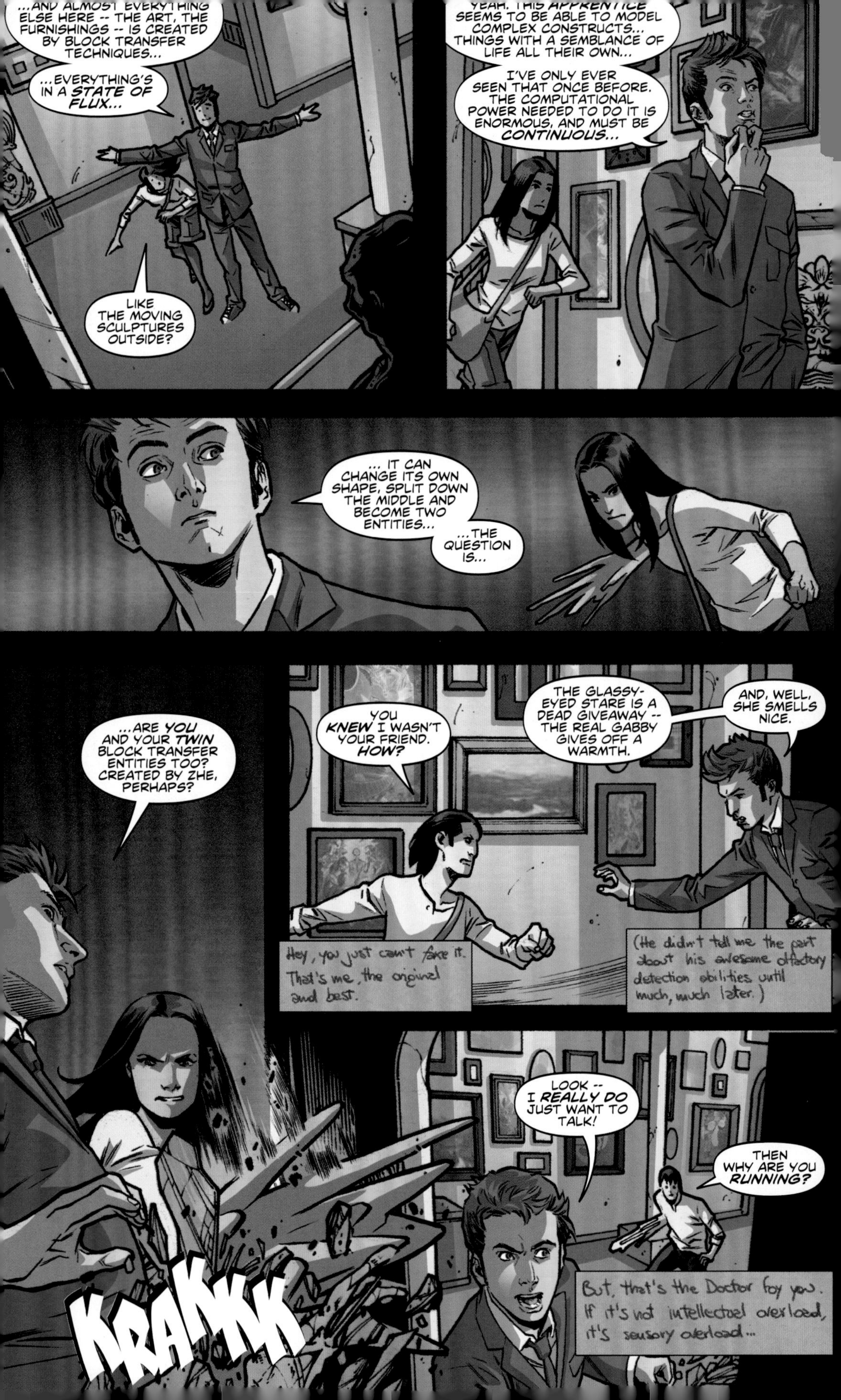

...AND ALMOST EVERYTHING ELSE HERE -- THE ART, THE FURNISHINGS -- IS CREATED BY BLOCK TRANSFER TECHNIQUES...
...EVERYTHING'S IN A STATE OF FLUX...
LIKE THE MOVING SCULPTURES OUTSIDE?
YEAH. THIS APPRENTICE SEEMS TO BE ABLE TO MODEL COMPLEX CONSTRUCTS... THINGS WITH A SEMBLANCE OF LIFE ALL THEIR OWN...
I'VE ONLY EVER SEEN THAT ONCE BEFORE. THE COMPUTATIONAL POWER NEEDED TO DO IT IS ENORMOUS, AND MUST BE CONTINUOUS...
... IT CAN CHANGE ITS OWN SHAPE, SPLIT DOWN THE MIDDLE AND BECOME TWO ENTITIES...
...THE QUESTION IS...
...ARE YOU AND YOUR TWIN BLOCK TRANSFER ENTITIES TOO? CREATED BY ZHE, PERHAPS?
YOU KNEW I WASN'T YOUR FRIEND. HOW?
THE GLASSY-EYED STARE IS A DEAD GIVEAWAY -- THE REAL GABBY GIVES OFF A WARMTH.
AND, WELL, SHE SMELLS NICE.
Hey, you just can't fake it. That's me, the original and best.
(He didn't tell me the part about his awesome olfactory detection abilities until much, much later.)
KRAKKK
LOOK -- I REALLY DO JUST WANT TO TALK!
THEN WHY ARE YOU RUNNING?
But, that's the Doctor for you. If it's not intellectual overload, it's sensory overload...

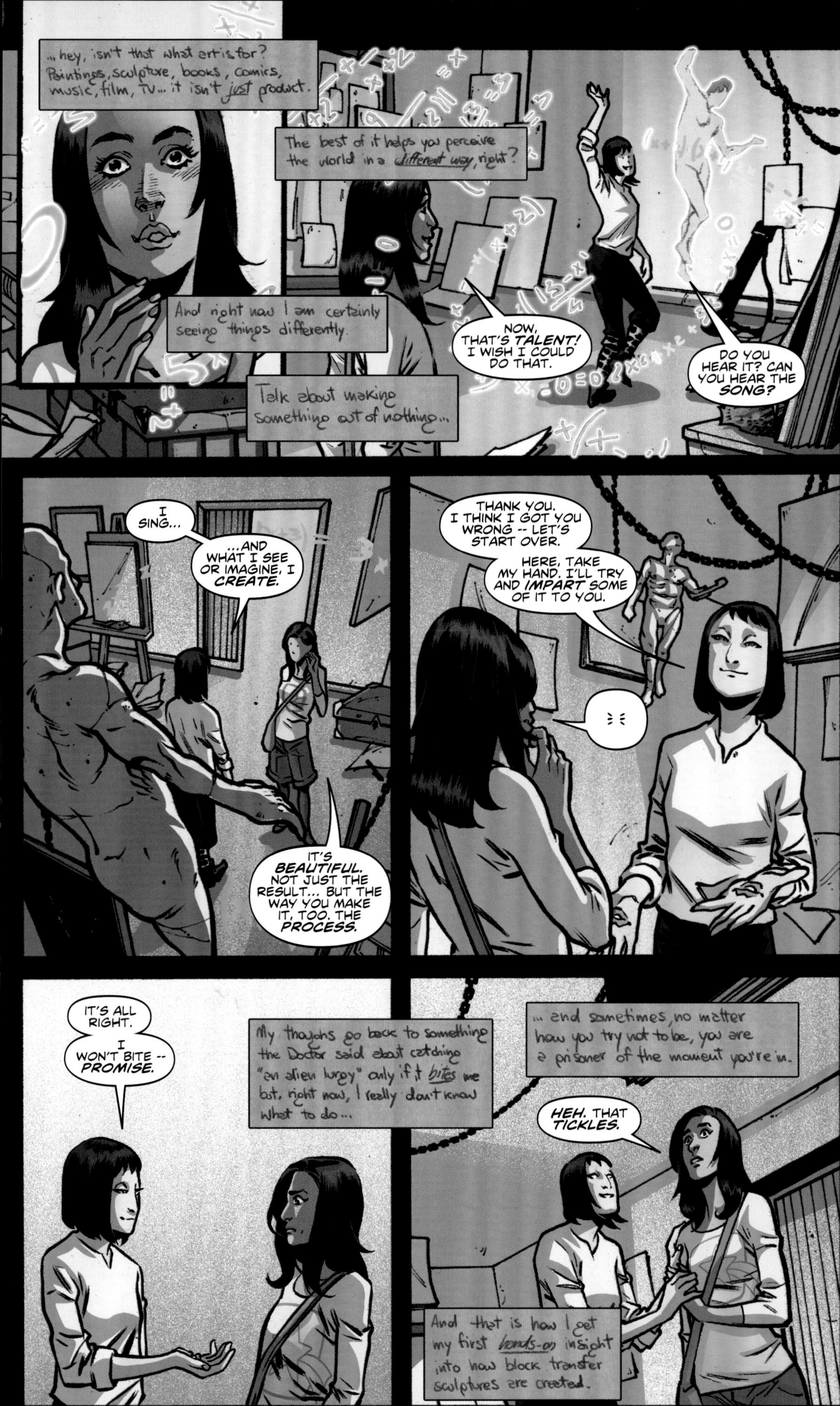
... hey, isn't that what art is for? Paintings, sculpture, books, comics, music, film, TV... it isn't just product.
The best of it helps you perceive the world in a different way, right?
And right now I am certainly seeing things differently.
Talk about making something out of nothing...
NOW, THAT'S TALENT! I WISH I COULD DO THAT.
DO YOU HEAR IT? CAN YOU HEAR THE SONG?
I SING...
...AND WHAT I SEE OR IMAGINE, I CREATE.
IT'S BEAUTIFUL. NOT JUST THE RESULT... BUT THE WAY YOU MAKE IT, TOO. THE PROCESS.
THANK YOU. I THINK I GOT YOU WRONG -- LET'S START OVER.
HERE, TAKE MY HAND. I'LL TRY AND IMPART SOME OF IT TO YOU.
IT'S ALL RIGHT.
I WON'T BITE -- PROMISE.
My thoughts go back to something the Doctor said about catching "an alien lurgy" only if it bites me but, right now, I really don't know what to do...
... and sometimes, no matter how you try not to be, you are a prisoner of the moment you're in.
HEH. THAT TICKLES.
And that is how I get my first hands-on insight into how block transfer sculptures are created.

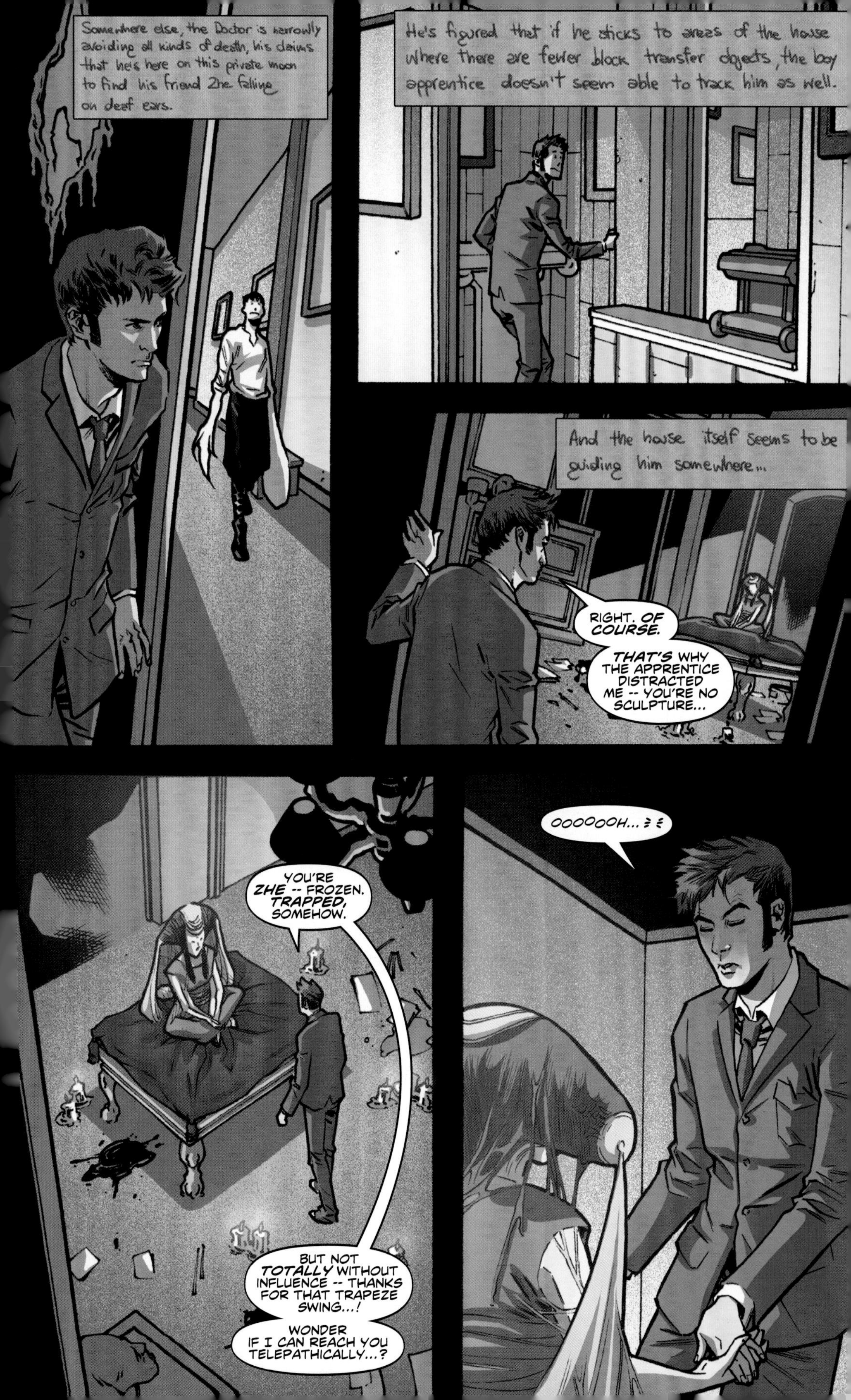
Somewhere else, the Doctor is narrowly avoiding all kinds of death, his claims that he's here on this private moon to find his friend Zhe falling on deaf ears.
He's figured that if he sticks to areas of the house where there are fewer block transfer objects, the boy apprentice doesn't seem able to track him as well.
And the house itself seems to be guiding him somewhere...
RIGHT. OF COURSE.
THAT'S WHY THE APPRENTICE DISTRACTED ME -- YOU'RE NO SCULPTURE...
YOU'RE ZHE -- FROZEN. TRAPPED, SOMEHOW.
BUT NOT TOTALLY WITHOUT INFLUENCE -- THANKS FOR THAT TRAPEZE SWING...!
WONDER IF I CAN REACH YOU TELEPATHICALLY...?
OOOOOOH...

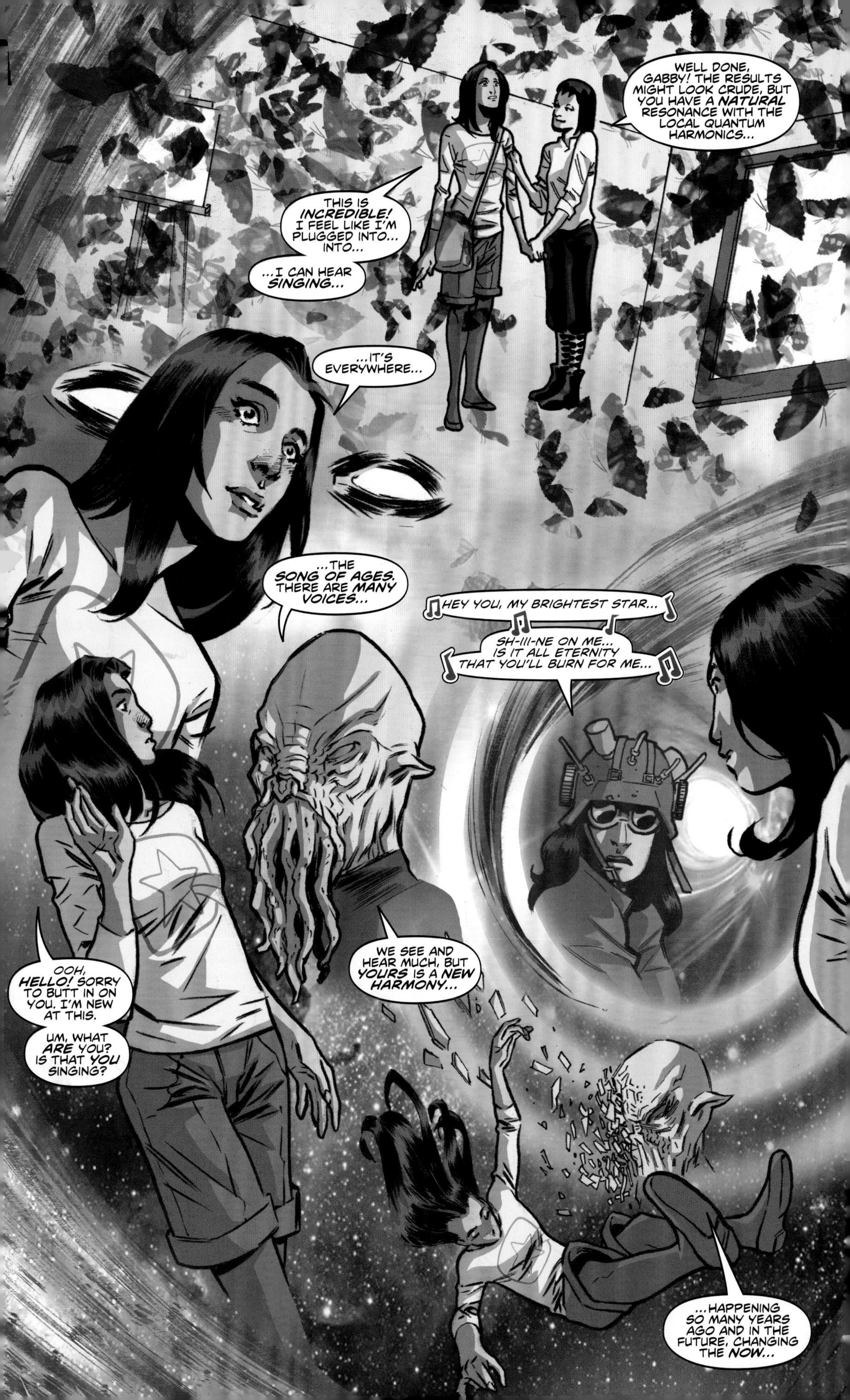
WELL DONE, GABBY! THE RESULTS MIGHT LOOK CRUDE, BUT YOU HAVE A NATURAL RESONANCE WITH THE LOCAL QUANTUM HARMONICS...
THIS IS INCREDIBLE! I FEEL LIKE I'M PLUGGED INTO... INTO...
...I CAN HEAR SINGING...
...IT'S EVERYWHERE...
...THE SONG OF AGES. THERE ARE MANY VOICES...
HEY YOU, MY BRIGHTEST STAR...
SH-III-NE ON ME... IS IT ALL ETERNITY THAT YOU'LL BURN FOR ME...
OOH, HELLO! SORRY TO BUTT IN ON YOU. I'M NEW AT THIS.
UM, WHAT ARE YOU? IS THAT YOU SINGING?
WE SEE AND HEAR MUCH, BUT YOURS IS A NEW HARMONY...
...HAPPENING SO MANY YEARS AGO AND IN THE FUTURE, CHANGING THE NOW...

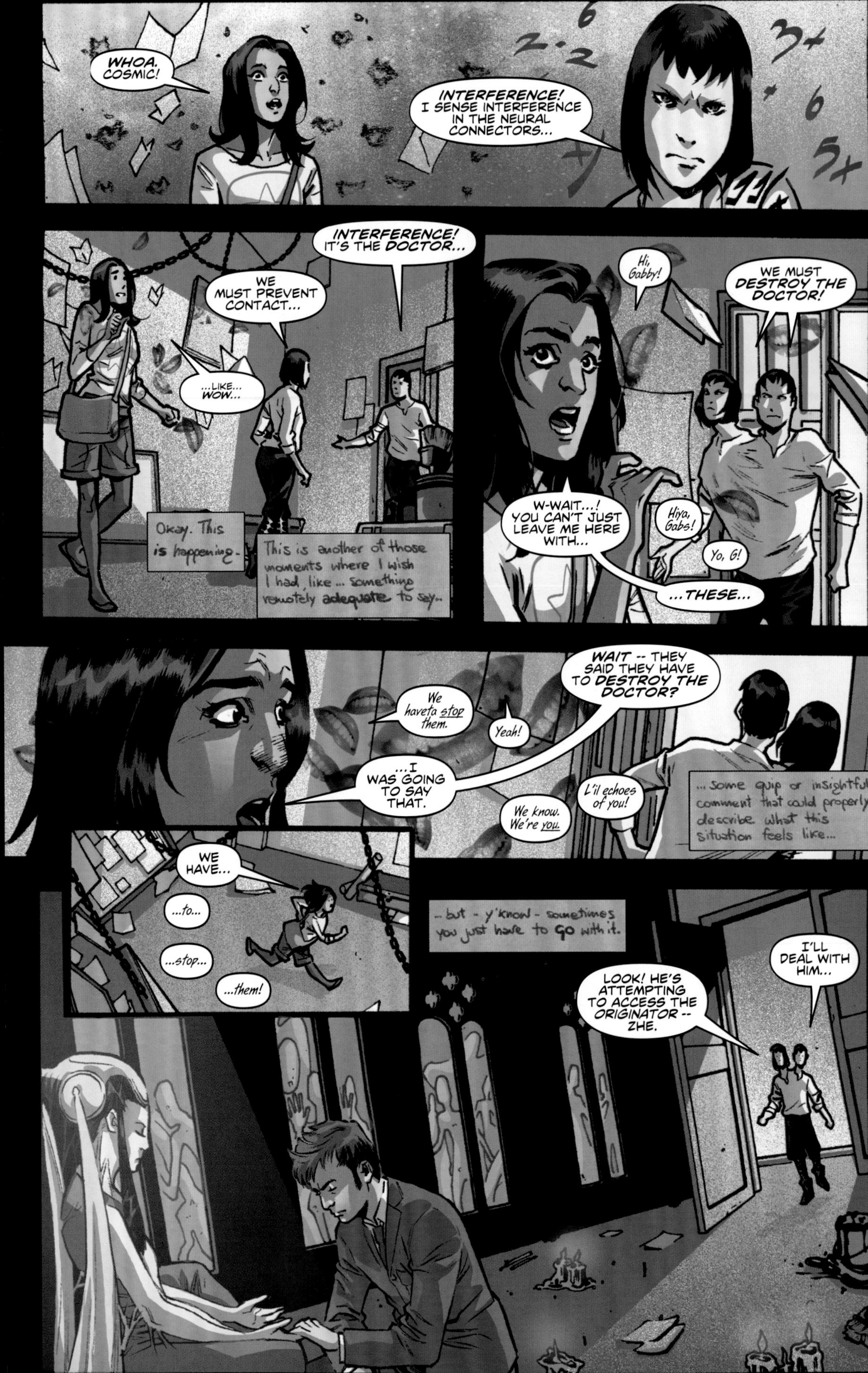
WHOA. COSMIC!
INTERFERENCE! I SENSE INTERFERENCE IN THE NEURAL CONNECTORS...
INTERFERENCE! IT'S THE DOCTOR...
WE MUST PREVENT CONTACT...
...LIKE... WOW...
Okay. This is happening.
This is another of those moments where I wish I had, like... something remotely adequate to say..
Hi, Gabby!
WE MUST DESTROY THE DOCTOR!
W-WAIT...! YOU CAN'T JUST LEAVE ME HERE WITH...
Hiya, Gabs!
Yo, G!
...THESE...
We haveta stop them.
Yeah!
WAIT -- THEY SAID THEY HAVE TO DESTROY THE DOCTOR?
...I WAS GOING TO SAY THAT.
We know. We're you.
L'il echoes of you!
... some quip or insightful comment that could properly describe what this situation feels like...
WE HAVE...
...to...
...stop...
...them!
-- but - y'know - sometimes you just have to GO with it.
LOOK! HE'S ATTEMPTING TO ACCESS THE ORIGINATOR -- ZHE.
I'LL DEAL WITH HIM...

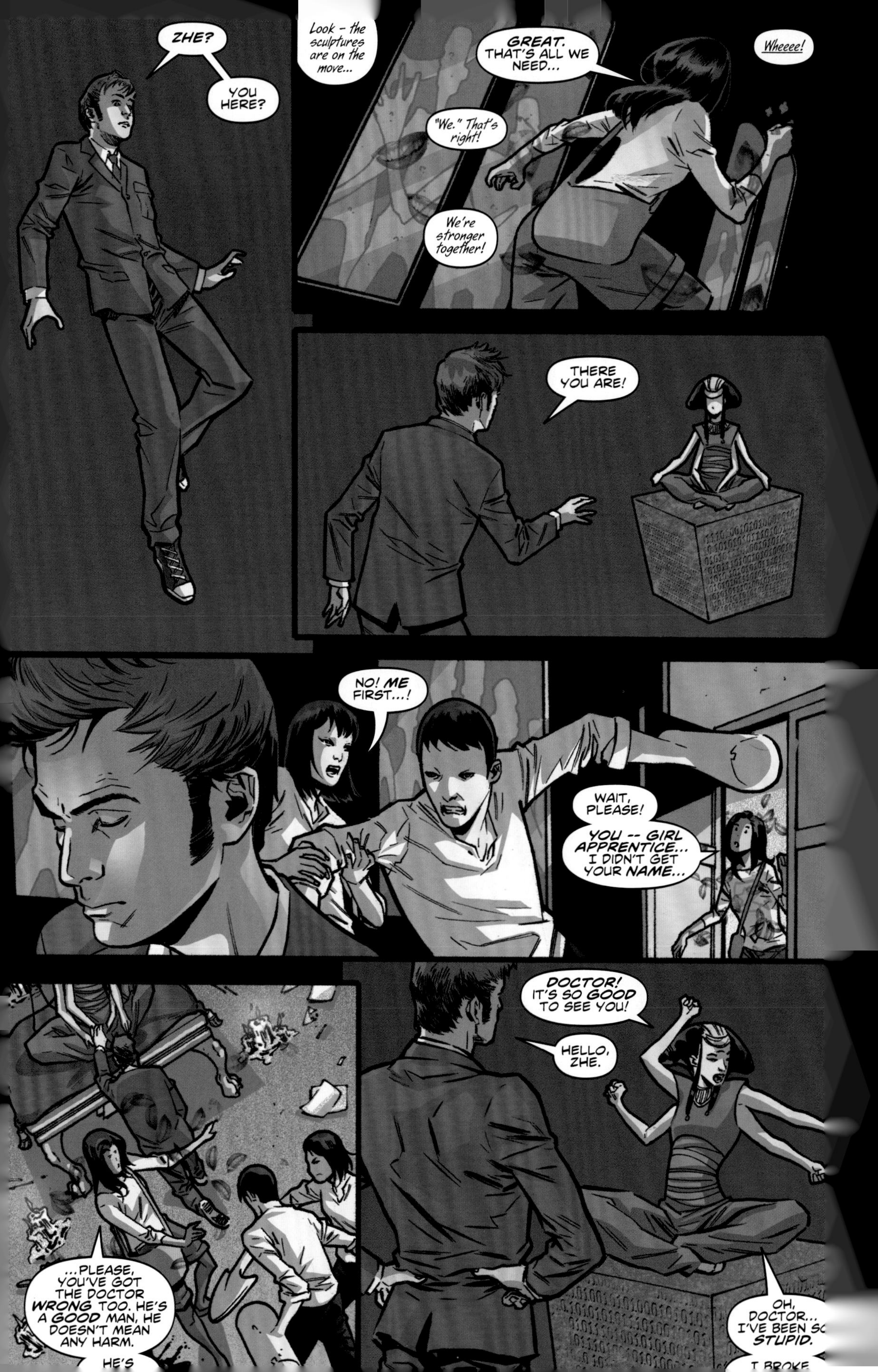
ZHE?
YOU HERE?
Look - the sculptures are on the move...
GREAT. THAT'S ALL WE NEED...
"We." That's right!
We're stronger together!
Wheeee!
THERE YOU ARE!
NO! ME FIRST...!
WAIT, PLEASE!
YOU -- GIRL APPRENTICE... I DIDN'T GET YOUR NAME...
...PLEASE, YOU'VE GOT THE DOCTOR WRONG TOO. HE'S A GOOD MAN, HE DOESN'T MEAN ANY HARM.
HE'S
DOCTOR! IT'S SO GOOD TO SEE YOU!
HELLO, ZHE.
OH, DOCTOR... I'VE BEEN SO STUPID.
I BROKE

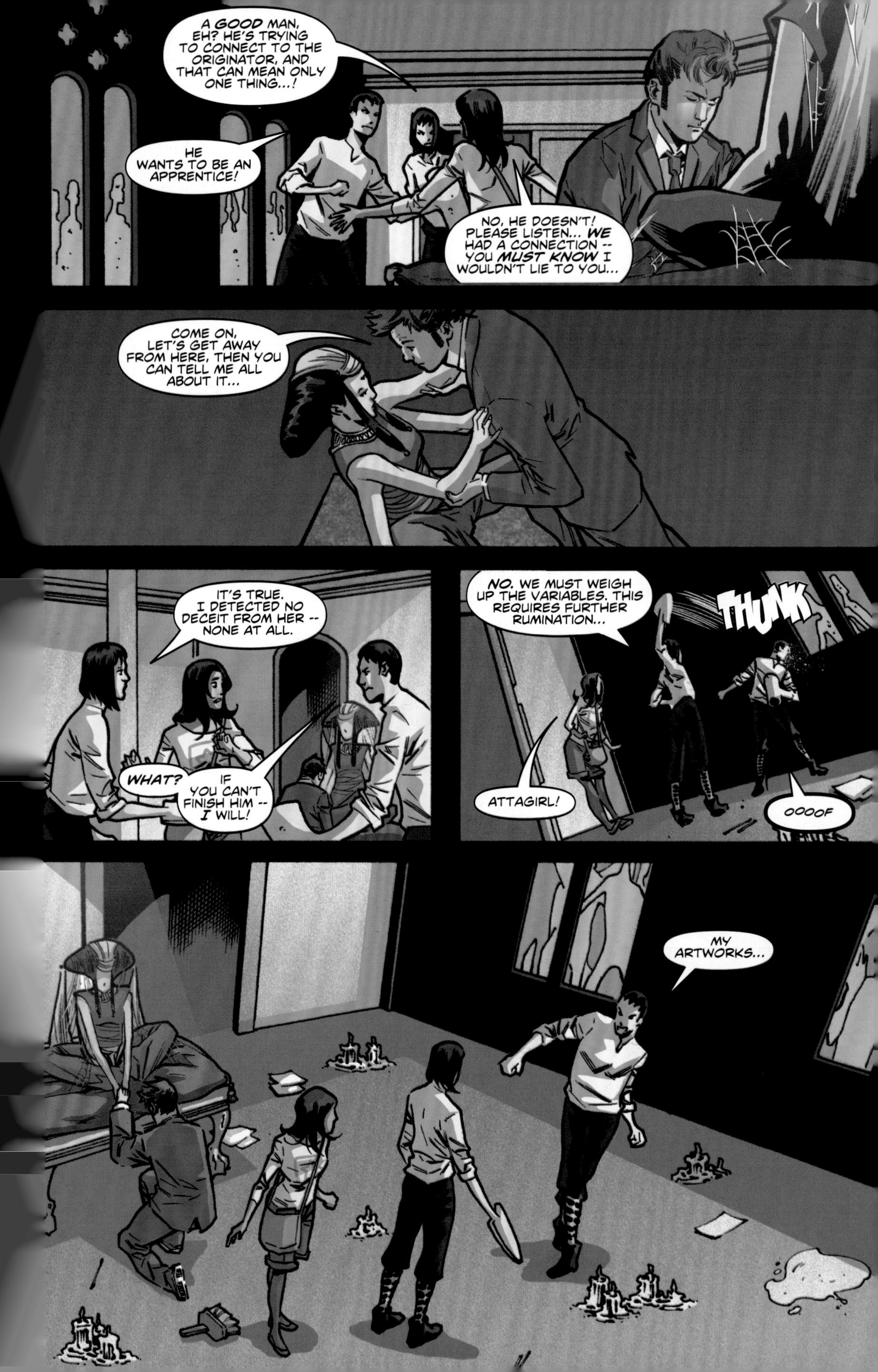
A GOOD MAN, EH? HE'S TRYING TO CONNECT TO THE ORIGINATOR, AND THAT CAN MEAN ONLY ONE THING...!
HE WANTS TO BE AN APPRENTICE!
NO, HE DOESN'T! PLEASE LISTEN... WE HAD A CONNECTION -- YOU MUST KNOW I WOULDN'T LIE TO YOU...
COME ON, LET'S GET AWAY FROM HERE, THEN YOU CAN TELL ME ALL ABOUT IT...
IT'S TRUE. I DETECTED NO DECEIT FROM HER -- NONE AT ALL.
WHAT?
IF YOU CAN'T FINISH HIM -- I WILL!
NO. WE MUST WEIGH UP THE VARIABLES. THIS REQUIRES FURTHER RUMINATION...
THUNK
ATTAGIRL!
OOOOF
MY ARTWORKS...

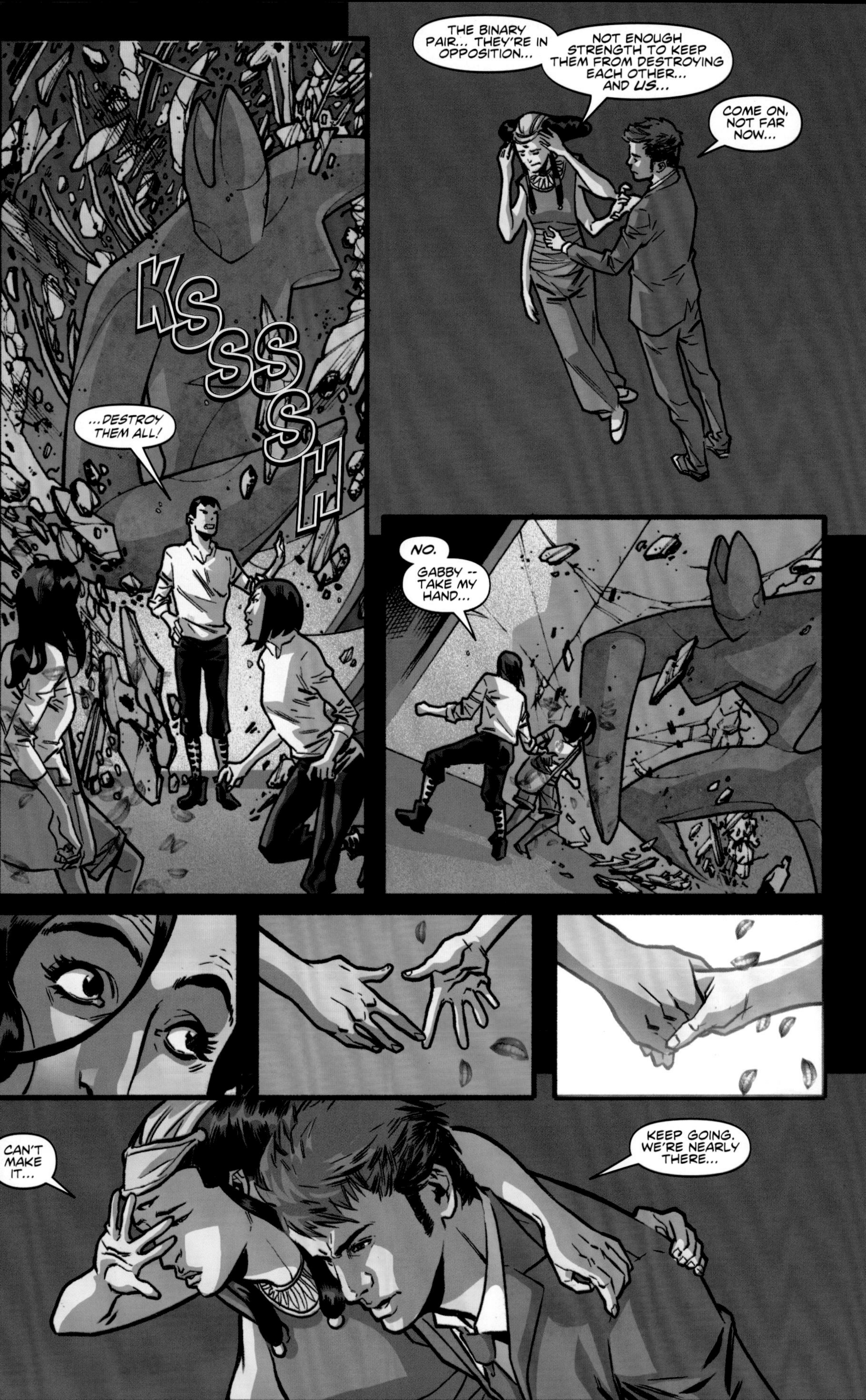
THE BINARY PAIR... THEY'RE IN OPPOSITION...
NOT ENOUGH STRENGTH TO KEEP THEM FROM DESTROYING EACH OTHER... AND US...
COME ON, NOT FAR NOW...
KSSSSH
...DESTROY THEM ALL!
NO.
GABBY -- TAKE MY HAND...
CAN'T MAKE IT...
KEEP GOING. WE'RE NEARLY THERE...

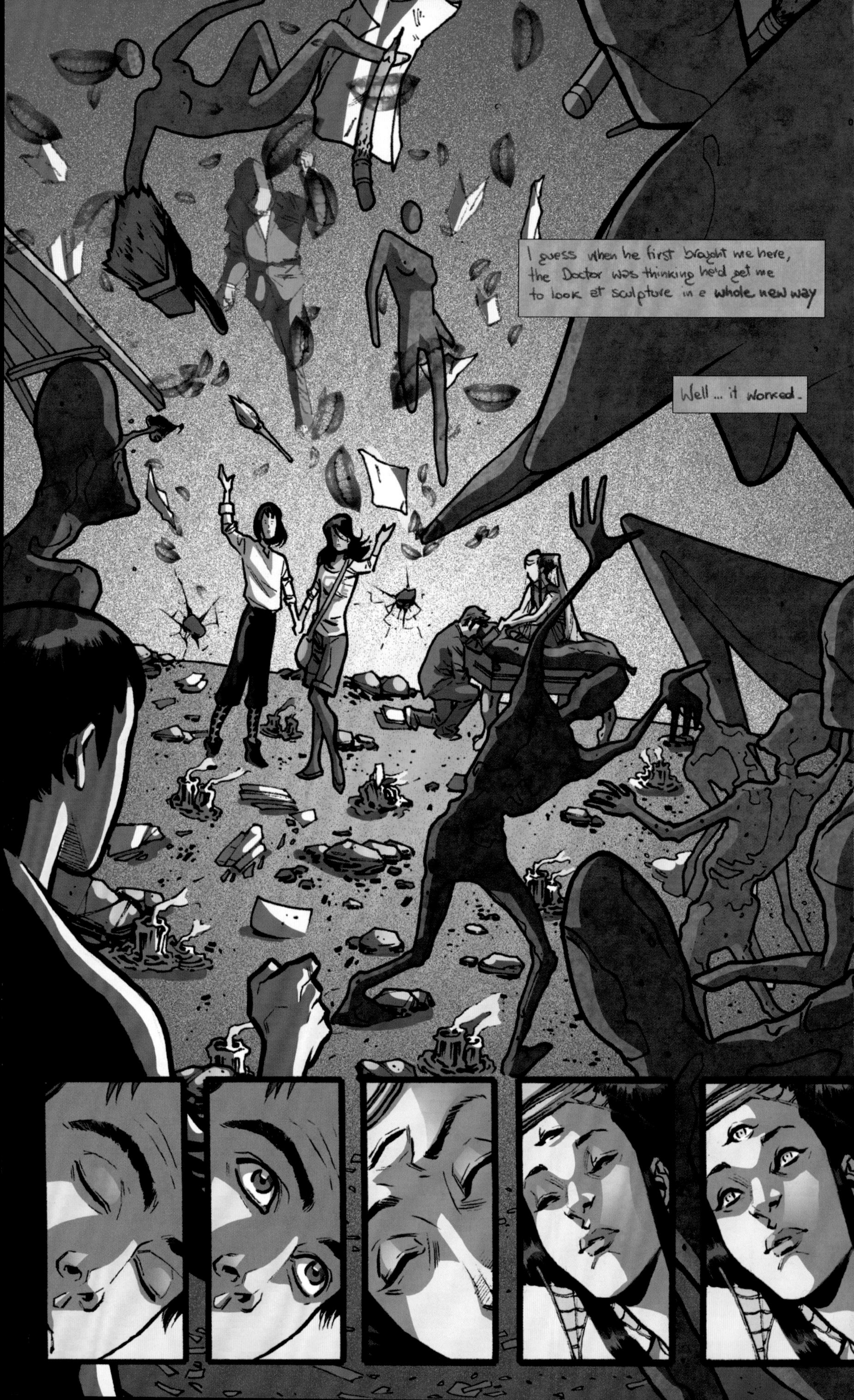
I guess when he first brought me here, the Doctor was thinking he'd get me to look at sculpture in a whole new way
Well ... it worked.

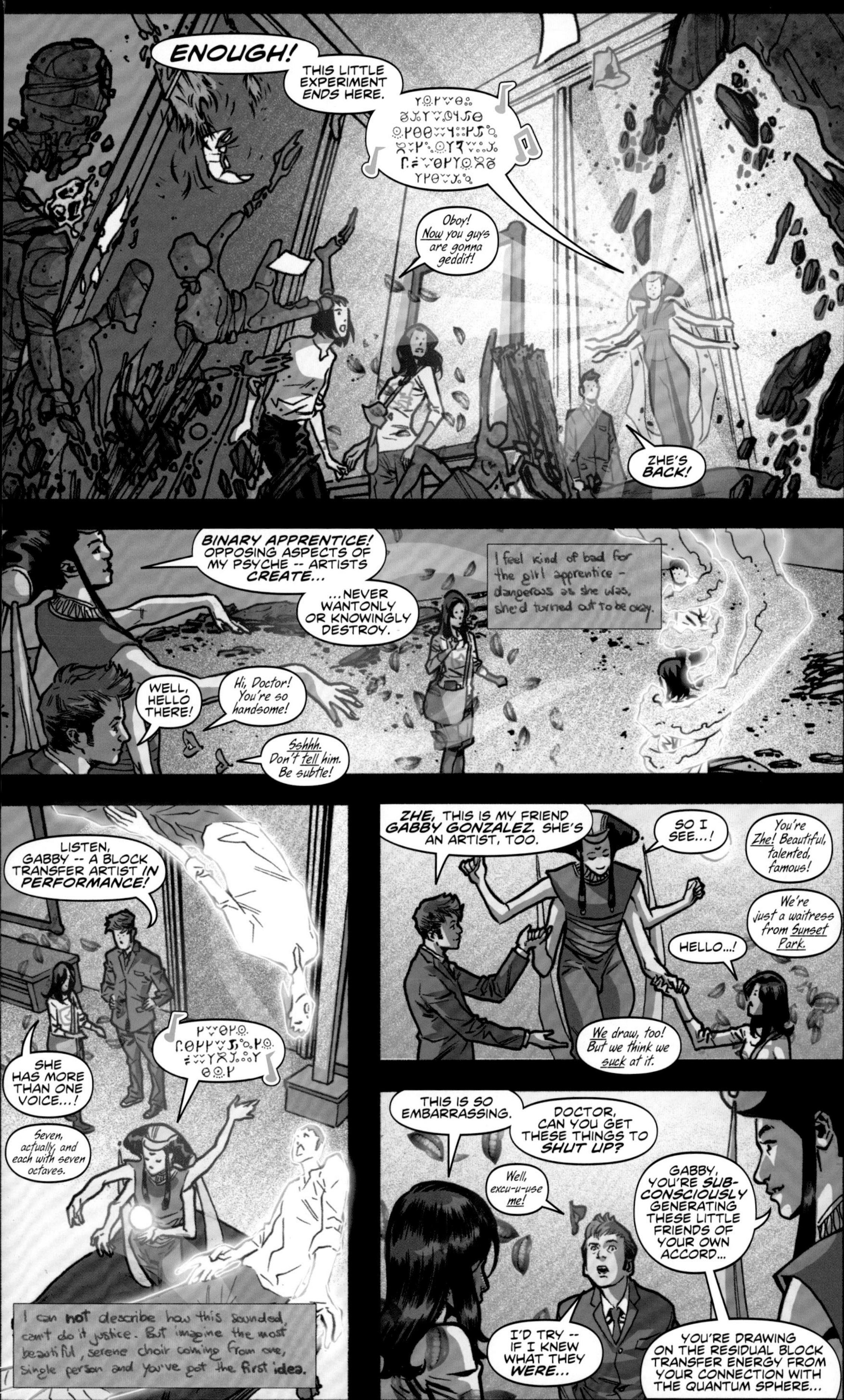
ENOUGH!
THIS LITTLE EXPERIMENT ENDS HERE.
Oboy! Now you guys are gonna geddit!
ZHE'S BACK!
BINARY APPRENTICE! OPPOSING ASPECTS OF MY PSYCHE -- ARTISTS CREATE...
...NEVER WANTONLY OR KNOWINGLY DESTROY.
I feel kind of bad for the girl apprentice - dangerous as she was, she'd turned out to be okay.
WELL, HELLO THERE!
Hi, Doctor! You're so handsome!
Sshhh. Don't tell him. Be subtle!
LISTEN, GABBY -- A BLOCK TRANSFER ARTIST IN PERFORMANCE!
SHE HAS MORE THAN ONE VOICE...!
Seven, actually, and each with seven octaves.
I can not describe how this sounded, can't do it justice. But imagine the most beautiful, serene choir coming from one, single person and you've got the first idea.
ZHE, THIS IS MY FRIEND GABBY GONZALEZ. SHE'S AN ARTIST, TOO.
SO I SEE...!
You're Zhe! Beautiful, talented, famous!
We're just a waitress from Sunset Park.
HELLO...!
We draw, too! But we think we suck at it.
THIS IS SO EMBARRASSING.
DOCTOR, CAN YOU GET THESE THINGS TO SHUT UP?
Well, excu-u-use me!
GABBY, YOU'RE SUB-CONSCIOUSLY GENERATING THESE LITTLE FRIENDS OF YOUR OWN ACCORD...
I'D TRY -- IF I KNEW WHAT THEY WERE...
YOU'RE DRAWING ON THE RESIDUAL BLOCK TRANSFER ENERGY FROM YOUR CONNECTION WITH THE QUANTUM SPHERE...

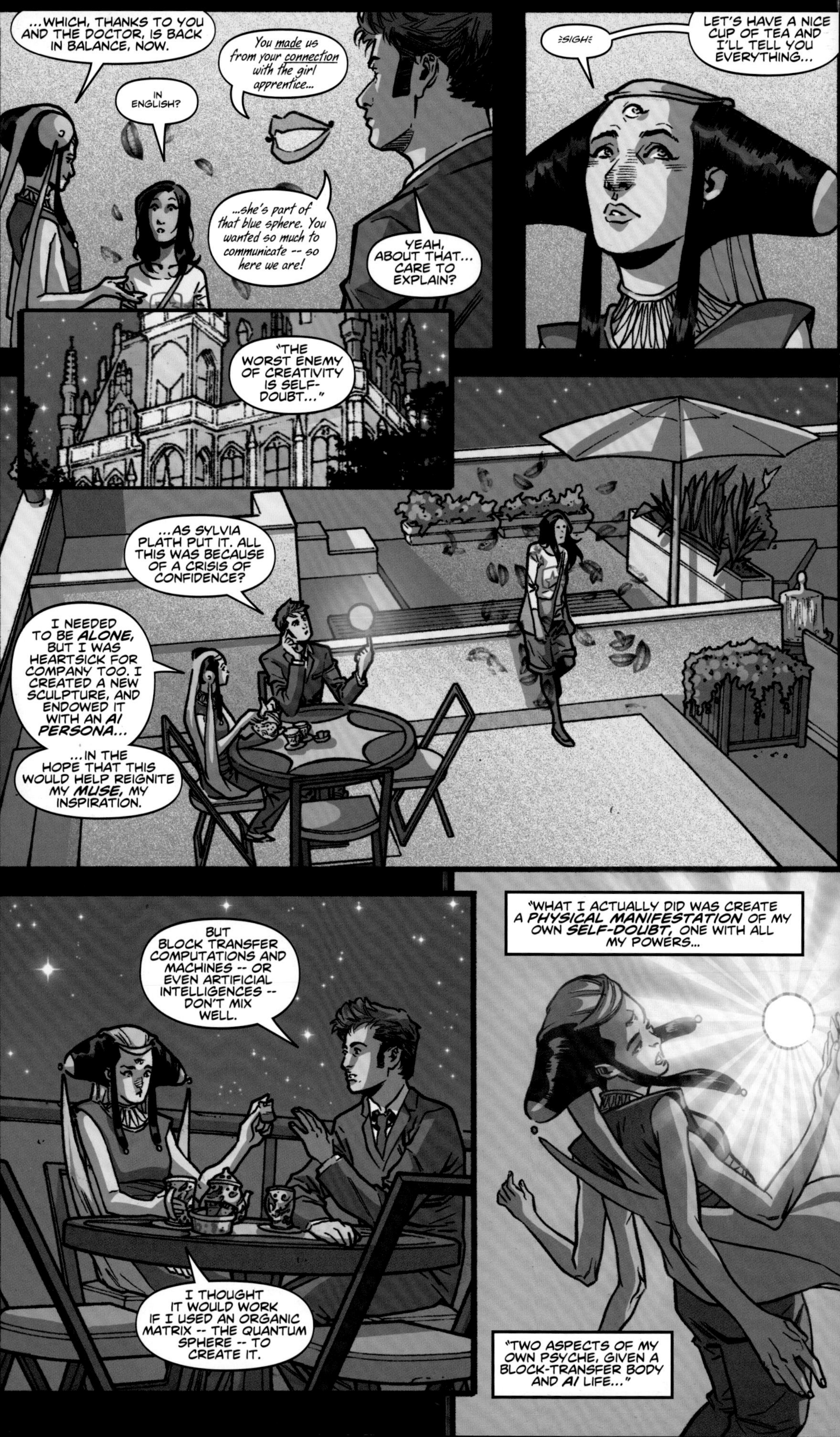
...WHICH, THANKS TO YOU AND THE DOCTOR, IS BACK IN BALANCE, NOW.
IN ENGLISH?
You made us from your connection with the girl apprentice...
...she's part of that blue sphere. You wanted so much to communicate -- so here we are!
YEAH, ABOUT THAT... CARE TO EXPLAIN?
SIGH
LET'S HAVE A NICE CUP OF TEA AND I'LL TELL YOU EVERYTHING...
"THE WORST ENEMY OF CREATIVITY IS SELF-DOUBT..."
...AS SYLVIA PLATH PUT IT. ALL THIS WAS BECAUSE OF A CRISIS OF CONFIDENCE?
I NEEDED TO BE ALONE, BUT I WAS HEARTSICK FOR COMPANY TOO. I CREATED A NEW SCULPTURE, AND ENDOWED IT WITH AN AI PERSONA...
...IN THE HOPE THAT THIS WOULD HELP REIGNITE MY MUSE, MY INSPIRATION.
BUT BLOCK TRANSFER COMPUTATIONS AND MACHINES -- OR EVEN ARTIFICIAL INTELLIGENCES -- DON'T MIX WELL.
I THOUGHT IT WOULD WORK IF I USED AN ORGANIC MATRIX -- THE QUANTUM SPHERE -- TO CREATE IT.
"WHAT I ACTUALLY DID WAS CREATE A PHYSICAL MANIFESTATION OF MY OWN SELF-DOUBT, ONE WITH ALL MY POWERS...
"TWO ASPECTS OF MY OWN PSYCHE, GIVEN A BLOCK-TRANSFER BODY AND AI LIFE..."

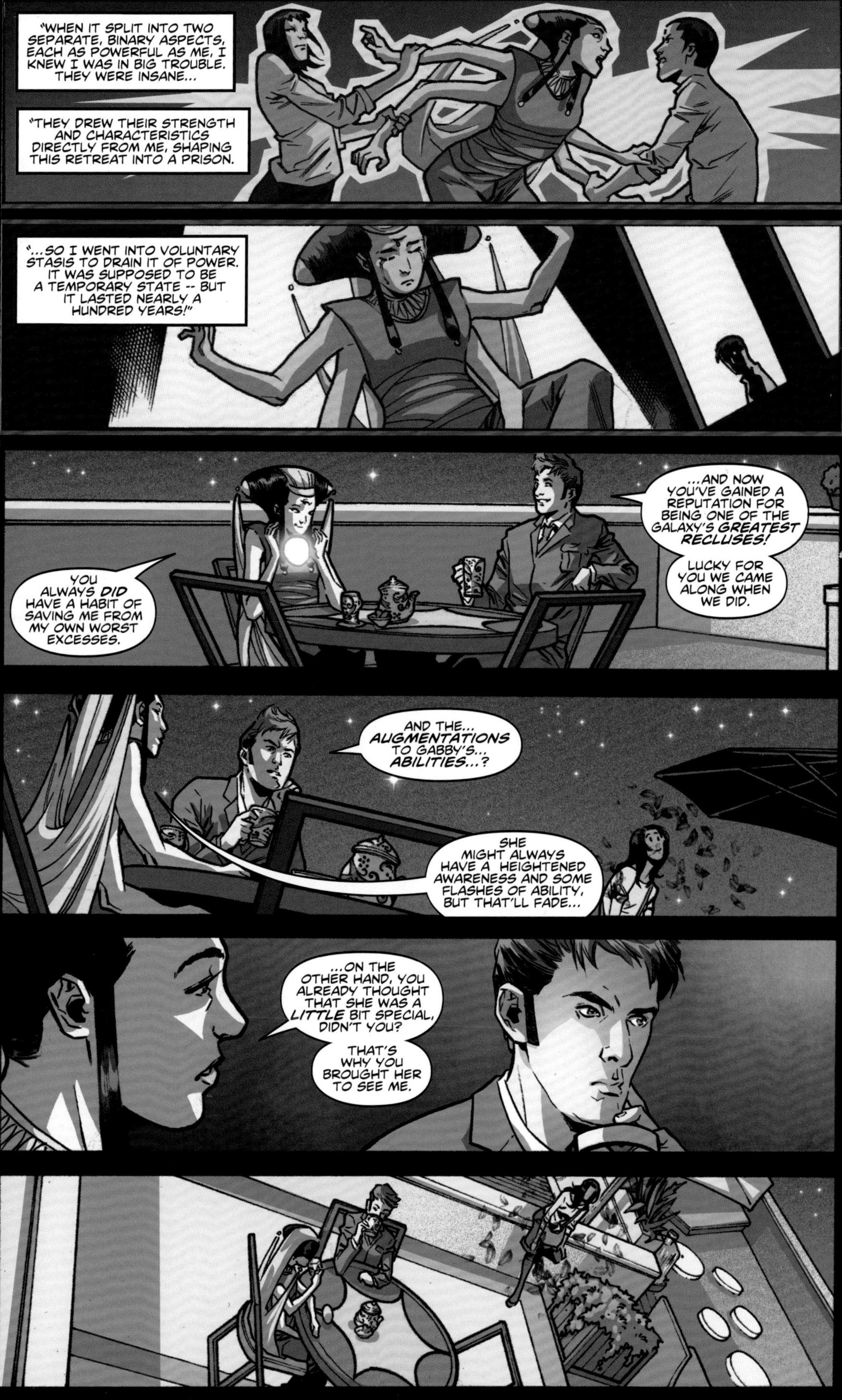
"WHEN IT SPLIT INTO TWO SEPARATE, BINARY ASPECTS, EACH AS POWERFUL AS ME, I KNEW I WAS IN BIG TROUBLE. THEY WERE INSANE...
"THEY DREW THEIR STRENGTH AND CHARACTERISTICS DIRECTLY FROM ME, SHAPING THIS RETREAT INTO A PRISON.
"...SO I WENT INTO VOLUNTARY STASIS TO DRAIN IT OF POWER. IT WAS SUPPOSED TO BE A TEMPORARY STATE -- BUT IT LASTED NEARLY A HUNDRED YEARS!"
...AND NOW YOU'VE GAINED A REPUTATION FOR BEING ONE OF THE GALAXY'S *GREATEST RECLUSES!*
LUCKY FOR YOU WE CAME ALONG WHEN WE DID.
YOU ALWAYS *DID* HAVE A HABIT OF SAVING ME FROM MY OWN WORST EXCESSES.
AND THE... *AUGMENTATIONS* TO GABBY'S... *ABILITIES...*?
SHE MIGHT ALWAYS HAVE A HEIGHTENED AWARENESS AND SOME FLASHES OF ABILITY, BUT THAT'LL FADE...
...ON THE OTHER HAND, YOU ALREADY THOUGHT THAT SHE WAS A *LITTLE* BIT SPECIAL, DIDN'T YOU?
THAT'S WHY YOU BROUGHT HER TO SEE ME.

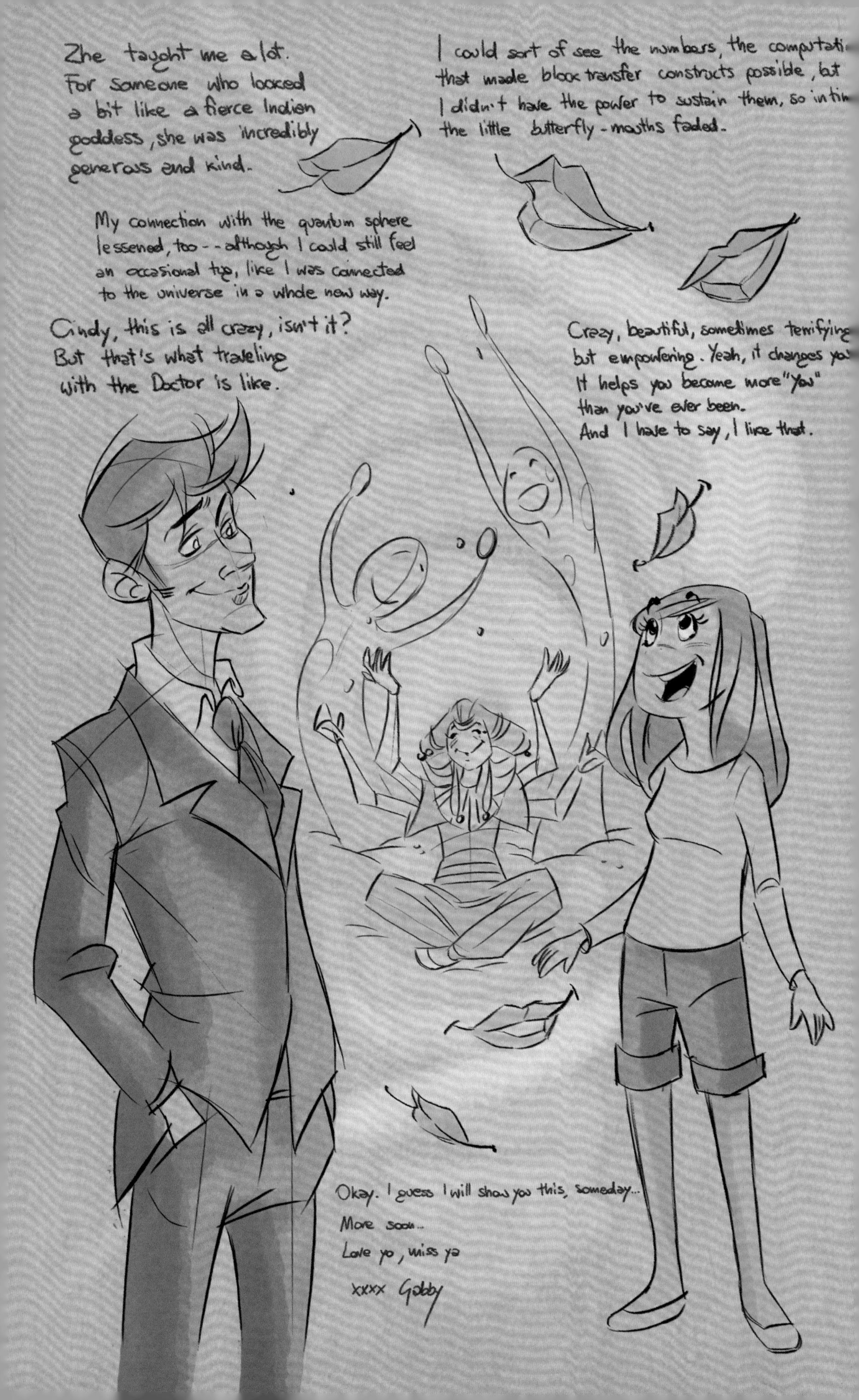
Zhe taught me a lot. For someone who looked a bit like a fierce Indian goddess, she was incredibly generous and kind.
I could sort of see the numbers, the computati
that made block transfer constructs possible, but I didn't have the power to sustain them, so in tim
the little butterfly-mouths faded.
My connection with the quantum sphere lessened, too -- although I could still feel an occasional tug, like I was connected to the universe in a whole new way.
Cindy, this is all crazy, isn't it? But that's what traveling with the Doctor is like.
Crazy, beautiful, sometimes terrifying but empowering. Yeah, it changes you. It helps you become more "You" than you've ever been. And I have to say, I like that.
Okay. I guess I will show you this, someday...
More soon...
Love ya, miss ya
xxxx Gabby

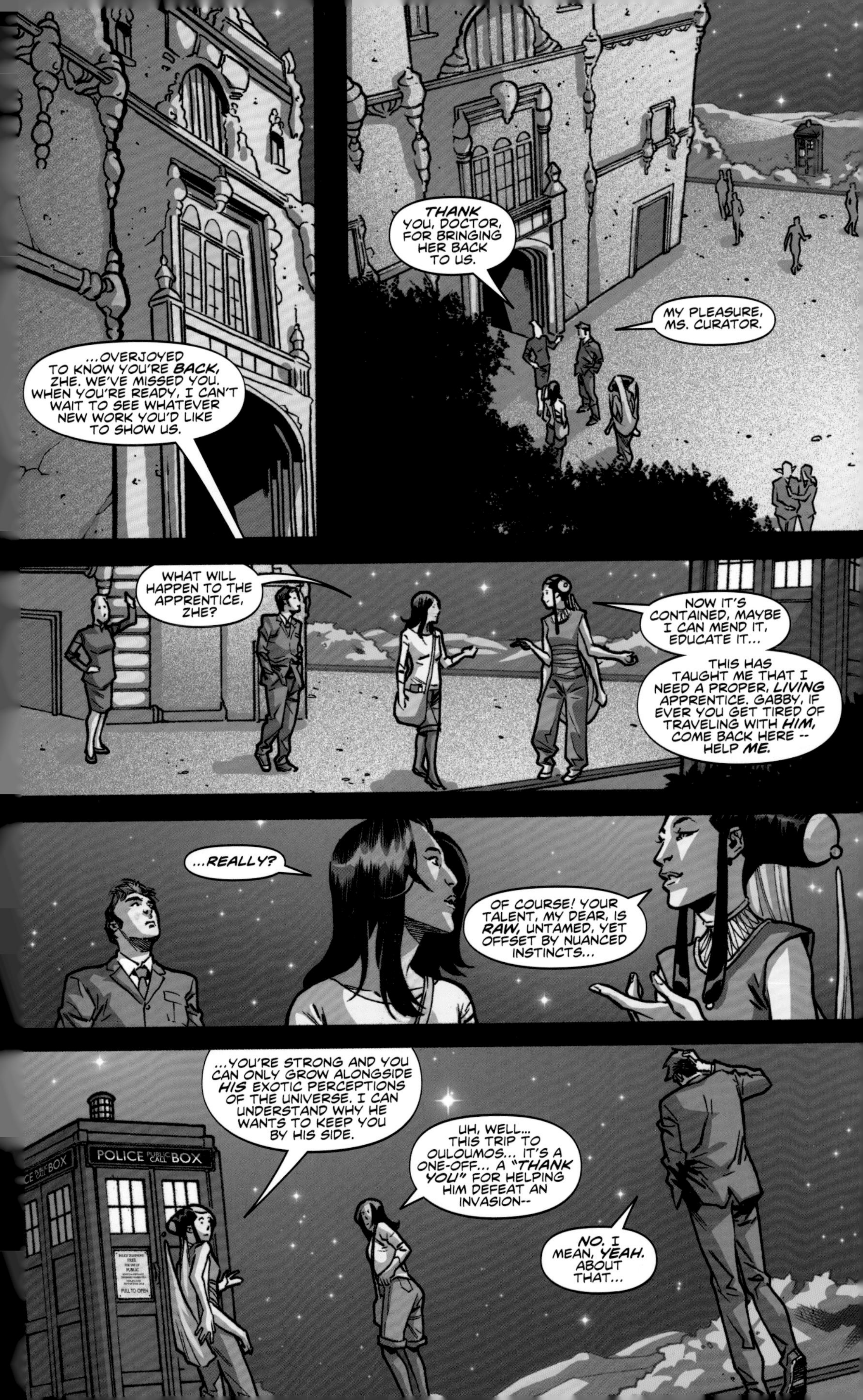

...OVERJOYED TO KNOW YOU'RE *BACK,* ZHE. WE'VE MISSED YOU. WHEN YOU'RE READY, I CAN'T WAIT TO SEE WHATEVER NEW WORK YOU'D LIKE TO SHOW US.
THANK YOU, DOCTOR, FOR BRINGING HER BACK TO US.
MY PLEASURE, MS. CURATOR.
WHAT WILL HAPPEN TO THE APPRENTICE, ZHE?
NOW IT'S CONTAINED, MAYBE I CAN MEND IT, EDUCATE IT...
THIS HAS TAUGHT ME THAT I NEED A PROPER, *LIVING* APPRENTICE. GABBY, IF EVER YOU GET TIRED OF TRAVELING WITH *HIM,* COME BACK HERE -- HELP *ME.*
...*REALLY?*
OF COURSE! YOUR TALENT, MY DEAR, IS *RAW,* UNTAMED, YET OFFSET BY NUANCED INSTINCTS...
...YOU'RE STRONG AND YOU CAN ONLY GROW ALONGSIDE *HIS* EXOTIC PERCEPTIONS OF THE UNIVERSE. I CAN UNDERSTAND WHY HE WANTS TO KEEP YOU BY HIS SIDE.
POLICE PUBLIC CALL BOX
PULL TO OPEN
UH, WELL... THIS TRIP TO OULOUMOS... IT'S A ONE-OFF... A *"THANK YOU"* FOR HELPING HIM DEFEAT AN INVASION--
NO. I MEAN, *YEAH.* ABOUT THAT...

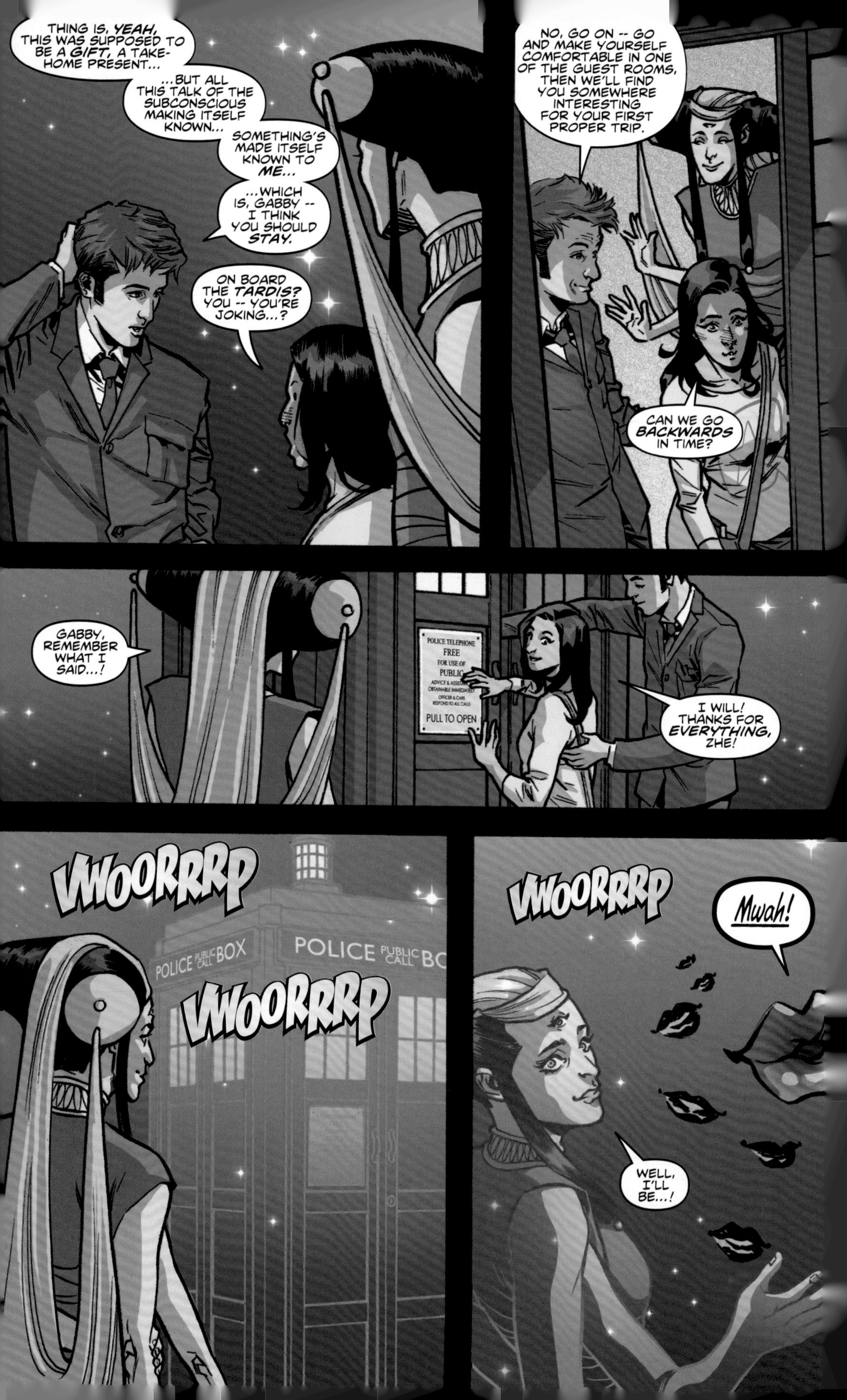
THING IS, YEAH, THIS WAS SUPPOSED TO BE A GIFT, A TAKE-HOME PRESENT...
...BUT ALL THIS TALK OF THE SUBCONSCIOUS MAKING ITSELF KNOWN...
SOMETHING'S MADE ITSELF KNOWN TO ME...
...WHICH IS, GABBY -- I THINK YOU SHOULD STAY.
ON BOARD THE TARDIS? YOU -- YOU'RE JOKING...?
NO, GO ON -- GO AND MAKE YOURSELF COMFORTABLE IN ONE OF THE GUEST ROOMS, THEN WE'LL FIND YOU SOMEWHERE INTERESTING FOR YOUR FIRST PROPER TRIP.
CAN WE GO BACKWARDS IN TIME?
GABBY, REMEMBER WHAT I SAID...!
POLICE TELEPHONE
FREE
FOR USE OF
PUBLIC
PULL TO OPEN
I WILL! THANKS FOR EVERYTHING, ZHE!
VWOORRRP
POLICE PUBLIC CALL BOX
POLICE PUBLIC CALL BO
VWOORRRP
VWOORRRP
Mwah!
WELL, I'LL BE...!

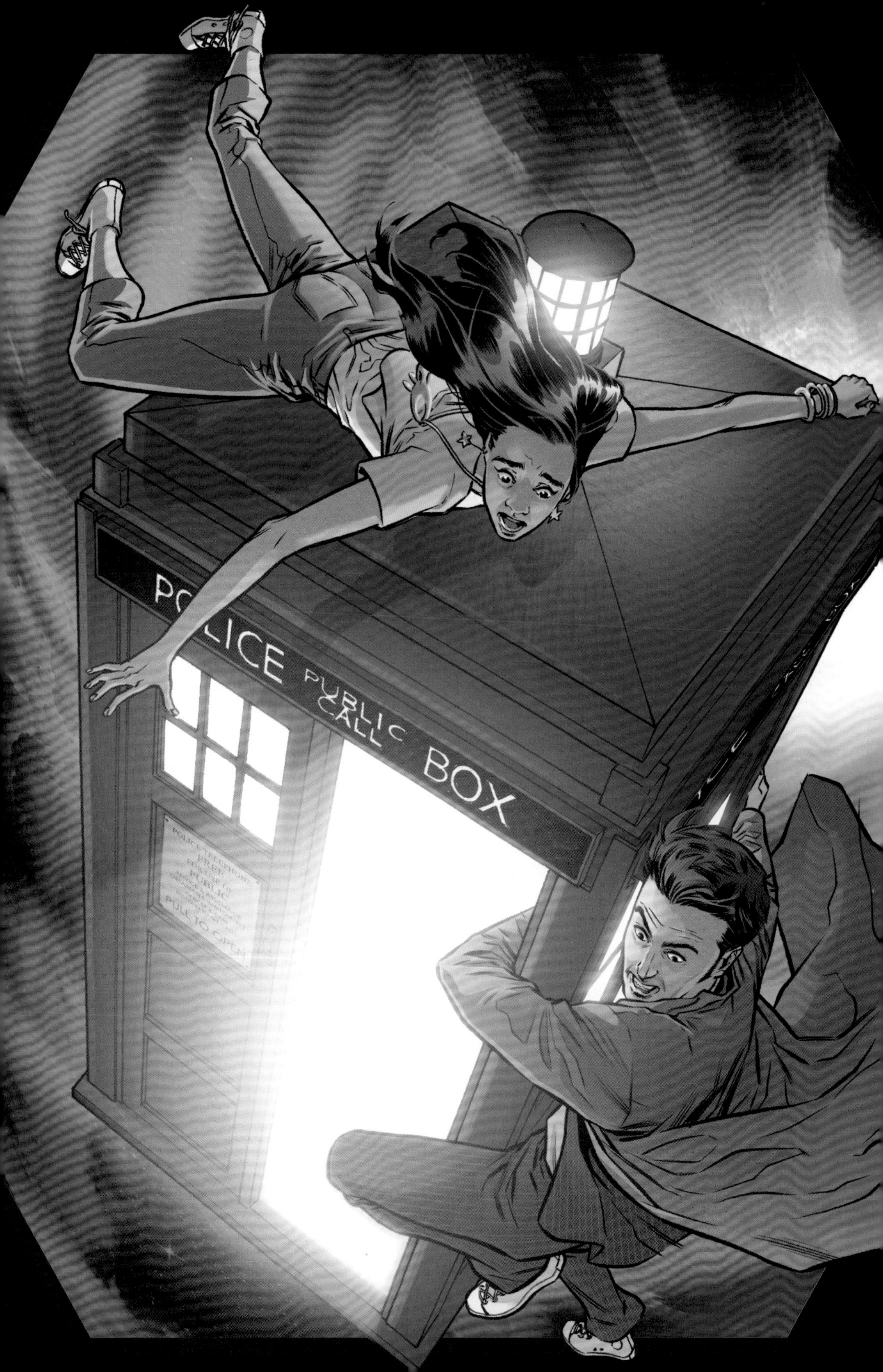
POLICE PUBLIC CALL BOX
FREE
PUBLIC
PULL TO OPEN

COVER GALLERY

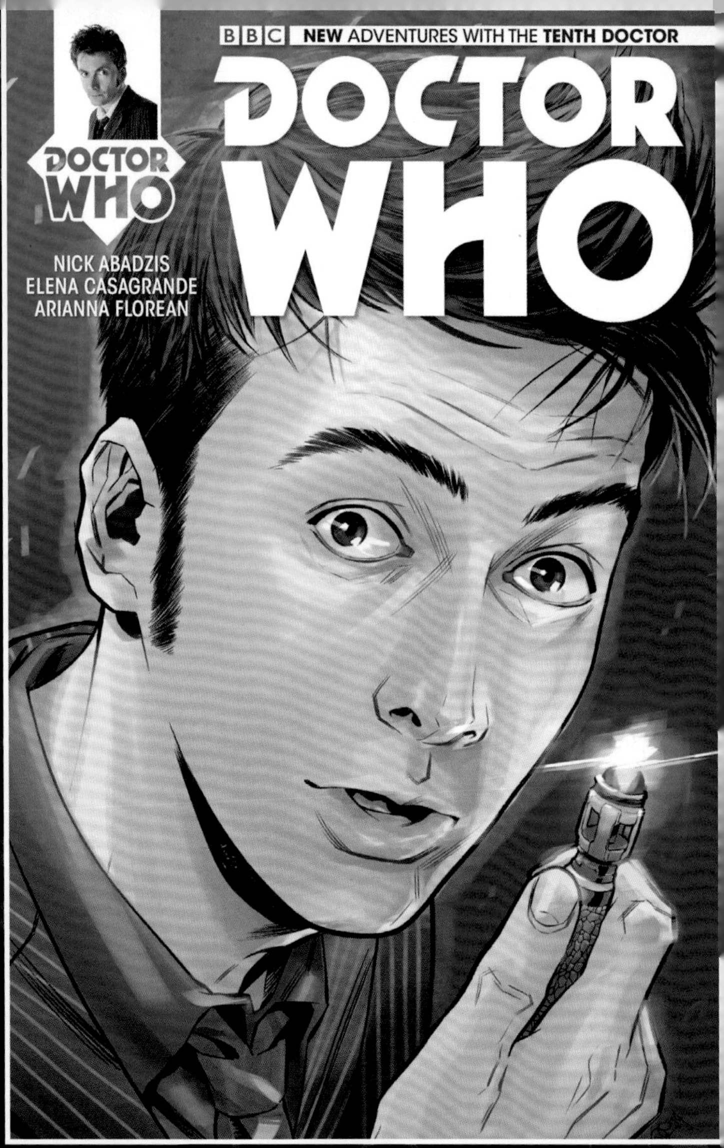

BBC NEW ADVENTURES WITH THE TENTH DOCTOR
DOCTOR WHO
DOCTOR WHO
NICK ABADZIS
ELENA CASAGRANDE
ARIANNA FLOREAN

B

A

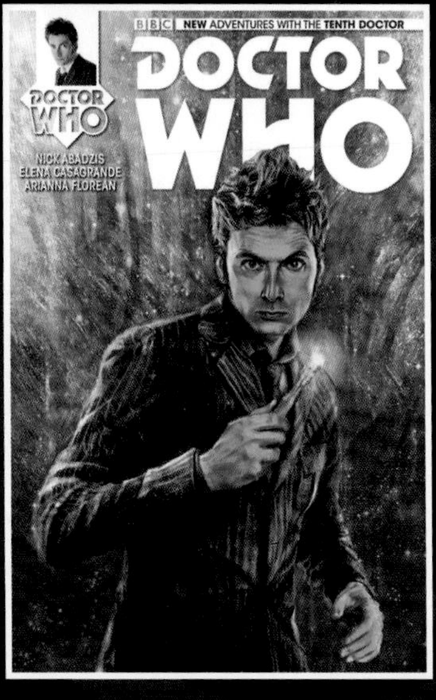

BBC NEW ADVENTURES WITH THE TENTH DOCTOR
DOCTOR WHO
DOCTOR WHO
NICK ABADZIS
ELENA CASAGRANDE
ARIANNA FLOREAN

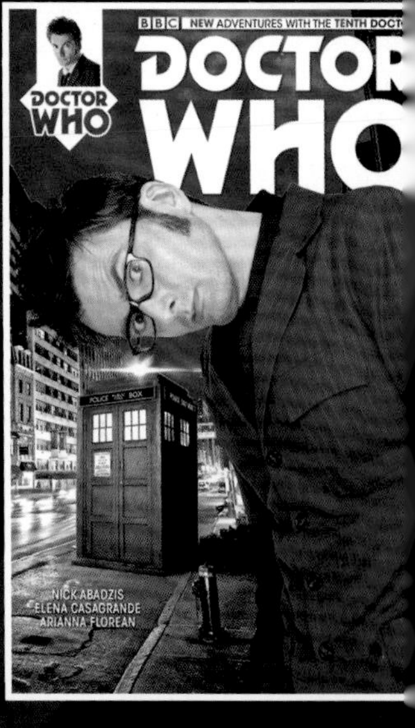

BBC NEW ADVENTURES WITH THE TENTH DOCTOR
DOCTOR WHO
DOCTOR WHO
NICK ABADZIS
ELENA CASAGRANDE
ARIANNA FLOREAN

C

ISSUE 1 Cover A: Alice X. Zhang Cover C: Rob Farmer

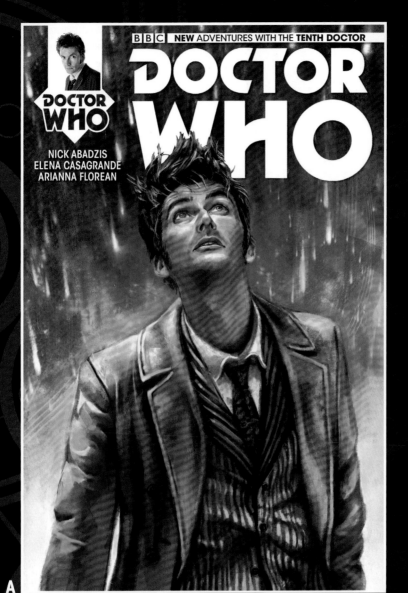

ISSUE 2 Cover A: Alice X. Zhang
Cover B: Rob Farmer

Cover C: Elena Casagrande
& Arianna Florean

COVER GALLERY

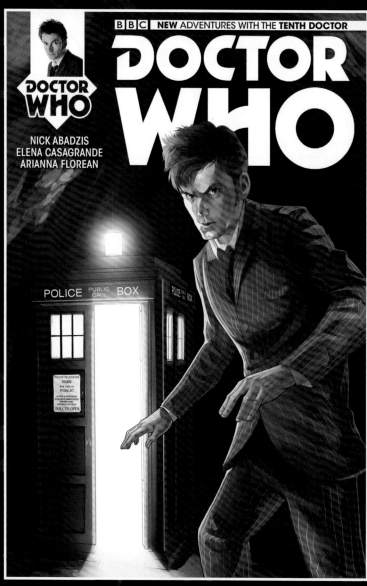

ISSUE 3   Cover A: Verity Glass
               Cover B: AJ

Cover C: Elena Casagrande
& Arianna Florean

ISSUE 4

Cover A: Verity Glass
Cover B: AJ
Cover C: Elena Casagrande
& Arianna Florean

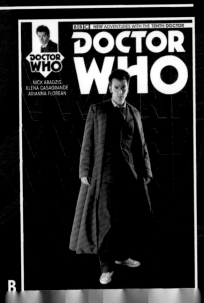

DESIGNING GABBY

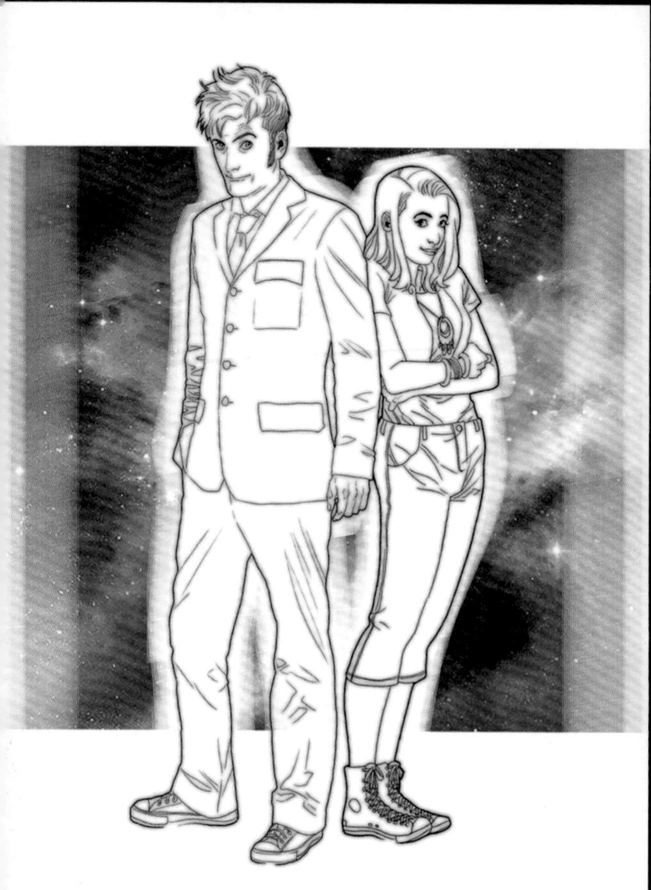
GABBY AND THE DOCTOR

ORIGINS

Gabby came to life in an email chain between Tenth Doctor writers Nick Abadzis and Robbie Morrison, artist Elena Casagrande, and editor Andrew James.

Nick led the hometown charge for this unique new American companion!

After settling on her characteristics – Mexican-American; arty, but frustrated by her job and her family; small, but stronger than she looks – Elena got started on the sketches you can see over the page.

SUNSET PARK

The place chosen as Gabriella's home turf is only a short bike ride away from where Nick Abadzis lives in Brooklyn, so he knows the area well. He kept the rest of the team well-supplied with photos of the area, to help them bring it to vivid life!

In October 2014, Elena and Arianna finally had the opportunity to visit Gabby's neighborhood for real, after the New York Comic Con, and returned home loaded with even more reference!

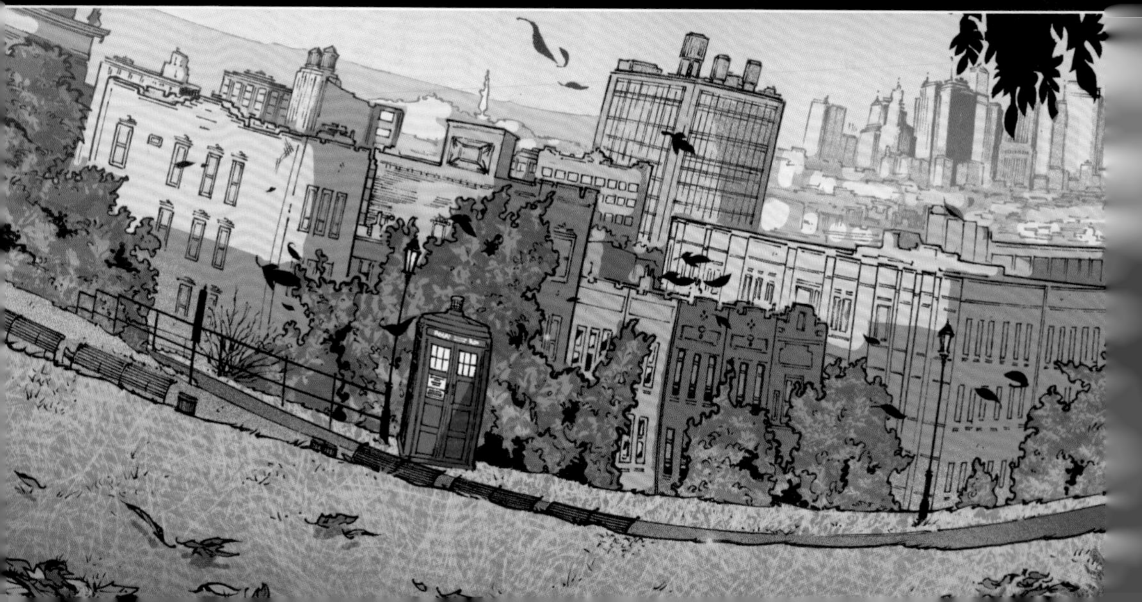

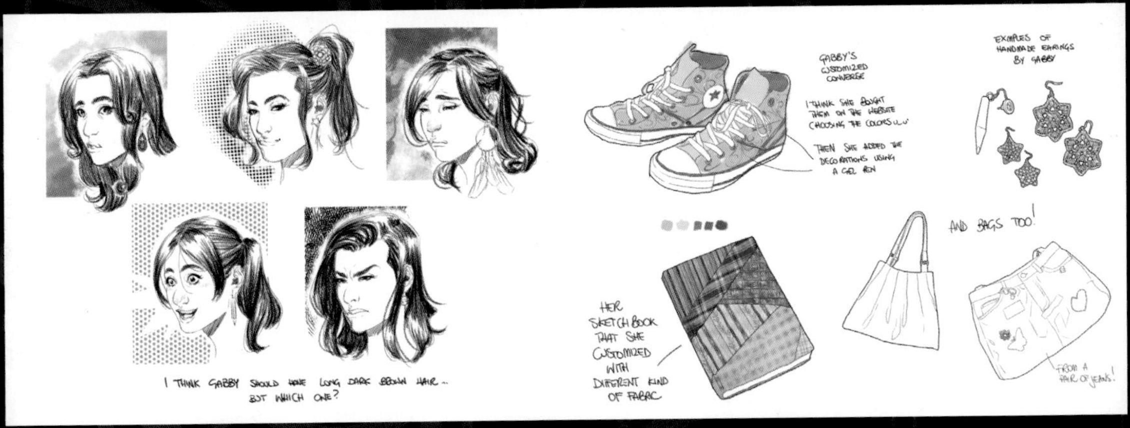
GABBY'S CUSTOMIZED CONVERSE
I THINK SHE BOUGHT THEM ON THE WEBSITE CHOOSING THE COLORS
THEN SHE ADDED THE DECORATIONS USING A GEL PEN
EXAMPLES OF HANDMADE EARINGS BY GABBY
AND BAGS TOO!
HER SKETCH BOOK THAT SHE CUSTOMIZED WITH DIFFERENT KIND OF FABRIC
FROM A PAIR OF JEANS!
I THINK GABBY SHOULD HAVE LONG DARK BROWN HAIR...
BUT WHICH ONE?

Above – a few expression and attitude sketches by Elena, and some quick glimpses into Gabby's wardrobe. Gabriella's deeply personal fashion sense, as well as her beloved sketchbook – in which she writes and draws her impressions of the Doctor – were intrinsic to her character from the very start.

Elena's full-body costume turnarounds (below) were subsequently rendered in hi-res color by Arianna.

These outfits, and several others, are now available as costumes for Gabriella's character in the popular *Doctor Who Legacy* game from Tiny Rebel Games!

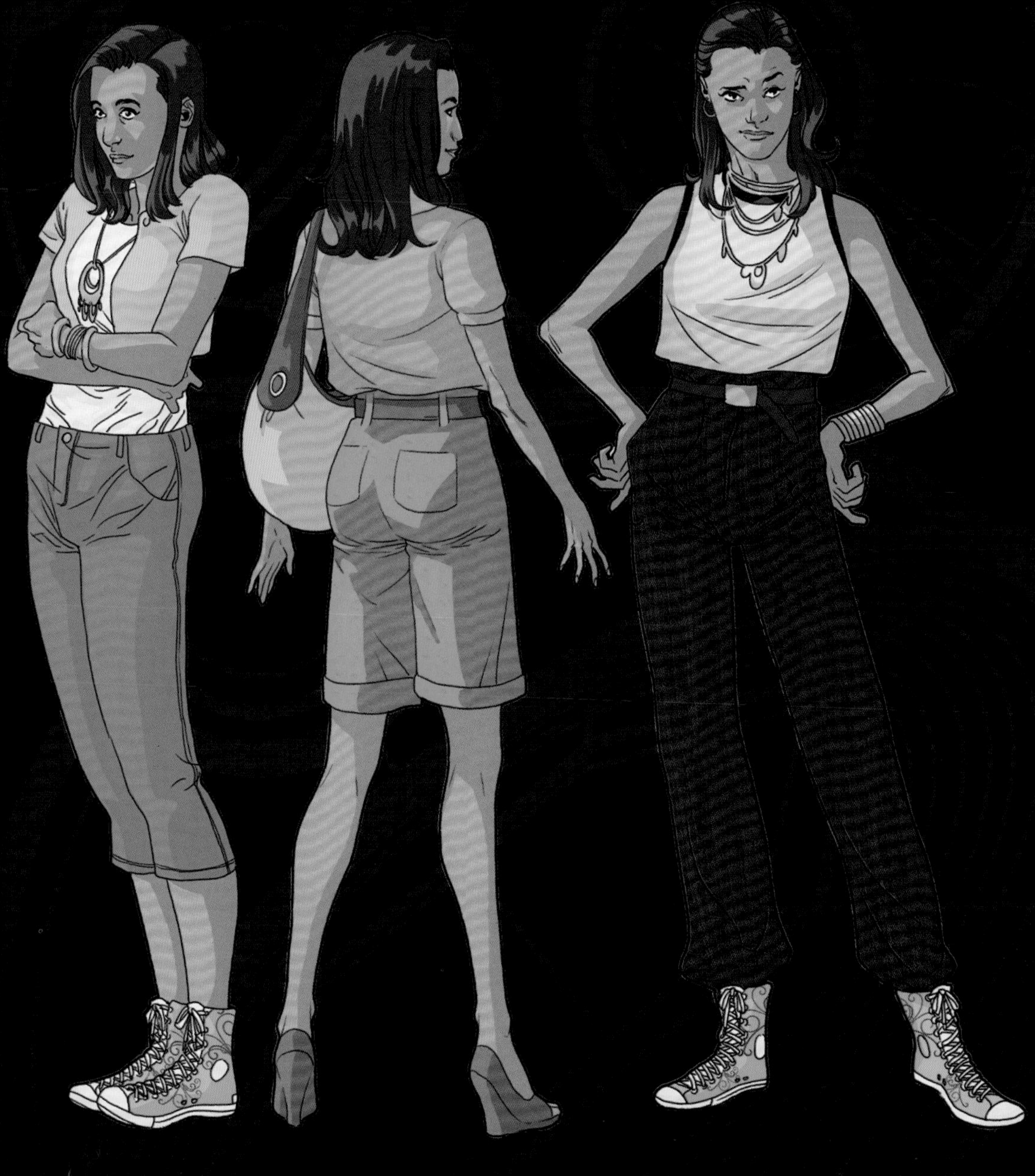

DOCTOR WHO: THE TWELFTH DOCTOR VOL. 1: TERRORFORMER

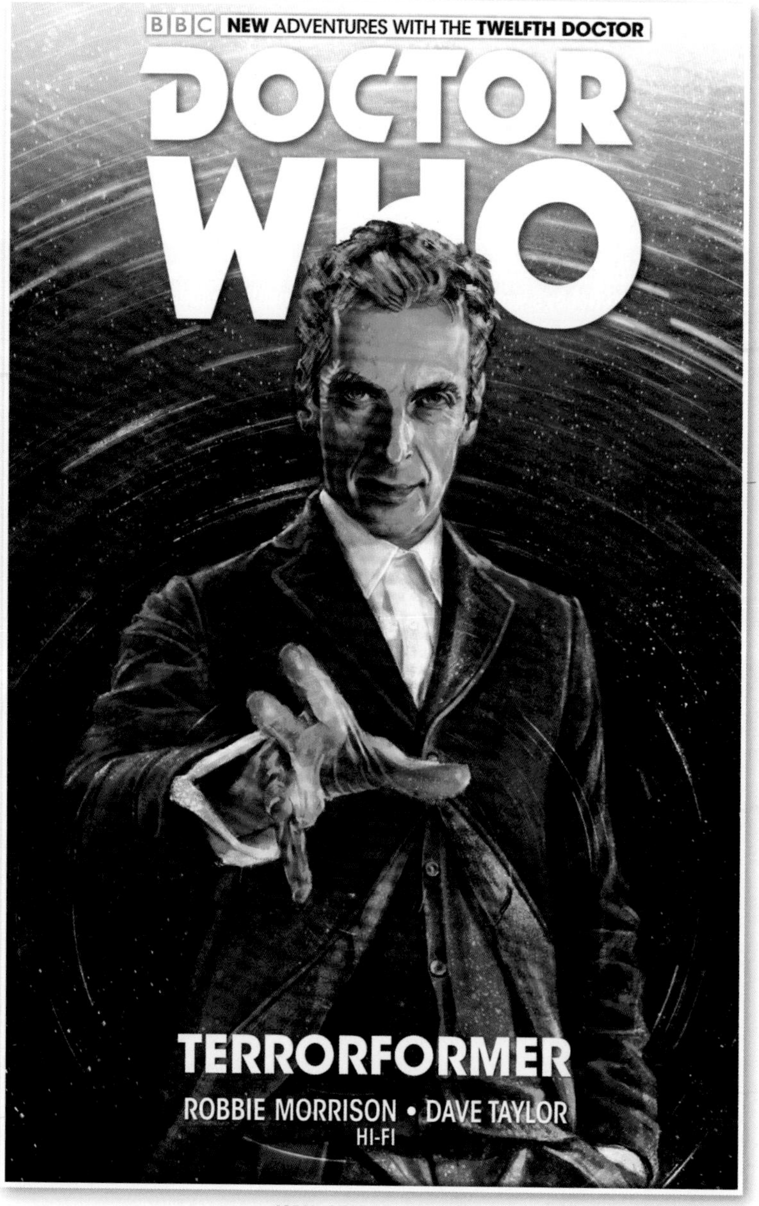
BBC NEW ADVENTURES WITH THE TWELFTH DOCTOR
DOCTOR WHO
TERRORFORMER
ROBBIE MORRISON • DAVE TAYLOR
HI-FI

ISBN: 9781782761778

ROBBIE MORRISON
(DROWNTOWN, NIKOLAI DANTE)

DAVE TAYLOR
(BATMAN: DEATH BY DESIGN)

COLLECTS DOCTOR WHO: THE TWELFTH DOCTOR ISSUES #1-5

COMING SOON $19.99 / $22.95 CAN

TITAN COMICS

For information on how to subscribe to our great Doctor Who titles, or to purchase them digitally for your favorite device, visit:

WWW.TITAN-COMICS.COM

BIOGRAPHIES

Nick Abadzis was born in Sweden to Greek and British parents and was brought up in England and Switzerland. He has been writing and drawing comics and graphic novels for all ages for over twenty-five years. His work has appeared in numerous books, newspapers, magazines and other periodicals around the world and he has been honored with various international storytelling awards, including an Eisner for his 2007 graphic novel, *Laika*. He also works as a publishing consultant, visual facilitator for corporate business and speaker on visual communication in culture. He lives in Brooklyn, New York, with his wife and daughter.

Elena Casagrande was born in 1983, and has worked on titles as varied as *Hulk, Hack/Slash, Angel, Star Trek* and *The X-Files*. As well as drawing the adventures of the Tenth Doctor in *Doctor Who*, she is best known for *Suicide Risk*, her creator-owned series with Mike Carey. She lives in Italy, where she works forty-eight hours a day and never sleeps.

Arianna Florean is Elena's preferred colorist, and has joined her on her many art adventures, as well as coloring series such as *GI Joe: Cobra, GI Joe: Origins, Jericho* and many more. A talented artist and cartoonist in her own right, Arianna lives and works in Rome, Italy, where she somehow keeps pace with Elena without complaint.

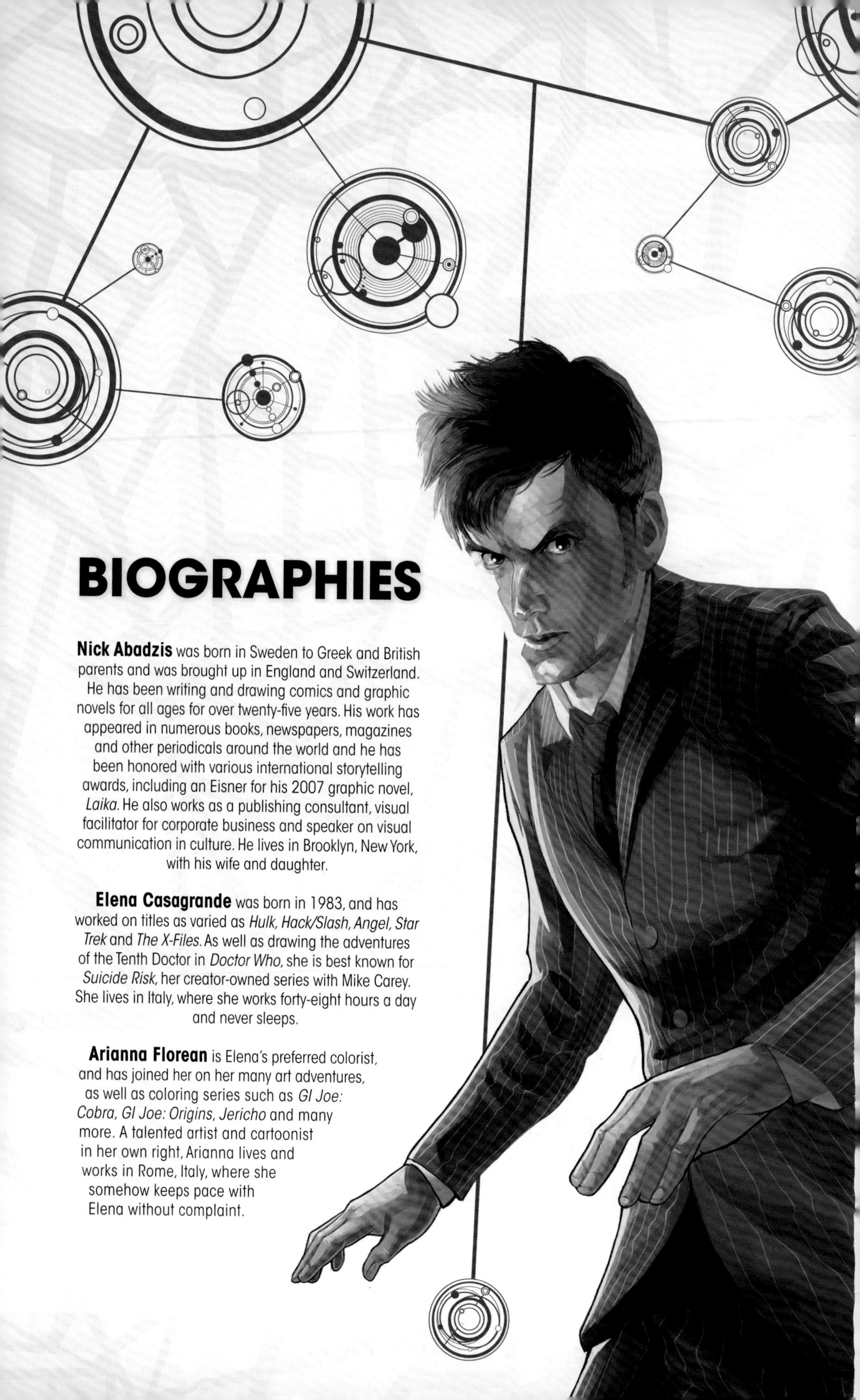